A WARRIOR DYNASTY

The Growth of an Empire

ARCTIC OCEAN

Norwegian
Sea

SWEDEN

RUSSIA

Trondhelm•

Jämtland &
Härjedalen
1645

FINLAND
(Swedish for Centuries)

Karelia
1617

NORWAY

Baltic
Sea

Viborg•

•Bergen

Oslo•

SWEDEN

Ingria
1617

•Fredrikstäd

Estonia
1561

Båhuslen
1645

•Stockholm

Öset
1645

Livonia
1629

North
Sea

•Göteborg

Gotland
1645

RUSSIA

DENMARK

Halland
1645

Öland

Säkne
1645

Bleklinge
1645

Copenhagen•

Bornholm

Pomerania
1648

EAST PRUSSIA

Bremen &
Verden 1648

POLAND

0	200 miles
0	200 km

A Warrior Dynasty

THE RISE AND FALL OF SWEDEN AS A MILITARY SUPERPOWER 1611–1721

HENRIK O. LUNDE

CASEMATE

Philadelphia & Oxford

First published in the United States of America and Great Britain in 2014.
Reprinted as a paperback in 2020 by
CASEMATE PUBLISHERS
1950 Lawrence Road, Havertown, PA 19083, USA
and
The Old Music Hall, 106-108 Cowley Road, Oxford, OX4 1JE, UK

Copyright 2014 © Henrik O. Lunde

Paperback edition: ISBN 978-1-61200-931-5
Digital edition: ISBN 978-1-61200-243-9

Cataloging-in-publication data is available from the Library of Congress and
the British Library.

Printed and bound in the United States of America
by Integrated Books International.

For a complete list of Casemate titles, please contact:

CASEMATE PUBLISHERS (US)
Telephone (610) 853-9131, Fax (610) 853-9146
Email: casemate@casematepublishers.com
www.casematepublishers.com

CASEMATE PUBLISHERS (UK)
Telephone (01865) 241249
Email: casemate-uk@casematepublishers.co.uk
www.casematepublishers.co.uk

Contents

Maps and Battle Sketches

This book is dedicated to

Dr. Enoch J. Haga

Friend — Adviser — Supporter

Preface and Acknowledgments

Magnanimity in politics is not seldom the truest wisdom,
and a great empire and little minds go ill together.
EDMUND BURKE

As a 13–14-year old student in Norway I first read Edward Gibbon's *The Decline and Fall of the Roman Empire* as a special assignment. I found this 225-year-old work (published between 1776 and 1788) as fascinating then as I did recently when I read it again.

I have two reasons for writing this book. First, throughout my life I have wondered if the elements that Gibbon identified in the decline of Rome would be equally pertinent in our times. In this work I make an initial attempt to answer my own questions, particularly as they apply to my former profession as a military planner and practitioner. Some elements in the rise of a power are obvious, such as size, population, and resources, but others are more difficult to identify.

Sweden is a good place to begin because in many ways Sweden breaks the commonly perceived mold when we talk about national and military power. Factoring in Finland and Sweden's holdings along the eastern shores of the Baltic, Sweden had something like 1.3–1.5 million inhabitants at the time it intervened in the Thirty Years War. There was virtually no industrial base except for mining; the country was a poor agrarian society. Nevertheless, Sweden was able to defeat powers or combinations of powers with more than ten times her population and with much greater resources.

It is important to get some terms and definitions out of the way at the very outset. I look upon national power as the aggregate capacity of a state to achieve its national interests and to influence the behavior of other states. This definition involves several distinct yet interrelated elements—population, geography, economics, technology, socio-psychological, and military. The focus of this book is on the military element, but since all elements of national power are interrelated it is impossible to deal in a meaningful way with just one to the exclusion of all others.

The unlikely rise and decline of Sweden as the pre-eminent European military power in the 17th and 18th centuries comprises a neglected aspect of military history, and thus is my second reason for writing this book. My hope is to partially fill the gap that exists in the military historiography for central, eastern, and northern Europe during this period.

Covering a period of more than 100 years, it is an exceedingly complicated and confusing time in European history when the political map of Europe looked much different than today. With respect to the Thirty Years War (1618-1648) Professor Peter H. Wilson (who wrote the latest comprehensive history in English in 2009) makes the following observation in his preface:

The history of the Thirty Years War is rich in specialist studies, but poor in general accounts. Few authors provide more than short overviews intended for students. It is easy to see why. To cover all aspects would require knowledge of at least fourteen European languages, while there are sufficient archival records to occupy many lifetimes of research. Even the printed material runs to millions of pages; there are over 4,000 titles just on the Peace of Westphalia that concluded the conflict. [1]

I have found that Professor Wilson is exactly right as far as military history is concerned. B.H. Liddell Hart reached a similar conclusion in 1929 when he wrote:

Considering that he [Gustav Adolf] *stands on the threshold of the modern world . . . the dearth of military studies of him in this country* [England] *is remarkable, the more so that the epoch of transition in which he lived is so well known and widely studied in its political and religious aspects.* [2]

The last book I know about in English with the military history of the

Thirty Years War as its prime focus was written by Trevor N. Dupuy in 1969. He deplores Anglo-Saxon insularity when he writes:

> *There is perhaps no more striking example of this insularity than the lack of attention that has been paid in the English literature of political and military history to the impact of Gustavus Adolphus in his time, and on subsequent eras.*[3]

This is especially true considering that the period under study was one of revolutionary changes in weaponry and tactics, many of Gustav Adolf's making, and which led to modern war as we know it.

There are a number of good books in German on military operations during this period. Surprisingly, there are few recently in Swedish, where the military is for the most part covered as just one element of general histories of the war.

The Thirty Years War became the benchmark for measuring all later wars. In his radio broadcast on 4 May 1945, Hitler's armament minister, Albert Speer, announced that the "the destruction that has been inflicted on Germany can only be compared to that of the Thirty Years War. The decimation of our people through hunger and deprivation must not be allowed to reach the proportion of that epoch." Public opinion surveys carried out in the 1960s revealed that Germans placed the Thirty Years War as their country's greatest disaster, ahead of the world wars, the Holocaust, and the Black Death.[4]

Even in the twenty-first century German authors assert that "never before and also never since, not even during the horrors of the bombing during the Second World War, was the land so devastated and the people so tortured" as between 1618 and 1648.[5]

If we fast-forward to the Great Nordic War (1700–1721), which brought the Swedish Empire into virtual collapse, we find a similar problem in historiography. There exist enormous numbers of archival records and again we find millions of pages dealing not only with that war but also with the wars between 1648 and 1700, but very little in English. Military operations are again normally covered among other subjects. The lack of adequate coverage in English of this important war is difficult to understand. It took place at the same time as The War of the Spanish Succession and is completely overshadowed by that event in the military literature. It can be argued persuasively that the outcome of the Great Nordic War was of greater importance than The War of the Spanish Succession since it led directly to the rise of Russia and Prussia, with enormous consequences for the history of the world.

For both the period marking the rise of Sweden as a great military power and for the period when that power declined, one is forced to be selective in research since as Professor Wilson said, it would take several lifetimes to carry out thorough original research. That much time is not available to me and I have therefore relied primarily on secondary sources in English, Swedish, German, and French. Because of my language limitations, I have not been able to use Russian or Polish sources unless they have been translated into a Western European language.

There are some books that I have relied on more than others and they are all listed in footnotes, in the bibliography, and in Appendix I. I am grateful to those authors, as well as others who are mentioned less frequently, since their excellent works spared me much research or at least pointed me to useful sources. Without their writings this would have been a "mission impossible" project. There are also two additional appendices, one listing rulers in selected countries and the other being a list of field marshals, or equivalent ranks, mentioned in the book.

The historians Will and Ariel Durant note the traditional difference in outlook on history's driving forces between philosophers (I assume some of the mainstream academic historians are included in that term) and military writers. *In the military interpretation of history war is the final arbiter, and is accepted as necessary . . .*[6] A military writer will question where our civilization and heritage would be if it had not been protected by arms at various critical times in history. The philosophers, on the other hand, point out—as they should—that war has reached a level of destructiveness that threatens the very foundations of that civilization. In some of my comments I shall try to steer clear of these arguments except where I find it necessary to fall back on my own lifetime of research and military experiences.

I am grateful to the library systems in Collier and Lee counties in Florida. Their helpful staffs were always ready to help find obscure references that were provided via the excellent Inter-Library Loan Program.

Dr Enoch Haga in California has assisted with advice and editing as he did for my previous books. The same is true for Dr. Loislane Lowe, who assisted in the editing and proofing process. Finally, it is obvious that I could not have completed this work without the tireless understanding, encouragement, and support of my wife Truong.

Despite the diligence of those who provided assistance, comments and advice, I must stress that I take full responsibility for all conclusions and such errors as this book may inadvertently contain.

NOTES

1. Peter H. Wilson, *The Thirty Years War: Europe's Tragedy.* (Cambridge, Massachusetts: Harvard University Press, 2009), p. xxi.
2. B. H. Liddell Hart, *Great Captains Unveiled.* New Introduction by Max Hastings (Novato, California: Presidio Press, 1990), p. 77.
3. Trevor Nevitt Dupuy, *The Military Life of Gustavus Adolphus: Father of Modern War* (New York: Franklin Watts, Inc., 1969), p. xi.
4. Wilson, *The Thirty Years War*, p. 6.
5. See for example, Wilson, *The Thirty Years War,* p. 6 and Volker Buchner and Alex Buchner, *Bayern im Dreissigjährigen Krieg* (Dachau: Bayerland GmbH, 2002), p. 7.
6. Will and Ariel Durant, *The Lessons of History* (New York: Simon and Schuster, 1968), pp. 82–83.

Introduction

A resolve not carried out at the right moment
resembles a cloud without rain in a great drought.
GUSTAV I'S ADVICE TO HIS SONS

ORGANIZATION OF THE BOOK

In writing a book the first problem is organization. This is important for the author but more significantly, for the reader. It can spell the success or failure of a project.

The chronological instead of the thematic approach is used in this book. After the introduction, which contains a very brief summary of Swedish history before 1600, the book is divided into nine chapters.

Chapter 1 deals with Gustav Adolf's Danish and Baltic campaigns. The foundations of Sweden's Baltic empire had already been laid by Gustav Adolf's Vasa predecessors, but there was a definite expansion of Swedish aims and power after Gustav Adolf's ascension. The importance of this chapter is that it highlights the differences between Gustav Adolf's earlier campaigns, when most of the innovations in weaponry and tactics had not been fully implemented, and those that followed in Germany a relatively short time later. By then Gustav Adolf had instituted most of the changes that are referred to as the Military Revolution. Those changes had a great impact on Swedish military power. The Danish and Baltic campaigns served as a testing ground and learning experience for the Swedish king.

Chapter 2 describes the changes in weaponry and tactics instituted by both Maurice of Nassau and Gustav Adolf. It demonstrates why things changed in a relatively short period of time.

15

Chapter 3 is basically an explanation of Sweden's reasons for intervening in the Thirty Years War, its war aims, and its establishment of a beachhead in Germany. It also addresses the twin problems of manpower and finances.

Chapter 4 describes the new Swedish military system in actions leading up to Breitenfeld, the first decisive battle in military history covered in this book.

Chapter 5 covers the strategic maneuvering by two of the great captains in military history—Gustav Adolf and Field Marshal Albrecht von Wallenstein (1583–1634)—that led to the second decisive battle, at Lützen, and the death of Gustav Adolf. In these first five chapters the questions of how Sweden overcame its shortfall in national power are addressed.

Chapter 6 summarizes Swedish operations in Germany from the death of Gustav Adolf in 1632 to the Peace of Westphalia, pointing out the strains on Swedish power.

Chapter 7 covers, also in summary, the period from the Peace of Westphalia and the Swedish withdrawal from most of Germany to the ascension of Karl XII in 1697. It encompasses the reigns of three Swedish monarchs—Kristina, Karl X, and Karl XI. In this period Sweden was under great financial strain as it tried to rebuild its military and defend its empire.

Chapter 8 covers the early campaigns of young Karl XII until 1707. It also deals with the friction between the king in the field and the political leaders in Stockholm.

Chapter 9 begins with highlights of the changes that had taken place in warfare since 1648 and examines Karl XII's strategy in his final campaign against Russia: his defeat at one of the world's most decisive battles at Poltava, his exile in Turkey, his campaign against Norway, and his death.

NAMES AND DATES

Spelling names of a location is always a problem in dealing with countries that have undergone as many changes as those in northern and eastern Europe, the greatest problem being with Livonia and Estonia. I have tried to use the German spelling or the accepted English form rather than the Latvian or Estonian forms.

I have made some changes to the normal spelling of certain Scandinavian names. In the literature we often find the spellings Christian, Frederick,

Charles, Erick, and Christopher. There were many leaders in Europe at the time covered by the book with those names. In order to avoid confusion I have used the Scandinavian spellings such as Kristian, Fredrik, Karl, Erik, and Kristoffer. I have avoided using the Latinized "Gustav Adolphus" and instead used his Swedish name, Gustav Adolf. I have also used the Scandinavian spelling of some geographic locations such as Skåne instead of Scania.

Researchers encounter a problem with dates during this period of history, as states were switching from the use of the Julian to the Gregorian calendar. While the Gregorian calendar was introduced in the late sixteenth century, it required time to take effect. Pope Gregory XIII had the authority to impose the new system on the Catholic Church, but not on the civil authorities. The new system therefore took years to implement even in Catholic countries. Protestant countries resisted because they viewed the change as a Catholic plot to bring them back into the fold.

While the change to the Gregorian calendar in the Protestant countries was slow, Sweden presents probably the most difficult case to understand. Sweden did not begin making the change to the Gregorian calendar until 1700 and, to make matters worse, it was done in a confusing and halting manner. The Swedish calendar was therefore out of step with both calendars for forty years. The common rule that you add 10 days to the Julian calendar to arrive at the Gregorian date is therefore not applicable in the case of Sweden during the period 1700–1740.

How have other authors handled this problem? Swedish sources and some English sources, such as Michael Roberts, use the Julian calendar. Most make no mention of it and one therefore doesn't know which calendar they are using. Both Robert I. Frost and Ragnhild Hatton address this problem in their books. Frost tried to use the Gregorian calendar (New Style or NS) but admits that there probably are mistakes.[1]

Hatton, in her note at the end of her preface, has this to say:[2]

But in 1700 Sweden opted for a modified form of the Julian calendar in the hope of a gradual progress to the Gregorian one: they dropped leap-year of that year and thus remained ten days behind N.S. but at the same time one day ahead of O.S. [Old Style]

To make this confusing situation even more bewildering, in 1712 Karl XII decided that the system in place gave the Swedes the worst of both worlds and switched back to the Julian calendar.

While I have tried to use the Gregorian calendar wherever I knew which calendar was used by my source, there will no doubt be numerous inconsistencies since most of the sources did not specify which calendar they used. After spending a long time trying to figure out how to handle a problem that two eminent professors had so much difficulty with, I decided to change dates when I knew they needed to be changed but to leave them as found in whatever source I was using when I was not sure.

BRIEF HISTORICAL OVERVIEW OF
SWEDEN BEFORE THE VASA DYNASTY

While this book begins with the birth of Gustav II Adolf of the Vasa dynasty, Swedish interest in the Baltic area pre-dates the Viking Age from 793 to 1066.[3]

There was undoubtedly a lively trade between the Nordic countries and the Romans well before the Viking period as attested to by archeological finds, such as jewelry, weapons and coins. Scandinavians also had an impact –on the Roman Empire in that murky period.

The Goths may have had a distant Scandinavian origin. The *Getica of Jordanes*, written in the middle of the sixth century AD, recounts how the Goths sailed across the Baltic from Scandinavia to what is believed was the Vistula Delta, from where they spread along the Baltic coast expelling the Rugii and subduing the Vandals.[4]

By the end of the first century AD, the Roman writer Publius Cornelius Tacitus had credible knowledge of Scandinavia and some of its people. He relates that the Svear (Swedes) used their fleets and soldiers to expand their holdings in the Baltic region.[5]

Swedish settlements during the Viking age—and before—were mostly in Russia and the Baltic littoral. There is great uncertainty about the dates and progress of the settlers in the east due to the shortage of historical records. The Scandinavian migrants who went east eventually became known as Varangians, and according to the oldest Slavic sources, these Varangians founded Kievan Rus, the major east European state prior to the Mongol invasions. They eventually penetrated to Constantinople and the trade routes to Asia.[6]

Christianity came later to Sweden than to most parts of Europe, including its neighbors where Christianity had been introduced about 150 years earlier. Vilhelm Moberg refers to the long conversion period as *The Three Hundred Years War*.[7] By the mid-twelfth century, the Christian faction appeared to have triumphed.

One factor in the rather late conversion was that the relative independence of the Swedish provinces resulted in a weak central government. Norway and Denmark were centralized at a much earlier date. One reason for this is that the monarchies in Denmark and Norway were mostly hereditary by law while in Sweden the rulers were elected. In a society where rulers were elected they could be dethroned and replaced if they lost the allegiance of the people, and this contributed to a lack of stability and almost continuous civil wars.[8] There were also frequent wars between the Scandinavian countries in the first centuries of the second millennium.

Sweden had a form of compulsory military service early in the Viking period. This obligation was based on the principle that all free men had the right to bear arms as well as a responsibility to defend their land.[9] This provincial system called for the raising and maintenance of fleets and the soldiers to man them, and which could be *nationalized* by the king for defensive and offensive purposes. These military forces were often used to embark on crusades to Finland and other areas along the Baltic littoral. It is safe to assume that the motivation for the crusades was heavily influenced by the opportunity for plunder and the seizure of land.

These crusades laid the foundation for the Swedish Baltic Empire. Finland was basically conquered in the twelfth century. This warfare was not a one-way affair as the Finns and the inhabitants of the Baltic littoral also raided Swedish and Danish possessions.[10]

A change in the military system came at the beginning of the thirteenth century. Swedish rulers were increasingly plagued by popular uprisings and the king needed a system more reliable than the provincial levies for use in internal conflicts. Under the new system, the duty to serve was replaced by a tax. These revenues were used to hire mercenary soldiers and to build forts at strategic locations. This was the beginning of a class system and the creation of privileged nobility. It led to continual internal wars that did not end until the beginning of the Vasa dynasty. Sprague observes that the new rules *forced the farmers to pay taxes to the king, the king used the money to equip soldiers, and the soldiers kept the farmers under control . . .*[11]

In the fourteenth and fifteenth centuries the history of Sweden was characterized by continuous friction between the various layers of society: church and state, farmers and nobility, and within the ruling families. The result was one violent revolution after another. These conflicts were often fought with mercenaries, and that type of warfare was exceptionally expensive. Most of the resulting tax burden fell on the commoners.

The higher nobility was not about to let an opportunity go to waste. They bought up lands from the struggling peasants—lands that had been taxable. When the nobility became owners those lands became non-taxable and a further heavy burden fell on the remaining farmers and workers.

The Black Death in the late 1340s wiped out one-third of Sweden's population in a single year. The nobility again saw an opportunity to profit from the misfortunes of others by buying deserted farms. Those nobles who were unable to increase their wealth became the lower nobility, which often sided with the citizenry and farmers in conflicts.

King Magnus Eriksson of Sweden also became king of Norway when his maternal uncle and king of Norway, Håkon V, died in 1319 and the two countries became united for a short period. King Magnus had a son named Håkon and when he became of age, the Norwegians selected him to become king as Håkon VI. In 1363, Håkon VI married Margaret, the daughter of King Valdemar IV of Denmark.

Margaret and Håkon had one child, Olav. When his father died in 1363, Olav inherited the Norwegian crown and was also selected king of Denmark after his maternal grandfather, Valdemar. This is how the two countries were joined in a union that lasted until 1814. In the beginning, it was a dual monarchy, each governed according to its laws and each with its own Council of State. This changed to an absolute rule by Denmark in the sixteenth century, around the time of the Reformation.

In the fourteenth century, the Swedish kings mortgaged so much land to Danes and Germans that it appeared Sweden might break up. The higher nobility broke with the king, Magnus Eriksson, and requested support from a German noble, Albrekt of Mecklenburg, who was the king's son-in-law. As a result of this rather unpatriotic move the upper nobility was awarded large tracts of land. In the process, Sweden lost much of its independence to foreign powers.

The rule of Albrekt was unpopular and the Swedish nobility requested help from Denmark to dethrone him. Queen Margaret I Valdemarsdtr sent an army into Sweden that decisively defeated Albrekt and his German allies at the Battle of Falan on 24 February 1389. Margaret became the governess of Sweden.

Queen Margaret I was undoubtedly the most far-sighted ruler in Scandinavia in the pre-Vasa period. Vilhelm Moberg calls her *Scandinavia's Greatest Monarch.*[12] She was truly a remarkable woman—politically astute, strong-minded, and resourceful. She had witnessed the continual warfare between the Scandinavian countries and was determined to end this situation by uniting them.

She was also set on curbing the power of the Hansa League. The League had strong footholds in the Nordic countries, forced concessions from their governments, and dominated the trade in that part of Europe. Swedes and Norwegians were especially treated brutally by the Germans who established their own societies in important ports and refused to obey local laws. It was Margaret's goal that a united Scandinavia would be able to eliminate the Hansa monopoly and the threat from Germany.[13]

Margaret's only child, Olav IV (Oluf III in Denmark) died when he was only 17 years old in 1387. He was the last of the old Norwegian royal family dating back to the ninth century. Margaret ended up governing both countries as well as being governess of Sweden.

With no living heirs, Margaret became preoccupied with the question of succession. Her eventual choice fell on her niece's son Bogislav. The name Bogislav was found unsuitable for a Nordic monarch, and his name was changed to Erik of Pomerania.

Margaret summoned the Norwegian, Swedish, and Danish nobility to a meeting in Kalmar in 1397, at which Erik was crowned king in all three Scandinavian countries. This act is known as the Union of Kalmar. All three countries were to have the same king; each kingdom had the right to self-rule domestically, but should act as one entity in foreign relations. Margaret continued to rule all three Scandinavian countries for King Erik until she died in 1412.

Both she and her successor considered Denmark the prominent country in the union[14] and, in violation of the spirit of the Kalmar agreement, appointed Danes and Germans to the most important positions in both Norway and Sweden. This gave rise to nationalism and a drive for independence in Sweden and caused a revolt in 1434. The Norwegians and Danes had also grown tired of Erik's leadership and he was forced to abdicate. Kristian of Oldenburg was chosen king in 1448, and the Oldenburg dynasty ruled Denmark and Norway until 1814. Sweden, still nominally part of the Union, was ruled by Karl Knutson Bonde. His regent from 1470–1495 was Sten Sture the Elder.

Kristian I of Denmark tried to reassert his power in Sweden by force of arms. Sten Sture met the Danish king in the decisive battle of Brunkensberg Ridge near Stockholm. The Swedes prevailed in this fierce battle.

Sten Sture the Elder held the political power in Sweden for almost three decades until his death in 1503, and is credited with laying much of the groundwork in the drive for Swedish independence. He was followed as regent by Svante Nilson Sture and later by Sten Sture the Younger, who held power during the culminating events in the Swedish struggle for independence.

Kristian II of Denmark tried to bring Sweden back into the fold and had the support of several Swedish nobles. Sten Sture the Younger had a conflict with Archbishop Gustav Trolle which ended in the archbishop's imprisonment. The Pope excommunicated Sten Sture and his supporters and directed Kristian II to punish the culprits. Sten Sture was fatally wounded in January 1520 in a battle with the invading Danes, leaving the Swedes leaderless.

Kristian II was crowned king in Stockholm in November 1520. Before the ceremony many of the Swedish nobility were summoned to meet the king in the palace, and those who had fought against him were given unrestricted letters of amnesty. In a double-cross, these Swedish nobles were then summarily accused of being heretics and after a perfunctory trial by church leaders, led to the main square in Stockholm and executed. In less than two hours, Sweden lost at least 82 of its most prominent nobles. This incident came to be known as the *Stockholm Bloodbath*.

The bloodbath provoked the Swedes to a new rebellion, which eventually led the Swedish nobleman Gustav Vasa to seize power. He served as regent until 1523 when he was crowned as King Gustav I and ruled until 1560. The date of his coronation—6 June 1523—became Sweden's national holiday. Vilhelm Moberg deplores the failure of the Union, since *for four hundred years to come the three peoples were to be always at war.*[15]

BRIEF OVERVIEW OF THE FIRST
TWO GENERATIONS OF VASA KINGS.

The first two generations of Vasa kings was a turbulent period in Swedish history. It was a time of transition from an aristocratic-based de-centralized society to one based on a hereditary monarchy and the growth of democracy. The relatively lengthy reign of Gustav I saw the last popular uprising (the Dracke rebellion in 1542) and great administrative changes. Foreign wars continued and the second generation of Vasa rulers saw Sweden become mired in wars with Russia and the Polish-Lithuanian Commonwealth.

There were also bitter sibling rivalries among Gustav I's children—Erik XIV who ruled from 1560 to 1569, Johan III who ruled from 1569 to 1692, and Karl IX who ruled from 1602.[16] This rivalry led to a brief civil war from 1599 to 1604 and the rivalry continued among Gustav I's grandchildren. There are traces of both genius and insanity in the Vasa family. Erik XIV was forced from office because of insanity and spent the rest of his life locked up under deplorable conditions.

Gustav I's most lasting contributions were the establishment of hereditary monarchy and the institution of a firmer financial foundation for the country. The ever-present problem in warfare—finance—resulted in a nearly bankrupt country by 1526.

Gustav I solved the financial problems in various ways. First, he imposed tolls on all foreign trade. Second, he supported and invested in mining and eventually turned that into the country's largest industry. He demanded strict bookkeeping to keep officials honest, probably less for the benefit of those taxed than for the crown.

Most importantly, Gustav I grasped the opportunity to increase the power of the crown by championing the Protestant faith. The Lutheran Church denied the authority of the Pope and supported the right of the crown to draw on the church's considerable resources. It is estimated that the Catholic Church in Sweden owned about 21 percent of the country's land in 1500 and collected the tithe. At the same time crown land amounted to five percent, but by adopting the Protestant religion, the church's property was reduced to zero while the crown properties increased to 28 percent.[17] Moberg states flatly that *it is quite possible that, but for Gustav Vasa's monetary straits, the Swedes would have remained Catholics to this day.*[18]

By turning the country into a Protestant state, Gustav I gained not only enormous wealth for the state but eliminated the power of the church to interfere in politics. This, in turn, strengthened the king's hand in dealing with the nobility. Through such means as making provinces smaller and appointing men from the lower nobility as administrators, Gustav reduced the land under control of the nobility by 16 percent and increased the share of peasant farms—which paid taxes to the crown—by 21 percent.[19]

Gustav I established in 1544 what has been described as the first national standing army in Europe.[20] At first, this defensive/offensive force was voluntary and served mostly in a standby capacity with an elite permanent training regiment. By 1560 it became obvious that the voluntary system was not working and an apportionment system was instituted whereby every ten peasants throughout the country had to provide one recruit. Sweden became embroiled in two short wars during Gustav I's reign: a war with the German Hanseatic city of Lübeck from 1534 to 1537 and a war with Russia from 1554 to 1557.

Gustav I was followed on the throne by his oldest son, Erik XIV, who ruled from 1560 to 1569. He may have been brilliant, but was also brutal to those who he believed were scheming against him, including his own siblings. He was eventually dethroned because of insanity. Erik XIV became deeply involved in wars in the Baltic, and instead of seeking an alliance with Poland he followed the disastrous policy of stubbornly and unsuccessfully seeking an alliance with Ivan the Terrible of Russia. Erik also became involved in a long war with Denmark and Norway, countries allied with Russia from 1562. Poland soon joined that alliance.

Erik XIV was so persistent in seeking the goodwill of Ivan the Terrible that he shamelessly agreed to a Russian demand for the extradition of Katarina of Poland who was married to his imprisoned brother Johan. Erik was removed from power before the extradition was carried out. He had no children that were considered legitimate and the crown passed to his brother Johan.

Johan III, who ruled from 1569 to 1592, inherited a kingdom beset by problems, many of them created by his brother. First and foremost was the fact that the nation was involved in a war with four countries and the city of Lübeck. Johan was determined to extricate Sweden from these conflicts without jeopardizing the national interest and to improve relations with other countries.

Johan III, while reversing his brother's policy by seeking friendship with

Poland, continued to be embroiled in the never-ending wars in the Baltic. He had both a strategic and personal reason for his policy. He was convinced that the best policy for Sweden was an alliance with Poland rather than Russia. His marriage to the daughter of Polish King Sigismund II Augustus of the Jagiellonian Dynasty gave him the personal reason. Sigismund II died in 1572 and there was a struggle over his succession—there was a short one-year rule by Henry of Valois followed by a ten-year rule by the Pole Stefan Batory. When Batory died in 1586, Johan III lobbied hard and successfully to have his son Sigismund selected as the new king of Poland and Lithuania. Under the name Sigismund III, he had a long reign terminated by his death in 1632.

The war in Livonia dragged on. But when Johan III, Sigismund II's brother-in-law, became king relations between the two countries immediately improved and the coalition against Sweden collapsed. Peace negotiations began that resulted in the Treaty of Stettin on 30 November 1570. The Swedes had little to show for seven years of war and 200,000 casualties. It was a defeat for Sweden in almost all areas. The Stettin treaty inaugurated a period of relative peace but its terms left Sweden broke and resentful. The war with Russia continued. It was a brutal war of devastation, raids, minor sieges, but few battles of any consequences in a starving countryside. Both sides were guilty of massacres of the vanquished and barbarous atrocities.[21]

Johan III's dogged determination to hang on in Livonia finally paid off in 1578. The Polish and Swedish armies, in improvised battlefield cooperation, inflicted a serious defeat on the Russians at Wenden. This led to a series of further Russian setbacks and by 1581 the Swedes had captured Estonia, Kexholm on the Finnish frontier, most of Ingria, and the city of Narva. The Russians lost all ports on the Baltic and Swedish possession of these ports helped alleviate some of her financial problems as she imposed tolls on merchandise passing through them. The Poles under King Batory also scored a number of victories over the Russians.

The Poles were alarmed, however, at Sweden's growing power and felt it was time to offer the Russians a truce. The truce of Jam Zapolski in 1582, mediated by the Papacy, was a great humiliation for Ivan the Terrible. Under these circumstances Johan III found it prudent to make a separate truce with the Russians. A three-year truce was arranged in 1583 on the basis of the existing status and was renewed in 1586 for another three years.

The inter-family quarrels did not disappear with the removal of Erik XIV. Michael Roberts writes that there is no doubt that Karl was involved in various conspiracies against his brother Johan: including a planned coup, and he also mentions that Johan exhibited some of the family's problems with mental illness.[22]

Ivan the Terrible died in 1584 and Batory died two years later. Ivan was succeeded by his son Theodore I who turned out to be a weak ruler. The country was run by the nobility under the leadership of Boris Godunov and Nikita Romanov. Boris Godunov, elected tsar by the nobility after Theodore in 1598, ruled Russia until 1605.

The successor to Batory in Poland was, as mentioned earlier, Johan III and Katarina's son, Sigismund III. Katarina was a devout Catholic and had brought her son up in that faith. The people in both Poland and Sweden were hoping that Sigismund's election as king of Poland would solve their problems, since Sigismund was also heir to the Swedish throne. Despite having agreed in 1568 that his brother Johan III should be succeeded by his son Sigismund, Karl now saw an opportunity to claim the Swedish crown for himself using Sigismund's religion as pretext. Peter Wilson refers to Karl *as in many ways the least attractive of the three brothers*.[23] There is no doubt that Karl was a manipulator, schemer, and selfish to the core.

Karl was able to have Sweden formally declared a Lutheran country in 1593. When Sigismund came to Sweden that year he was forced to accept the new laws and to leave Karl as the head of the government in his absence. Religion and personal rivalry led to the formation of rival groups, one supporting Karl and the other his nephew.

Sigismund III returned to Sweden in 1598 at the head of a small army of mercenaries, and he defeated a much larger Swedish force at Stegenborg. In the decisive battle of Stångebro a month later, Karl launched a treacherous attack while a parley was in progress and defeated Sigismund's army.[24] Sigismund returned to Poland but never gave up his claim to the Swedish throne, and this was to haunt the Swedes for more than two generations. Karl prevailed in the Riksdag (Parliament) to depose Sigismund, but waited until 1604 before accepting the crown as Karl IX.

Moberg believes that the early Vasa kings may have been influenced by a contemporary, Nicolo Machiavelli. It appears that Machiavelli's writings were influential throughout Scandinavia in both the political and military arena.[25] Moberg notes that according to "The Prince," *force, treachery, guile, lies, hypocrisy and dissimulation are all necessary and defensible instruments of policy.*[26] Most rulers of the day followed the same rules and, unfortunately, so do many current politicians.

Karl IX continued Sweden's war in the Baltic with disastrous consequences. If one had to summarize the results of this war in one sentence it would be: Karl IX, an amateur military strategist, lost in five years of war all that which his brother Johan III had gained during the previous reign.

The Polish generals that Karl IX came up against were excellent military leaders, and the enemies were Poles and Lithuanians rather than Russians. The Battle of Kircholm was the most important battle of the war and a devastating defeat for the Swedes by any measure, although the Poles, under Field Marshal Jan Karol Chodkiewiz, were outnumbered three to one. Frost, using Polish sources, reports that the citizens of Riga who buried the Swedes and their mercenaries in mass graves counted over 8,900 fallen. That constituted an amazing 82 percent of the Swedish army while the Poles lost 100 killed.[27] Roberts reports that the Swedes had at least 7,600 casualties as opposed to 900 among the Poles.[28] Whatever the true casualty count, there is absolutely no doubt that it was a disaster for Karl IX.

Except for another defeat of a Russian-Swedish army at Klushino in July 1610, where the Poles and Lithuanians were led by Field Marshal Stanislaw Zólkiewski, the war was practically over after the Battle of Kircholm in 1605. The subsequent period was marked by periodic fighting and intermittent truces until it resumed in earnest in the 1620s. There will be more said about Karl IX's wars against Russia in the Baltic and against Denmark and Norway in chapter 1.

Alan Axelrod writes *Think of war, and the country of Sweden does not come readily to mind.*[29] Alexlrod is correct in that current thinking about Sweden views that country as a very pacifist society. Historically, this is a false view as the reader should glean from this brief overview and the rest of this book. It is difficult to find more warlike Western societies than the Scandinavians in the first millennium of their recorded history. They were involved in internal conflicts, war among themselves, or with other European nations nearly on a continuous basis until well into the eighteenth century. The vestiges of the old Norse religious beliefs prior to the conversion to Christianity may have had something to do with this situation since heavy emphasis was placed on battle, honor, and on the idea of Valhalla, a mythical home with the gods for fallen warriors.

While Sweden opted for armed neutrality after 1815, the other countries in this region—Finland, Denmark, and Norway—continued their involvements in wars through the middle of the twentieth century. Those involvements have persisted into the current century with their limited contributions in Iraq and Afghanistan.

NOTES

1. Robert I. Frost, *The Northern Wars 1558–1721* (London: Longman, 2000), p. 330.
2. R. M. Hatton, *Charles XII of Sweden* (New York: Weybright and Talley, 1969), behind p. XVII.
3. These dates are not universally accepted. Karsten Alnæs, *Historien om Norge*. Five volumes (Oslo: Gyldendal Norsk Forlag, 1996–2000), volume 1, pp. 89–116 uses the dates about 700 to about 1050 based on archeological finds.
4. Gwyn Jones, *A History of the Vikings*, (New York: Oxford University Press, 1968), p. 21–28.
5. Martina Sprague, *Sweden: An Illustrated History* (New York: Hippocrene Books, Inc., 2005), pp. 21–28.
6. Robert Ferguson, *The Vikings: A History* (New York: Penguin Group, 2009), pp. 108–117.
7. Vilhelm Moberg, *A History of the Swedish People*. Two volumes. Translated by Paul Britten Austin (Minneapolis: University of Minnesota Press, 2005), volume 1, pp. 73–85.
8. Sprague, *op. cit.*, p. 71.
9. *Ibid*, p. 69.
10. Erich Christiansen, *The Northern Crusades* (New York: Penguin Books, 1997), pp. 93–113.
11. Sprague, *op. cit.*, p. 74.
12. Moberg, *op. cit.*, volume 1, p. 198.
13. *Ibid*, volume 1, pp. 204–205.
14. Kristian Erslev, *Dronning Margrethe og Kalmarunionens grundleggelse* (Kjøbenhavn: J. Erslev, 1882) estimates the population of Denmark at that time as about equal to the combined population of Sweden, Norway, and Finland.
15. Moberg, *op. cit.*, volume 1, p. 206.
16. From 1592 to 1599 Sweden's legal ruler was Gustav I's grandson Sigismund, the son of Johan III.
17. Andrina Stiles, *Sweden and the Baltic 1523–1721* (London: Hodder & Stoughton, 1992), p. 18,

18. Moberg, *op. cit.*, volume 2, p. 169.

19. Wilson, *The Thirty Years War*, p. 178.

20. Stiles, *op. cit.*, p. 30.

21. Michael Roberts, *The Early Vasas: A history of Sweden 1523–1611* (London: Cambridge University Press, 1986), p. 258.

22. *Ibid*, pp. 216–217.

23. Wilson, *The Thirty Years War*, p. 180.

24. Frost, *op. cit.*, p. 45.

25. Geir Atle Ersland and Terje H. Holm, *Norsk Forsvarshistorie*. Three volumes (Bergen: Eide Forlag, 2000), volume 1, pp. 151–152.

26. Moberg, *op. cit.*, volume 2, pp. 180–184, particularly p. 181.

27. Frost, *op. cit.*, p. 65.

28. Roberts, *The Early Vasas*, p. 401.

29. Alan Axelrod, *Little-Known Wars of Great and Lasting Impact: The Turning Points in Our History We Should Know More About* (Beverly, Massachusetts: Fair Winds Press, 2009), p. 129.

1
Gustav Adolf's Danish and Baltic Campaigns

It is my nature not to believe well done
except what I do myself: it is also necessary
that I see everything by my own eyes.
GUSTAV ADOLF'S REPLY TO AN ADMONITION
THAT HE NOT RISK HIS LIFE NEEDLESSLY.

THE FORMATIVE YEARS

Gustav II Adolf was born in Stockholm on 9 December 1594. He was the oldest son of King Karl IX and Kristina of Holstein-Gottorp, though Karl was not yet king when Gustav was born. The legal king was Sigismund (crowned in 1593), King Karl's nephew.

Being the son of a royal duke and duchess, Gustav II Adolf had an opulent and sheltered upbringing. There were no indications that he would be a future king, as the Swedish crown was in a different branch of the family when he was born—his father, Karl IX, was not crowned king until 1604. Gustav Adolf had private tutors for every aspect of his education, and he was no idle child, being gifted with a considerable intellect combined with a great eagerness to learn.

It is reported that by the time Gustav was twelve he spoke perfect German—not surprising since his mother was a German princess—and was fluent in Latin, Italian, and Dutch. He also showed early signs of becoming an inspiring orator.

But it was in the study of diplomacy and military affairs that he really excelled. Young Gustav apparently read everything he could lay his hands on dealing with military art and science, and Maurice of Nassau became his hero. He was a strong athlete and became adept at horse riding and the use of various weapons. He displayed an early contempt for physical danger, a trait we find repeated in his later life and which eventually led to his death.

There was a truce in the Dutch War of Independence in 1609 and, according to Colonel Dupuy, many veterans from that war came to Sweden seeking employment in the Baltic wars. Gustav paid great attention to their description of the new method of warfare introduced by Maurice.[1] These conversations and his own readings profoundly affected his life.

Sigismund was deposed by the Riksdag in 1599 and his uncle Karl became de facto king. Sigismund, the rightful heir, refused to accept the parliamentary decision engineered by his uncle, declared war in early 1600, and hostilities soon commenced in Livonia. This war, interrupted occasionally by truces, was to last until 1629.

Karl IX's formal period as king was relatively short (1604-1611), but he began to have Gustav Adolf participate in the affairs of state at an early date. Gustav often attended meetings of the Council of State and met many foreign diplomats. In 1609, at the age of fifteen, Gustav took over the administration of the duchy of Vestmanland. The following year, he pleaded with his father to be allowed to participate in an expedition to Russia. His father refused.

The Polish-Swedish conflict was suspended after 1605 due to the implosion of the Russian government beginning with the death of Tsar Boris Godunov and ending with the reign of Michael Romanov in 1613—referred to as the *Times of Trouble*. A succession of pretenders claimed to be Dimitrii, the last Riúrik prince, who had actually died in 1591.[2] Both Poland and Sweden took advantage of the Russian turmoil to grab Russian territory. Sigismund intervened in the Russian power struggle in 1609 by supporting a group of rebellious nobles who had besieged Tsar Vasilii Shuiskii in Moscow. Sigismund's intent was to make his son Wladyslaw the new tsar.[3]

The besieged tzar requested help from Sweden. In return for the help he promised to cede control of the disputed region on the Gulf of Finland to Sweden. Karl IX agreed and dispatched a corps under Field Marshal Jacob de la Gardie.

De la Gardie's troops, in cooperation with troops loyal to Tsar Shuiskii, relieved the Russian capital and forced the rebels to retreat.[4] After the success at Moscow, de la Gardie marched with his Russian allies to the rescue of the fortress of Smolensk, which was besieged by a Polish army. However, halfway between Moscow and Smolensk, the Russo-Swedish army was badly defeated at the battle of Klushino on 4 July 1610 by a much smaller Polish force under one of Poland's greatest commanders, Field Marshal (hetman) Stanislaw Zolkiewski.

Zolkiewski thereupon marched on Moscow, captured the city and deposed Tsar Vasilii (Basil). Having sustained a serious defeat at Klushino and with Russia now under virtual Polish control, King Karl IX decided that the wisest course of action was to withdraw northward. He also decided that with the turmoil going on in Russia, this was the right time to seize some of the properties promised by Vasilii for Swedish help. De la Gardie captured the region around Kexholm as well as the city of Novgorod.

There may also have been a dynastic motive by Karl IX, similar to that of his nephew Sigismund. The Swedish historian Nils Ahnlund (1889–1957) writes that in the early summer of 1611, *the Russian national militia assembled in Moscow, despairing of the chances of its native rulers, had chosen Gustav Adolf of Sweden as their tsar and grand duke.*[5] When Jacob de la Gardie concluded a treaty with the authorities in the captured city of Novgorod, Karl IX is referred to as the protector of the city and it was indicated that one of his sons would become tsar. It appears that Karl IX, who was trying to cope with the progress of the Poles, was surprised by the Russian offers.

Anhlund maintains there is evidence to show that in the summer of 1612 Gustav Adolf was still considering the Russian offers, possibly for tactical reasons in dealing with his Polish enemy.[6] In the end he decided that it was not a good idea because of Sweden's and Russia's conflicting interests.

However, Karl IX had a younger son Karl Filip who might rise to the challenge. Gustav Adolf was not too enamored of this idea either. He realized that the conflicting future interests of Russia and Sweden had the potential to create animosity between himself and his younger brother. He undoubtedly had the Polish situation in mind where he was fighting his cousin.

Nevertheless, the project was apparently favored by Queen Kristina. Considerable time passed, however, before Karl Filip headed to Russia. An event which took place before he reached the Russian frontier, however, destroyed any hope of establishing a junior Vasa line in Moscow. This event was the election of Michael Romanov as tsar in 1613—and he was to rule

Russia until 1645. Sweden continued her struggle against Russia until the Peace of Stolbova in 1617.

THE KALMAR WAR (1611–1613)

Kristian IV of Denmark decided to take advantage of Sweden's deep involvement in Russia and Livonia to settle old scores. It was a crafty move on the part of Kristian since all of Karl IX's best troops were in the Baltic region and these could not be brought back to Sweden if the powerful Danish fleet could blockade the ports in the eastern Baltic from where it was logical they would embark. Kristian also appears to have known that Karl IX had come down with apoplexy. What we do know is that Gustav Adolf considered the attack treacherous and that he and Kristian IV remained bitter rivals until Gustav died in 1632.

Let us take a quick look at the reasons for this war, which began just forty-one years after the bloody Northern Seven Years War had been settled by the Treaty of Stettin. This treaty was a defeat for Sweden's King Erik in virtually every area. The Treaty of Stettin only led to bitterness for the losing side and increased ambition on the part of the winning side.

As a result, the leading power in the Baltic at the beginning of the seventeenth century was the kingdom of Denmark-Norway. Even if the distant territories of Iceland and Greenland are left out, the kingdom covered an immense area from northern Germany to the extremity of the European continent. The total length of the coastline was huge, providing easy access to both the Atlantic and the Baltic. To the south, the duchies in Jutland added a considerable German-speaking population. The nearby secularized bishoprics of northern Germany were attainable objectives for the ambitious Oldenburg dynasty. The entrance to the Baltic was completely in Danish hands, and this not only brought great wealth into the royal coffers but gave the Danes great leverage with the western maritime powers. The islands of Gotland and Ösel, off the southeast coast of Sweden, were controlled by Denmark and posed a threat to Sweden, since they were stepping stones to the eastern Baltic, and locations facilitating naval control of the Baltic.

Norway's contribution to the union was first and foremost the Norwegian genius for seamanship—their seamen provided the backbone for the navy as well as the merchant marine. The deep-sea fishery and the large export of timber benefited from high demands in an extensive market. Norway's northern coast made it possible to control trade coming from the White Sea. Meantime, there was only one power that Denmark-Norway needed to reckon with and that was Sweden, including Finland.

Sweden, on the other hand felt surrounded. The area to the west and north was controlled by Norway as well as two provinces east of the Scandinavian watershed. Conflict from there could reach the Baltic and separate the northern part of Sweden from the southern. Norway's geography also posed problems for Sweden's hoped-for outlet to the Arctic Ocean. To the east Sweden faced two great powers: Orthodox Russia and Catholic Poland. To the south she had to contend with Denmark, which occupied a large portion of the Swedish mainland, and the German Hansa League across the southern Baltic.

The mining industry had for centuries been one of Sweden's most important resources, but its full potential was far from being realized. Agriculture was undependable; in some years surpluses were produced while in others the country had to rely on imports. Sweden and Finland were extensively forested but their exploitation was mainly for domestic use and little was left for export. Swedish shipping was in no way comparable with that of Denmark-Norway. Sweden had no outlet to the west except for a sliver of land around the fortress and harbor of Älvsborg.

King Karl IX's policy of extending Swedish and Finnish territories to the Arctic Ocean as a way to interrupt Russian trade from the White Sea and provide the Swedes with an outlet to the Atlantic raised alarm bells in Denmark. This was at least one reason for Kristian IV's surprise attack on Sweden in 1611 that led to the two-year conflict known as the Kalmar War. There were many other animosities between the Scandinavian countries that the leaders could use to stir up the masses. The rivalries between the two kingdoms were the single greatest force determining their relations in the seventeenth century.[7]

The surprise Danish invasion from Skåne and Norway found Karl IX in sickbed. He had to gather whatever forces he could locally since most of the Swedish army was fighting in Russia and Livonia. While the king prepared to move to relieve the besieged Kalmar Castle he put his son Gustav Adolf—not yet 17 years old—in command of the forces in East Gotland.

Kristian IV had made good preparations before the attack, even concluding an alliance with Poland and Russia. The heavily fortified city of Kalmar was key to the defense of southeastern Sweden, and in August Kristian sailed into Kalmar. The Danes stormed and captured the town but were not able to take Kalmar Castle.

Gustav Adolf was not content to sit in East Gotland, and on his own initiative he assembled a small militia force and crossed to the island of Öland where the Danes had left only a small force. As a consequence, the Danish garrison, unprepared when the Swedes under Gustav Adolf appeared, withdrew to Borgholm Castle but was soon compelled to surrender.

The Swedish commander of Kalmar Castle surrendered despite the approach of a relieving force under Karl IX. Kristian IV, seeing that the Swedes had been able to assemble a militia army, realized that his earlier hopes of an unopposed march through southeastern Sweden had been frustrated. With winter approaching, Kristian left a garrison to hold Kalmar and withdrew the rest of his army to prepare for the 1612 campaign.

Gustav Adolf had returned from Öland and planned additional offensive action. He led his small force into the Danish province of Skåne—apparently only intending a quick raid. However, the Danish commander of the border fortress of Christianopol became nervous and sent an urgent message to Kristian requesting reinforcement by about 500 cavalry. The message never reached its destination because it was intercepted by the Swedes. Gustav Adolf saw an opportunity and grabbed it. He dressed a force of his militia to look like Danish cavalry and approached the fort after dark. The Danes, believing it was the force they had requested, opened the gates and after a short fight the fortress was captured, ending the war's first season with a success for the Swedes.

King Karl IX died a few weeks after the 1611 campaign came to a close. Swedish law required that a king had to be 24 years old before taking full control of the government. Gustav Adolf was not yet 17 so that a Regency Council, composed of his mother, Gustav's first cousin Duke John of East Gotland, and six nobles from the Council of Ministers, was therefore appointed. However, within two months the Riksdag amended the succession law, allowing Gustav to become king at the age of 17. Eight days after his birthday he became king of Sweden.

Gustav's first act in January 1612 was to appoint Axel Oxenstierna, age 28, as chancellor. It was a wise choice and Oxenstierna remained at Gustav's side until the king's death in battle. Thereafter, Axel took over the direction of affairs in Germany while also serving as guardian for Gustav's underage daughter Kristina. Oxenstierna's calm demeanor was a perfect match for a king who could be both impetuous and high strung.

Along with the crown, Gustav Adolf inherited three ongoing wars: against Denmark; against Poland; and against Russia. The opponents all enjoyed a considerable superiority over Sweden in power and it was obvious that he had to prioritize his efforts. He decided correctly that the war against Denmark was the most dangerous to Swedish interests and he gave that conflict the highest priority. He was eager to bring that conflict to an acceptable solution as quickly as possible.

THE 1612 CAMPAIGN AGAINST DENMARK AND NORWAY

Denmark began the 1612 campaign with the distinct advantages of having captured the cities of Kalmar and Älvsborg, the latter being Sweden's only outlet to the west. King Kristian IV may also have thought that he had another advantage: a young and inexperienced king on the Swedish throne. These real or perceived advantages may explain why he declined an offer of mediation by King James I of England.[8]

Gustav, rather than trying to recover the two lost cities in protracted siege operations, decided to take the war into Danish territory. He made his bold decision to invade Skåne against the advice of most of his advisers. His immediate objective was the town of Helsingborg, and here he displayed two weaknesses that were to repeat themselves several times in his campaigns in Poland and Germany: failure to acquire adequate intelligence about enemy movements and to take adequate security measures. Before reaching their objective, the Swedes were surprised by a sudden Danish attack. The result was an obvious Swedish defeat forcing Gustav to make a quick withdrawal. After this sharp setback, Gustav decided to try his luck against Norway.

No significant gains were made there either, but in a pattern that was to repeat itself often, the king's recklessness in leading from the front almost cost him his life. In a cavalry skirmish on a frozen lake, his horse fell through the ice. Since he was wearing body armor, he was rescued only with great difficulty. Gallantly leading from the front is a great troop motivator and something that Gustav Adolf repeatedly practiced. In so doing, however, he put his whole command in danger of becoming leaderless and thus losing battles—as happened during both the Polish and German campaigns. A leader's place in battle is where he can best control the action directed at winning and saving lives. Only when all resources have been committed in a set course of action and where the outcome hangs in the balance should a leader become personally involved so as to tip the scale in his favor.

While Gustav was campaigning in Norway, King Kristian IV prepared a bold stroke against Stockholm, the Swedish capital. To deceive Gustav as to his intention he made it appear that he was preparing for action against the fortress of Jönköping near the Norwegian frontier. This was a very believable feint as it would have placed the Danish army on Gustav's line of communication to Sweden. Kristian was hoping that by moving against Gustav's rear he could prevent him from interfering with the main operation against Stockholm.

It was a brilliant strategic move on the part of Kristian but its execution was not that spectacular. Gustav, as Kristian had hoped, moved to protect Jönköping while the main Danish force of 8,000 men, loaded on 30 ships, sailed against Stockholm without interference from the badly outnumbered Swedish navy. Kristian disembarked his troops successfully at a location only 19 kilometers from the capital.

When the news of the Danish threat to the capital reached him, Gustav quickly assembled a small force of 1,200 mercenaries and undertook a grueling forced march of circa 400 kilometers to the capital, accomplishing this task in less than a week. When he arrived in Stockholm, Kristian had advanced only 10 kilometers from his landing site and no significant encounters occurred. After Gustav's arrival, Kristian simply returned to Denmark.

This inconclusive two-year war was coming to an end without either side scoring any spectacular gains. The Swedes had overrun the two Norwegian provinces of Jämtland and Härjedalen but had not crossed the watershed, and most importantly, Gustav's hopes of driving the Danes out of southern Sweden had not come to fruition; in fact the capture of the two cities of Kalmar and Älvsborg had increased Danish holdings and robbed Sweden of her only outlet to the west. Both sides were therefore ready to call it quits and they accepted an offer by England and Holland, eager to maintain a balance of power in the north, to mediate a peace treaty. This mediation led to the signing of the Treaty of Knärad on 19 January 1613.

The terms of this treaty were more advantageous to Denmark than Sweden. Gustav Adolf had to renounce his father's policy of seeking an outlet to the sea in northern Norway and even to return the two conquered provinces to Norway. All of Sweden's attention was devoted to reclaiming the lands around the mouth of the Göta River which provided the only outlet to the west.[9] The treaty returned Kalmar and Älvsborg to Sweden but at a very heavy cost—1,000,000 riks-dollars to be paid in three installments, and the first installment had to take place before a Danish withdrawal. This was a steep price to pay for a relatively poor nation also involved in two other wars, but assurance of financial assistance from Holland cemented the deal. In fact, Holland was so eager to preserve a balance of power in the north that she concluded an alliance with Sweden in 1614. This also demonstrates that both Holland and England considered Denmark-Norway the preeminent power.[10]

WAR AGAINST RUSSIA

With the Danish war out of the way, Gustav Adolf could devote his energies to the wars on the other side of the Baltic. However, it appears that he was in no hurry since he delayed his departure until 1614. The Riksdag voted half a million riks-dollars for the Russian adventure. Fortunately, before Gustav arrived in the theater of war, his commander in Livonia, Gabriel Oxenstierna, the brother of Gustav's chancellor, had managed to conclude a truce with the Poles—one of many such truces in the years that followed.

Dupuy speculates that Gustav's delay in leaving Sweden had something to do with his infatuation with the beautiful Countess Ebba Brahe. It appears that he wanted to marry Ebba but his mother was against such a union. She told her son that he should not marry for love but for reasons of policy. She prevailed and Ebba later married Field Marshal Jacob de la Gardie, the king's military tutor when he was young. This turn of events does not appear to have affected the relations between the king and his field marshal. Another reason may have been the maneuvering involved in his younger brother's quest for the Russian throne (discussed earlier). Since Gustav and his advisers took a long time arriving at a decision, the Russians withdrew their offer and elected Michael Romanov. Dupuy views this as perhaps the most serious political mistake in Gustav's career.[11] However, Gustav worried that the contrary interests of Russia and Sweden would bring troubles between brothers.

When Gustav sailed for the war zone in 1614, his first destination was Finland. From there, he took personal command of the forces engaged with the Russians. These forces had been commanded by Field Marshal Gardie,

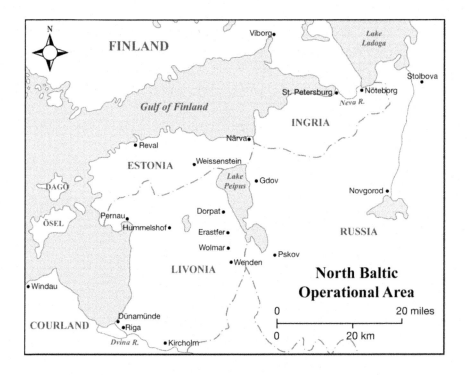

who now became the second in command. This was a wise decision since Gardie had been in the theater of operations for several years and was familiar with the situation. At this time Sweden held Karelia, much of Ingria, and Novgorod. De la Gardie's troops had defeated a Russian attempt to retake Novgorod in 1613.

Gustav Adolf began an offensive in early 1615 by moving from Finland into Ingria. He completed the conquest of that province by storming the city of Gdov. Gustav then tried to storm Pskov, the strongest fortress in northwest Russia, but the attempt failed. The Swedes then resorted to siege operations but after three months there were no signs that the siege would succeed. With winter approaching, Gustav retreated.

The Russian campaign of 1615 was as devoid of meaningful results as the campaign against Denmark in 1612. The Swedes had captured the rest of Ingria but had failed to make any progress against Pskov. Dupuy notes that the only significant change in the Swedish army was its strict discipline introduced by Gustav Adolf.

At the end of the 1615 campaign King Gustav had decided that Russia was such a backward country that it was not worth fighting over. He was ready to negotiate a peace. The Russians were also eager to terminate the war, since Tsar Michael needed time to rebuild after the devastating civil war. Gustav Adolf stayed in Finland, another war ravaged country, while the peace negotiations were in progress.

Russia accepted the harsh Swedish conditions for peace in early 1617, and the Treaty of Stolbova was signed on 27 February 1617. Russia accepted Swedish claims to the provinces of Karelia and Ingria, and on top of that, paid Sweden a large cash indemnity. Novgorod and four other captured towns were given back to the Russians. The acquisition of Karelia and Ingria gave Sweden, for the time being, a secure land connection between Finland and Estonia. Russia was again pushed away from the Baltic Sea, and most of Russian trade with the west was carried out under Swedish control.[12]

By the end of his first four years as king, there was really nothing that set Gustav Adolf starkly apart from his predecessors in the Vasa dynasty. There was nothing to indicate that within sixteen years his military accomplishments would lead him to be labeled, as late as the twentieth and twenty-first centuries, as the "father of modern warfare," worthy of a place among the great captains in history,

Gustav had not sat on his hands during this period. He had thought out his reforms, was to put some of them into practice during the war with Poland, and refine others because his campaigns had been important learning experiences for the young king.

He was also undertaking steps to modernize and strengthen the Swedish position in the world in other areas. He instituted governmental reforms that increased efficiency and undertook to create an economic system that laid the foundation for future prosperity. He encouraged the growth of commerce and entered into trade treaties with foreign countries. He founded a new port on Sweden's west coast—Gothenburg—which became the nation's second largest metropolis. He encouraged an increase in the Swedish merchant marine and started building a powerful navy that could, in the future, dominate the Baltic Sea. In all these efforts he sought the advice of leading scholars, businessmen, and nobles so that they became enthusiastic supporters of his reforms. However, as noted by Frost these reforms also resulted in giving increased power to the nobility and enlarging the role of the Council of Ministers and the Riksdag.[13]

THE POLISH-LITHUANIAN WAR

The Polish-Lithuanian Commonwealth was the largest and most powerful of the three contenders for Baltic domination at the beginning of the seventeenth century. Covering an area twice the size of France, this territory not only included modern Poland and Lithuania, but also Latvia, Belarus, and the western half of Ukraine. Although the commonwealth was sparsely populated, it had at least 11 million inhabitants, more than six times the population of Sweden at that time.

Sweden and Poland had entered into a truce in 1611 and it held until 1617 when full-scale war again broke out. Over the next twelve years the Poles and Lithuanians ground themselves down trying to expel the Swedes from Livonia.[14] I have chosen to give a summary account of these campaigns year by year. These campaign years were normally short as the warring armies went into winter quarters, sometimes for many months.

When Gustav Adolf decided to renew the war in 1617, Poland was badly distracted by wars against Russia and Turkey. Sweden may have decided to take advantage of this distraction, especially in view of the fact that Livonia and Lithuania were almost devoid of troops. The Swedes maintained superiority in numbers throughout the war.

Until now the future "father of modern war" had only faced mediocre opponents. However, Gustav was now about to meet some resourceful and experienced Polish commanders. The skill of his new opponents provided Gustav with excellent experience. For the most part, these generals, with an abundance of experience from their wars on the eastern and southern frontiers, avoided pitched battles with the Swedes. However, their cavalry-strong armies proved their ability to strike swiftly and successfully at isolated Swedish detachments and garrisons. The Swedish cavalry was inferior in the traditional use of that arm, primarily because they were mounted on the smaller Scandinavian horses that lacked the speed of their continental opponents. This was a severe drawback both in pursuit and in retreat, as we shall see. The Poles and Lithuanians also had a home-field advantage. That gave them accurate geographic and intelligence information, a problem the Swedes never fully overcame in either Poland or Germany.

Gustav Adolf landed in Livonia with reinforcements for the army in 1617. He took the offensive against the small detachments of Polish-Lithuanian forces in the area and quickly captured the ports of Pernau and Windau

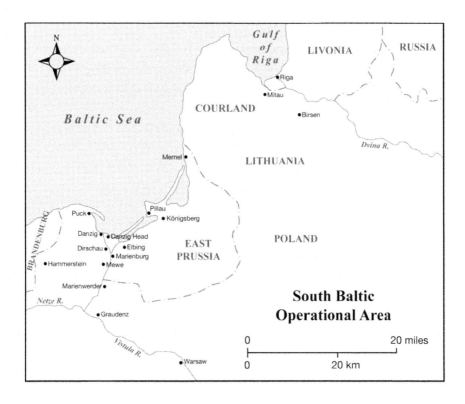

as well as the island of Dünamünde in the Dvina estuary. Gustav was not successful in capturing Riga, one of his main objectives. The Swedes encountered better fortifications in Poland than what they had been used to up to now. These forts could be adequately defended by a smaller number of troops and it took the Swedes time to improve their siege techniques.

When Field Marshal Krzysztof II Radziwill arrived with an army to relieve Riga in the spring of 1618, Gustav decided that it was time to seek a peace similar to the one that had recently concluded the war with Russia. However, since Sigismund III, Gustav's cousin, refused to relinquish his claim to the Swedish throne this prevented—as it did on later occasions—the attainment of a peace treaty. However, a two-year truce was arranged.

Gustav returned to Sweden and spent the next three years building, organizing, and training his army. Dupuy writes:

> . . . beginning in the early months of 1618, most of [Gustav's] personal at-

*tention and efforts were to be devoted to the development of new weapons, the
improvement of old, the designing of new equipment and new methods, and
the melding of all of this into an instrument of warfare that would fully take
advantage of gunpowder weapons and his own weapons refinements.* [15]

During this three-year interlude Gustav married Princess Maria
Eleonora, the sister of Elector George William of Brandenburg. It was, as his
mother had argued earlier, a marriage for policy reasons. In the end the marriage brought neither political advantages nor great happiness. [16]

THE CAMPAIGN OF 1621–22

Gustav landed in Pernau on 24 July 1621. The army and navy he had assembled to complete the conquest of Livonia were far cries from his earlier effort.
The fleet now consisted of 158 ships, including 25 warships, carrying 17,850
troops, including 3.150 cavalry. [17] The entry of the fleet into the Dvina estuary
was delayed until 14 August.

The Poles were still occupied with their war against Turkey and had
45,000 men defending Chocim. [18] The Turkish war showed signs of winding
down, however, and this state of affairs was obviously known by Gustav.
Therefore, he quickly moved against Riga, a large city with a population more
than twice that of Stockholm.

The Swedish army appeared before Riga on 29 August 1621. The city
was defended by a garrison numbering only 300, but the fortifications were
strong and the garrison was supported by a force of 3,700 city militia. The
city was well supplied. [19]

Gustav invested Riga and immediately began strong siege operations,
including bombardment by 22 heavy siege guns. Swedish engineers also dug
mines under the walls of the fortifications and the garrison was subjected to
continuous probes by Swedish infantry. The defenders mounted an excellent
defense, repelling numerous Swedish assaults, and even conducted sorties
against the besiegers.

The citizens of Riga were encouraged on 10 September when they heard
the sound of battle at a distance. This was Lithuanian Field Marshal Radziwill
who approached the city with 1,500 men and encountered a Swedish force.
The Lithuanian relief force was quickly driven away by the more numerous
Swedes. The Swedes pressed the siege vigorously and the garrison came to

realize that further resistance was pointless and negotiated surrender. Gustav entered the city on 16 September. The defenders were granted honorable terms and no reprisals were taken by the Swedish troops. Taking another advantage of the absence of the main Polish-Lithuanian army, Gustav quickly moved into the Duchy of Courland. Mitau, the capital, surrendered on 15 October without resistance.

Gustav Adolf offered peace to Poland now that he had added Riga and Courland to Swedish holdings, while knowing that a truce had been concluded between Poland and Turkey. Sigismund III again refused but authorized Radziwill to conclude another armistice. The truce became effective on 11 August 1622. The Swedes had to give up Courland but retained Riga and Livonia.

Gustav Adolf returned to Sweden, one of numerous times that he left his army in the Baltic region to return to his capital. Various reasons have been put forward by historians: tending to state business, raising new forces, and experimenting with new weapons. This is in sharp contrast to the actions of Karl XII who stayed with his army both during campaigning and in winter quarters and remained away from Sweden for most of the Great Northern War.

The Poles were not happy about Sigismund's claim to the Swedish crown and blamed the continuous warfare on that issue. While the Polish Diet refused to appropriate money for renewing the war against Sweden, that did not prevent Sigismund from making ambitious plans which included an agreement with Danzig for a fleet to invade Sweden. He also began negotiations with Spain for naval assistance.

Gustav learned what his cousin was up to. In June 1623 the Swedish king arrived off Danzig with a strong fleet. Gustav demanded that the city provide assurances that it would not support Sigismund's plans. After some initial reluctance, Danzig gave Gustav the requested assurance. This ended Sigismund's plans and he agreed to extend the truce entered into by Radziwill for another year.

THE CAMPAIGN OF 1625–1626

As the truce between Poland and Sweden was nearing an end, another attempt was made to arrive at a permanent agreement in late 1624. The European powers had already begun to form into two camps, one supporting the

Protestant cause and the other supporting the Catholics. Gustav enjoyed the support of two great powers in the Protestant camp—England and France, although the latter was a Catholic country. The Holy Roman Empire and its principalities advised Sigismund against concluding a permanent agreement with Sweden. This impasse caused the Swedish chancellor to break off negotiations.

Sigismund had good relations with the Austrian Hapsburgs despite their opposition to his election in 1587.

A formal treaty was entered into in 1613, basically the result of dynastic marriages. The treaty promised mutual assistance against rebels, which in Poland's definition implied the Swedish Vasas. However, when the Hapsburgs tried to invoke it at the time of the Bohemian Revolt in 1618, Poland recoiled.

Both Sweden and Poland prepared for a renewal of the war and Gustav took the initiative by landing his army of 20,000 troops near Riga in July 1625. Sigismund was unable to obtain wholehearted support of the war from the nobility, and was therefore ill prepared. He was unable to interfere as the Swedes consolidated their hold on Livonia and again captured Courland. By the end of the year Gustav Adolf had achieved all his objectives.

A small Polish army tried to surprise the Swedes in their winter camp, but were themselves surprised when the Swedes attacked in overwhelming strength at Walhoff on 17 January 1626. The Swedes pursued the defeated Poles into southwestern Lithuania. The Swedish king again returned to Sweden, leaving Field Marshal Gardie in charge in Livonia.

THE 1626 EAST PRUSSIAN CAMPAIGN

Gustav Adolf had no intention of carrying the war into Lithuania or the heart of Poland. His eyes were fixed on East Prussia with the objective of capturing or dominating the Baltic shores. This would cut Polish commerce and lead to economic strangulation by eliminating the outlets for their products, particularly grain. The resulting pressure was considered sufficient to bring Sigismund to make a lasting peace which for Gustav meant that the Polish king had to renounce his claim on the Swedish crown.

Gustav arrived at Pillau in East Prussia with 26,000 troops and 150 ships. The Duchy of Prussia was a feudal fiefdom of Poland and the duke was none other than Gustav's brother-in-law who was also the Elector of Brandenburg. Swedish troops quickly captured Königsberg and other nearby Prussian town.

Gustav crossed the Vistula River in mid-July and captured Dirschau. He demanded Danzig's neutrality but this was quickly refused as the future of the city depended on Polish trade. Like Gustav's brother-in-law it also owed feudal allegiance to Poland. The Swedish king had to settle for the capture of several towns in the Vistula delta that severed all roads between Danzig and Poland.

Sigismund and his Poles were finally galvanized into action. With a hastily raised army Sigismund moved to the lower Vistula near Graudenz. The first encounter between the two cousins took place in late September when the Poles attacked the Mewe castle, occupied by a small Swedish garrison. Dupuy writes that Gustav *hastened to the rescue of the castle and easily defeated Sigismund's larger army on the left bank of the Vistula River.*[20]

There is no doubt that the 3-day fight at Mewe was a Swedish victory but it was not that easy. The fighting took place over more than a week so it is probably not right to call it one battle. There were several engagements: one on 22 September, two Polish attacks on 29 September, and a final action on 1 October.

A Polish cavalry charge on 22 September was repelled. The same is true for two cavalry charges on 29 September. After the second day of failure the hussars were totally demoralized and Sigismund had a hard time convincing them to make another try on 1 October. This time they managed to drive the first line of Swedish musketeers off the ridge because they had not had time to reload after firing a salvo at the Polish infantry. The hussars were again forced to retreat in disorder after they were halted by a salvo from a second line of Swedish musketeers, apparently located some distance behind the one driven off the hill.[21]

The action at Mewe ended the 1626 campaign and both sides went into winter quarters. Gustav Adolf again returned to Sweden.

THE 1627 CAMPAIGN

An important shift in the Polish attitude about the war with Sweden took place between the 1626 and 1627 campaigns. Until 1627 many Poles had viewed the war with Sweden as a dynastic dispute between two cousins and they had been reluctant to lend Sigismund their full support. This attitude changed when Sweden laid siege to Danzig and moved into East Prussia. They realized that the struggle had become a struggle for Poland's very existence as a great power. The Polish Diet decided to give the king its full support and levied taxes to support the war.

Rather than taking the field himself, Sigismund assigned Field Marshal Stanislaw Koniecpolski to take over the front in Prussia. Koniecpolski was an outstanding field commander, and had distinguished himself in the recent war with Turkey and in battles against Tartars and Cossacks. He was a veteran soldier, an outstanding strategist, a resolute cavalry leader, and a skilled tactician. He arrived in Prussia toward the end of 1626, and in the following years he was to become Gustav's foremost instructor in the art of war. He not only taught him strategy, but he greatly contributed to the development of the king's genius as a battlefield tactician. He was unquestionably the most able opponent Gustav ever faced.[22]

Koniecpolski seized the initiative in the spring of 1627, and his first move was to reopen communications with Danzig. Faced with a double threat from land and sea, the Swedish garrison surrendered the fortified port of Puck. This opened a corridor from Danzig to Poland and Germany.

Five days after the capture of Puck, Koniecpolski received intelligence that a force of 4,000 German mercenaries was on its way to join the Swedish army. Leaving his infantry, artillery and baggage to join him later, Koniecpolski led his cavalry west as rapidly as possible and encountered the mercenaries at Hammerstein. He surrounded the town with a cavalry screen and when the infantry and artillery arrived, he began a bombardment of the surrounded Germans. The German troops mutinied against their commanders and surrendered to the Poles. Most entered Polish service but 1,500 who elected not to do so were escorted to the German border after taking an oath not to fight against the Poles for thirteen and a half months.[23]

Gustav Adolf was in Sweden when Koniecpolski began his offensive. As he began his return to the theater of war, unfavorable weather delayed his arrival in Pillau until 8 March. He brought 6,000 men as reinforcements, bringing the total number of Swedish troops in Poland and East Prussia to 35,000. This was the largest army Sweden had ever sent overseas.

Rather than seeking out Koniecpolski to try to end the war in a decisive battle, Gustav made the capture of Danzig his first objective. It is possible that he hoped that this would bring the Polish field marshal to the city's relief. After reestablishing the land blockade Gustav decided to capture Danzig Head, a fortified strip at the mouth of the Vistula, thereby also blockading the city from the sea in case the land blockade did not hold. Danzig Head was held by four hundred Poles and the king decided to cross the mouth of the river in open boats. In another example of recklessness he placed himself in the lead boat in order to pick the best landing place. Gustav received a bullet wound in the hip. The Swedes became discouraged without the king's leadership, and in the face of heavy musket fire they terminated the attack. Why the seaward blockade was not left to the Swedish navy is not known.

Gustav's wound was not life-threatening but he was laid up for several critical weeks before he could resume command. His reckless gallantry made him very popular among the troops but was becoming a concern to the Swedish government, and he was constantly urged not to be so careless. One such admonition was made by Captain Dumaine, a Scot in his service, to which the king simply replied: *It is my nature not to believe well done except what I do myself: it is also necessary that I see everything by my own eyes.*[24]

Koniecpolski took advantage of the Swedish king's absence from service to improve his strategic position. His constant harassment of the Swedish line of communication in swift cavalry raids was a continuing frustration for the Swedes. On 3 July 1627 he began a siege of Mewe, and the Swedish garrison capitulated on 12 July.

By the middle of July Gustav Adolf had recovered to the point where he could mount a horse, and he moved to Danzig to commence siege operations. Koniecpolski followed at a distance and established a fortified camp only eight kilometers from the Swedish headquarters at Dirschau.

When in the vicinity of Danzig, Gustav learned that his brother-in-law, the Elector of Brandenburg, had brought a force of 2,000 Prussians to assist Sigismund. Gustav crossed the Vistula and surrounded the Prussians near Mohrungen, whereupon the Prussians surrendered without resistance. Gustav's brother-in-law was among those captured and Gustav provided him a cavalry escort back to Brandenburg. The conversation between the brothers-in-law must have been interesting.

BATTLE OF DIRSCHAU

Having learned that Koniecpolski had taken up positions on the high ground west of the Motlawa River, overlooking the Swedish fortified camp, Gustav hurried back to Dirschau. It appears that the Swedes outnumbered the Poles.

A personal reconnaissance by King Gustav noted that the side of the river held by his own army was swampy, and movement was also restricted by causeways or dikes. The action opened around noon on 17 August when Swedish cavalry drove back some outposts that Koniecpolski had moved to the Swedish side of the river.

Gustav decided that it would be suicidal to attack Koniecpolski's prepared positions through the marshes and across the Motlawa. Much of the Swedish army was involved in the siege of Danzig but still he had numerical superiority at Dirschau. The Poles had 7,000 troops at Dirschau while the Swedes had 10,200.[25] Each army waited for the other to make the first move, Gustav put his Swedes to work digging entrenchments.

The Polish marshal, becoming tired of waiting when the Swedish army had not appeared after several hours, decided to make the first move. He led his army across the Motlawa stream, drove back some Swedish outposts, and deployed his army in battle formation on relatively firm ground east of the causeways. There he was surprised to discover the Swedish army, also in battle formation, protected by the hastily dug trenches.

Koniecpolski waited for two hours, hoping that the Swedes would leave their trenches. But Gustav refused to move. He knew that the Polish army was in a dangerous situation with the Swedish trenches to their front and with marshy terrain and a stream to their rear. Koniecpolski also realized this fact and felt he had to move before dark. He began a slow and cautious retreat towards the stream.

This was the moment Gustav had waited for and he ordered his army to attack. Koniecpolski's own regiment covered the Polish withdrawal and absorbed the brunt of the Swedish attack. In the ensuing melee, Koniecpolski's horse was killed and he was forced to fight on foot. The Polish cavalry regiments which had already reached the western bank of the Motlawa now returned via the narrow dikes, but there was no room to deploy. Swedish artillery swept the dikes, causing heavy casualties among the Polish cavalry. Koniecpolski was eventually able to withdraw his mauled army to the western bank under cover of his own artillery. Dupuy writes: *Total Polish casualties are unknown, but were extensive. The Swedes carried five hundred seriously wounded Poles to their camp. Their own losses had been negligible.*[26] Frost gives no figures for Swedish casualties but writes that the Poles had only 80 to 100 killed or drowned.[27]

The sources give various and conflicting conclusions about the Battle of

Dirschau. They range all the way from calling it a Swedish victory, to an inconclusive draw, to a Polish victory. It is often found that nationalist sentiments prevail in these conclusions. Academic writers on military history often fail to fully grasp that the "truth is the first casualty of war" and that the first battle reports are invariably wrong. If opposing sides give greatly different casualty figures, it is better to give both sets. The best gauge of the outcome of a battle is what each side did after the fighting ended.[28]

At Dirschau, Gustav was determined to continue the fight the following day. He crossed the Motlawa with nine infantry regiments, forty cavalry squadrons, and 1,600 musketeers. This does not appear to be the act of a vanquished commander. Frost describes the *near panic among the Polish cavalry as the Swedish foot marched purposefully on the Polish camp.*[29]

Gustav, in another example of reckless gallantry while still not fully recovered from his earlier wound, led his men in a reconnaissance of the village of Ronkitki where the Poles were hastily constructing field fortifications. The king was recognized by a Polish officer who directed two musketeers to fire at him. The first bullet missed, but the second found its mark. Gustav was wounded in the neck/shoulder area and tumbled from his horse.

Gustav Adolf believed he was mortally wounded, and ordered his army to withdraw. Although he remained in critical condition for a few days, he began to recover but was out of action for three months. Based on Frost's above description of the morale among the Polish cavalry, his own recklessness had lost him the best opportunity to perhaps decisively defeat his most formidable opponent.

It is true that the Swedish cavalry performed excellently at Dirschau, driving the Polish cavalry off the field, but that does not translate into them having achieved parity with the Poles in that arm.[30] The Swedish cavalry mounts were too small and slow to reach parity with the larger and faster enemy mounts.

A Swedish naval setback in its blockade of Danzig is worth mentioning. The Swedish squadron of six vessels was positioned in two groups when one group of two ships was attacked by nine smaller Polish ships under Admiral Arend Dickmann. Both he and the Swedish commander, Admiral Niclas Sternskiöld, were killed in the vicious fighting that followed. The Poles captured one Swedish ship and the Swedes blew up the second as it was about to be captured. The other four Swedish ships appeared on the scene and drove off the Poles. Nevertheless, it was an embarrassing affair for the Swedish navy.

The Polish conflict had become a stalemate in a war of attrition, with neither side having any hope of achieving a decisive victory. Meantime, while Gustav was nursing his wounds, Koniecpolski's demoralized troops were near mutiny from lack of pay. The 1627 campaign ended in another draw, and King Gustav returned to Sweden in late October.

THE 1628 CAMPAIGN

The Swedes sent additional reinforcements to East Prussia during the winter. They now had a clear superiority over Koniecpolski. This state of affairs was not due to any negligence on the part of the Polish command or the lack of human resources but to the inefficiency of the Polish government.

Gustav Adolf arrived in Pillau with 4,000 troops in late May, 1628. This brought the total Swedish field army to nearly 8,900 infantry and over 6,000 cavalry.[31] The Swedes had considerably more troops in the country but they were scattered in garrisons, a problem that was to take on greater significance during the campaigns in Germany. While the overall strength of the armies looked impressive, to achieve a concentration of force became more and more difficult. Gustav still had a fixation on capturing Danzig, not being content with a naval blockade. This led him to make a costly and unsuccessful assault on the city in early June, resulting in 1,400 Swedish casualties.

The Swedes captured Marienwerder in late August. Koniecpolski, who had his headquarters at Mewe, moved his army south and established a fortified position on the eastern bank of the Vistula near Graudenz. Gustav followed but found the Polish entrenchment too strong and established his own fortified camp several kilometers away. He tried to entice Koniecpolski to leave his entrenched positions by having part of his army make an unsuccessful attack on Mewe. Koniecpolski did not fall for the ruse.

The Swedes made several attempts to get Koniecpolski to leave his entrenchments but he refused to budge. After a month of this fruitless activity, the Swedes broke camp in late September and marched south into northern Poland. Koniecpolski followed, hanging on their flanks. The Poles intercepted Swedish supplies and attacked isolated detachments. The Swedish raid into Poland terrorized a large region but Koniecpolski's harrying had also taken its toll on the Swedes.

So did the twin specters of hunger and disease. While I have no accurate figures, I believe it is correct to conclude that more soldiers died from these twin causes than from actual battle.[32]

The 1628 campaign was probably the most inconclusive of this long war. The Swedish army went into winter quarters in Elbing and Gustav made his annual pilgrimage back to Sweden in early November. The campaign had shown a surprising lack of aggressiveness on the part of Gustav, and many reasons have been advanced to explain his behavior. The two that appear most logical and interlinked are:

1. That Sweden had reached a point in the Baltic where a peace with Sigismund was possible because of the economic pressure being applied. Poland's coast was sealed off and Sweden dominated the land routes both east and west from northern Poland.
2. That Gustav was becoming increasingly preoccupied by events in Germany where the forces of the Holy Roman Empire were winning and had reached the Baltic coast. This threatened Sweden's strategic objective of controlling that sea.

THE 1629 CAMPAIGN

The year 1629 is a bit unusual in that we witness a true winter campaign. In February, Field Marshal Hermann Wrangel mounted a strong drive to relieve pressure on Strasburg, under siege by Poles under Stanislaw Potocki. This happened while Gustav Adolf was still in Sweden. Wrangel launched a surprise attack on Potocki at Górzno. The battle was won by Wrangel's flanking attack that virtually destroyed Potocki's forces. The Poles sustained 2,000 casualties, which amounted to nearly half the force involved. However, while Górzno was a substantial victory, Wrangel was unable to exploit it. He made a dash for the town of Thorn, which his forces were inadequate to capture. Since his small force risked being destroyed deep in enemy territory, he wisely and quickly withdrew northward.[33]

In the meantime, Oxenstierna had managed to negotiate a truce with Poland. This truce lasted from February—after Wrangel's exploits—to June 1629, but all efforts at a permanent peace failed. Both sides therefore prepared for a resumption of hostilities.

THE BATTLE OF HONINGFELDE

The Swedes had established a triangular shaped base area that was anchored on the towns of Dirschau, Marienburg and the point where the Vistula River divides into its two principal estuaries. All forces not required for the still ongoing siege of Danzig were moved into this triangle. Gustav established himself further to the south, at Marienwerder with about 13,000 troops (8,000 infantry and 5,000 cavalry), leaving about 5,000 to hold the base area.

The Polish army had been increased in strength to about 20,000 by the arrival of an Austrian contingent of about 7,000 (5,000 infantry and 2,000 cavalry) under the command of Field Marshal Hans Georg von Arnim.[34] The emperor was apparently concerned that Gustav Adolf might make a move into Brandenburg. Gustav had tried to intercept von Arnim before he joined Koniecpolski, but failed to prevent their junction.[35] After they met on 25 June, Koniecpolski and von Arnim decided to attack Marienburg.

Frost writes that Koniecpolski and von Arnim decided to attack Marienwerder, but this must be an inadvertent mistake. The choices debated between Koniecpolski and von Arnim were either an attack on the Swedish naval base at Pillau or on Marienburg, which was part of the Swedish base area. If their intention had been to attack the fortified camp at Marienwerder, Gustav would surely have waited for them there and not moved north only to be caught in the open at Honingfelde.

Gustav, at Marienwerder, was informed of Koniecpolski's move to the north and guessed accurately the enemy's intended objective. He also moved towards Marienburg. Polish intelligence kept Koniecpolski well informed about Swedish activities and he decided to launch a surprise attack on the Swedes while they were en route. He moved quickly against Gustav with most of his cavalry—about 4,500 when the Austrian dragoons are included.

Koniecpolski intercepted the Swedish column near Honingfelde, south of Stum on 27 June after a small force of dragoons had beaten the Swedes to a crossing over the river Leibe. Koniecpolski immediately attacked a mixed detachment of 2,400 Swedish cavalry and mercenaries, commanded by Rhinegrave John William. He personally led a cavalry force in a flanking movement through a hidden valley against the Swedes who had taken up positions on a low ridge. The attack scattered the surprised Swedes. With the arrival of reinforcements, they rallied, but were again put to flight by another Polish attack.

Gustav now appeared on the battlefield with the remaining Swedish cavalry and the battle was joined near the village of Pulkowitz. Recklessly in the middle of the ensuing melee, Gustav barely escaped death or capture twice, and ended up being slightly wounded in the back. The Swedish cavalry were again beaten in this wild melee, but were saved from total defeat by the timely arrival of an infantry contingent led by Colonel Johan Wrangel, son of Field Marshal Hermann Wrangel.

The Swedes managed to disengage and withdraw to join the rest of the army at Stum. The Poles did not press their victory by a pursuit. It had been a costly battle for the Swedes as they lost 1,500 killed. Among the dead were Rhinegrave John William and Colonel Johan Wrangel. They also lost 15 field guns along with several hundred prisoners. The Polish losses were relatively light.[36]

After assuring himself that Koniecpolski was not going to pursue, Gustav continued his withdrawal to Marienburg, and after satisfying himself that the city was strong enough to withstand a siege, he proceeded to his headquarters at Dirschau. Koniecpolski, who had received reinforcements, moved north to besiege Marienburg after learning that Gustav had left. This fortified town was well defended, and after several weeks of fruitless efforts to take it, Koniecpolski gave up and moved southward, possibly hoping that Gustav would follow.

But Gustav Adolf stayed in the north. He was busy trying to make arrangements that would bring this unsuccessful eight-year war of attrition to an acceptable conclusion. As noted by Roberts, the situation in late summer of 1629 was very much like it had been three years earlier.[37]

THE TRUCE OF ALTMARK

Sigismund had also come to the realization that he could not drive the Swedes out of East Prussia. He was also well aware that the Polish nobility was opposed to his war with Sweden, which brought only increased devastation and financial burdens. However, Sigismund still stubbornly refused to abandon his claim to the Swedish crown.

Gustav Adolf was also ready to end the protracted and costly war, although it was less costly to Sweden than to Poland, since Poland was the battlefield. The Swedish situation was probably not as bleak as depicted by Frost.[38]

Gustav was now anxious to plunge into the more important war in Germany as soon as possible. Cardinal Armand Jean Richelieu (1585–1642) of France, who had already been instrumental in engineering a truce between Sweden and Poland in early 1629, had promised to subsidize the Swedish army if it intervened in the war in Germany. We are getting a little ahead of ourselves, but Sweden and France signed the Treaty of Bärwalde in January 1631 whereby France promised Sweden 400,000 riks-dollars per year for financing the Swedish expeditionary force.

Swedish-Polish negotiations began at Altmark (near Stum), and a six-year truce was signed on 26 September 1629. The terms of the armistice were very advantageous to Sweden:

1. All ports in Prussia, except for Puck, Danzig, and Königsberg were retained by Sweden.
2. In return for the loss of Pillau and Memel, the Elector of Brandenburg was given temporary possession of the Polish towns of Marienburg, Stum, Danzig Head, and the fertile region around Marienburg. These were to be returned to Sweden if no peace was achieved by the time the truce expired.
3. Sweden retained all of Livonia north of the Dvina.
4. Sweden had to evacuate the Duchy of Courland.
5. Sweden received an additional 3.5 percent duty on exports through Danzig, bringing the total to which she was entitled to 5.5 percent.
6. Poland was forbidden to build ships in Danzig.
7. The Elector of Brandenburg agreed to Sweden receiving tolls on goods passing through the Courland ports as a price for the lands temporarily held by him.

The Treaty of Altmark, and associated treaties, gave Sweden virtual total control of Poland's outlets to the sea. Furthermore, Sweden was guaranteed to receive enormous income from the tolls on exports and imports passing through Danzig, the Courland ports, and those ports held by Sweden. Poland and Brandenburg were in effect forced to pay Sweden's war costs as well as much of her expenditures in the early years of her involvement in the Thirty Years War.

Sweden would not have received all these favorable terms if it had not been for strong pressures exerted on the Poles by France, England, and Holland. These countries were alarmed at the expansion of the Empire to the Baltic and North seas. Imperial Field Marshal Wallenstein had reached Stralsund in 1626 and begun a siege of that important Baltic seaport. The powers mentioned above needed Swedish arms to try to stop the imperial forces and Poland paid for it by the terms of the Truce of Altmark. That this was the case is shown by the different attitude they took when the truce came up for renewal in 1635. It was renewed for 26 years but Sweden lost much of what she had gained at Altmark. Swedish arms and blood had by this time removed the danger from the Empire. In the world of international relations there are permanent interests but no permanent friends.

NOTES

1. Dupuy, *Gustavus Adolphus*, p. 7.
2. Wilson, *Thirty Years War*, p. 195.
3. *Ibid*, p. 196.
4. Dupuy, *Gustavus Adolphus*, p. 10.
5. Nils Ahnlund, *Gustavus Adolphus the Great*. Originally published in 1940. Translated from Swedish by Michael Roberts. (New York: History Book Club, 1999), p. 50.
6. *Ibid*, p. 51.
7. *Ibid*, p. 220.
8. Depuy, *Gustavus* Adolphus, p. 13.
9. Ahnlund, *op. cit.*, p. 221.
10. *Loc. cit.*
11. Dupuy, *Gustavus Adolphus*, pp. 16–17.
12. See Ahnlund, *op. cit.*, pp. 231–233 for an in-depth reasoning by Gustav Adolf in support of the Treaty of Stolbova.
13. Frost, *op. cit.*, p. 102.
14. Lukowski, Jerzy and Zawadzki, Hubert, *A Concise History of Poland*, Second Edition. (New York: Cambridge University Press, 2006), p. 93.
15. Dupuy, *Gustavus Adolphus*, p. 22.
16. Ahnlund, *op. cit.*, pp. 78–82 and 84–89.
17. Generalstaben, *Sveriges Krig 1611–1632 II Polska Kriget* (Stockholm: V. Petterson, 1936), pp. 75–76; Dupuy, *Gustavus Adolphus*, p. 25 and Philip J. Haythornthwaite, *Invincible Generals* (Bloomington: Indiana University Press, 1192), p. 29 give the same figures but these are slightly different from those by Generalstaben.
18. Frost, *op. cit.*, p. 102.
19. *Ibid,* p. 103.

20. *Ibid*, p. 32.

21. *Ibid*, pp.104–105.

22. Dupuy, *Gustavus Adolphus*, p. 33.

23. *Ibid*, pp. 33–34. There is some confusion in the sources both as to the size of the German force and its fate. While Dupuy and Haythornthwaite puts it at 5,000, Frost, *op. cit.*, p. 109, states that its size was 2,500. Frost also reports that those who refused to take service in the Polish army were massacred by peasants in Pomerania on their way home.

24. As quoted in Liddell Hart, *Great Captains*, p. 97.

25. Generalstaben, *Polska Kriget*, pp. 356–357 and Frost, *op. cit.*, p. 129, note 15.

26. Dupuy, *Gustavus Adolphus*, p. 39.

27. Frost, *op. cit.*, p. 108.

28. I have personally experienced the truism that initial battle reports are invariably way off the mark. Furthermore, in examining battle reports by various participants for my book on the German invasion of Norway in 1940, I was amazed at the discrepancies. It was at times difficult to believe they were describing the same event. A losing side is most often the one that tries to put the best face on an outcome, but not always.

29. Frost, *op. cit.*, p. 105.

30. Michael Roberts, *Gustavus Adolphus: A History of Sweden 1611–1632*. Two volumes. (New York: Longmans, 1958) volume II, p. 248.

31. Generalstaben, *Polska Kriget*, pp. 414–15.

32. For a detailed discussion of the pestilence and plagues during campaigning in the seventeenth century, see R. S. Bray, *Armies of Pestilence: The Impact of Disease on History* (New York: Barnes & Noble Books, 2000).

33. Frost, *op. cit.*, p. 111.

34. Dupuy, *Gustavus Adolphus*, p. 49 and Haythorntwaite, op. cit., p. 31. Not surprisingly, other sources give different figures. Frost, *op. cit.*, gives the total strength of the force as barely 5,000. He claims that the Swedes exaggerated the size of Arnim's force—referring to Roberts, *Gustavus Adolphus*, volume II, p. 392—by stating it was 12,000 or 10,000, the former number being what Wallenstein had agreed to send and the latter being the number Sigismund agreed to accept.

35. Frost, *op. cit.*, p. 111.

36. Dupuy, *Gustavus Adolphus*, p. 51.

37. Roberts, *Gustavus Adolphus*, volume II, P. 395.

38. Frost, *op. cit.*, pp. 112–113.

2

The Military Revolution —
Dutch and Swedish Reforms

*My troops are poor Swedish and Finnish peasant
fellows, it's true, rude and ill-dressed; but they
smite hard and they shall soon have better clothes.*
GUSTAV II ADOLF

I n Chapter 1 we detailed the early campaigns of Gustav Adolf and the beginning of Sweden's rocky rise to power. This was a time when some of his innovations in weapons and tactics were in the embryonic stages and he fought the campaigns with a mixture of old and new. It was therefore a training ground and educational experience for the young king. In this chapter we see the widespread improvements in armaments and tactics, the products of a military genius, which were to ultimately make Sweden a formidable military power.

The transition from the Middle Ages to the modern era that took place mainly in the seventeenth and eighteenth centuries brought momentous changes to almost every aspect of life. These changes affected the arts, literature, politics, economics, science, technology, and the military.

Because of the focus of this book, our main concern is with the military changes—or the military revolution as it is most frequently called in the literature. It can be argued persuasively that military changes were the driving force behind the political and we will see examples of this throughout the book.

War was almost continual during the sixteenth and seventeenth centuries. This state of affairs resulted, as was to be expected, in developments

59

in weaponry, tactics, and extended durations of wars.[1] The military changes, primarily in technology and weapons, started in the mid-fifteenth century on an evolutionary scale. However, as John Childs points out, changes that took place over several centuries cannot be labeled as revolutionary.[2] It is only when these changes picked up speed in the seventeenth and eighteenth centuries that they became revolutionary in nature.

The advances in technology in the late middle ages led—gradually at first—to modifications of all aspects of war by the early 1700s. During this period military operations devastated the population and countryside, and, as the monopoly of violence rested securely with the Crown, the accompanying increase in the size of armies and costs led to the rise of absolutism and autocracy across the continent.

THE MILITARY REVOLUTION

The armies prior to the Thirty Years War were relatively small and they were primarily mercenary based. Because of the expenses involved in training, nations increasingly moved toward permanent military establishments and away from the use of militia forces which were disbanded during the winter. Roberts has pointed out that the quick spread of technology was influenced by the use of mercenary forces that learned new technology in the service of one nation and then took that knowledge with them when they shifted employers.[3]

Rapid growth in the size of armies characterized the seventeenth and eighteenth centuries. This stemmed from a number of factors such as the proliferation of wars, rise in population, sophisticated armament, increased specialization, and a large expansion of the support base.[4]

The imperial forces numbered approximately 20,000 at the beginning of the Thirty Years War while the Protestant opposition amounted to some 12,000. A little more than a decade later the Catholic forces numbered over 150,000 and those under Swedish command were even larger.[5]

New armaments, the move toward large standing military establishments, growing requirements for a large and sophisticated support base, and prolonged wars resulted in a steep rise in military expenditures and this led to major political changes in most countries. Downing has pointed out that the cost of a single cannon was equivalent to the feeding of 800 soldiers for a whole month. The whole transition in armament involved large expenses.[6]

Economic considerations, then as now, dictated strategy. Countries were unwilling to risk the destruction of their armies—expensive investments—and therefore wars were for the most part short and indecisive in nature. Major engagements were avoided. The rare attempts to mount rapid and decisive campaigns usually failed because of poor communications and consequent lack of speed.

The solution adopted by most continental powers to deal with the steep increase in the costs of war was to raise standing armies. This transition took place in most countries in the last half of the seventeenth century. This did not mean that mercenaries disappeared from the scene. They continued to account for a sizable portion of a nation's army, even into the nineteenth century. In the Thirty Years War, Sweden switched the burden of maintaining its armies to the territories in which they operated through what became known as the "contribution system."

Since the 1950s we have entered a similar period with respect to advances in technology. The standing armies in most Western countries have been severely curtailed in size since the 1970s as we went to an all-voluntary system where personnel costs increased at the same time as there was an explosion in high cost technology. The cost of most military hardware has skyrocketed. The cost of a modern fighter or ground support aircraft as compared to similar aircraft in World War II tells the story, and this problem is prevalent across the board. It seems evident that we are now facing changes similar to those of the seventeenth century—increased centralization, heavy tax burdens, and the possible loss of individual freedoms.

The sixteenth and seventeenth centuries witnessed a decline of the cavalry arm of most armies (Russia, Poland/Lithuania, and Turkey being notable exceptions). This change had been in progress well before that time period. The battlefield became more and more infantry dominated as the weapons of foot soldiers improved and became more effective. This required organizational and tactical changes.

In grappling with this problem in the early 1500s, Spain opted for an organizational structure resembling the Greek phalanx. The troops were armed with a mixture of pikes and firearms. The infantry, which gained prominence on the battlefield, was organized into units of 3,000 men (*tercio*), perhaps better known to the English reader as the "Spanish square." It was devised, partially, as a means of making the matchlock handgun a more effective infantry weapon. Like the Greek phalanx, the "Spanish square" was expected to sweep everything before it.

The pikemen were in the center of these 100 by 30 man squares and the musketeers on the flanks. However, these formations reduced tactical flexibility because of their unwieldiness on the battlefield. Despite these shortcomings the Spanish square dominated the battlefields of Europe for over a century.

The heavy cavalry which had been in decline for centuries underwent a further decline as infantry weapons and artillery became deadlier. In the seventeenth century the ratio of cavalry to infantry had declined to about 25 percent. The light cavalry, however, was still very useful for pursuit, skirmishing, screening, and the interdiction of lines of communication.

MAURICE OF NASSAU'S REFORMS

It gradually became obvious that the Spanish system needed to be modified to make it more flexible and to make better use of manpower. The first important steps in the modification process were taken by Maurice of Nassau and Prince of Orange (1567–1625) who was a general in the United Provinces in their ongoing rebellion against Spain. He had an excellent theoretical and practical knowledge of warfare, and used the Roman legion as the model for his organizational reforms.[7] The reforms that Maurice initiated resulted in a revolution of military organization and tactics during the seventeenth century.[8]

Maurice's primary contribution to the art of war can be found in the tactical employment of manpower. He sought battlefield flexibility by a reduction in both the size and depth of the infantry formations. Maurice modified the tercios by subdividing them into units of 580 men in ten ranks.[9]

This new formation became the beginning of the modern linear formation. The companies were organized into battalion-size units with pikemen in the center and musketeers on the flanks. The objective was to allow the musketeers to deliver continuous fire by ranks before countermarching to the rear to reload. We thus see that the musketeers and pikemen were still linked in one unit but were no longer mixed so that a large number of soldiers were ineffective. With a maximum battalion front of about 250 meters this formation avoided the waste of manpower found in the Spanish square. The number of soldiers who could effectively use their weapons was virtually doubled.

While the pikes were supposed to protect the musketeers from cavalry attacks, the smaller units were more vulnerable to attacks on their flanks and rear than in the Spanish square. Maurice attempted to avoid this danger by adopting a checker-board battle formation, *the spaces between battalions of the first line covered by echeloned battalions in the second line* and by trying to rest the flanks on natural obstacles.[10] If this was not possible, the flanks were protected by cavalry. The battalions were grouped into "brigade" formations in three distinct lines.

As Childs notes, the army reforms of Maurice of Nassau required extensive training and a high level of discipline—contributing factors leading to standing national forces. The success of the system required intensive training over all kinds of terrain and this is one of Maurice's most important contributions. This training also made officers adept at handling and changing formations, and it was an effective way to keep troops busy between campaigns. Such practices as marching in step date from this period.[11]

Maurice was also ahead of his time in experimenting with new weapons such as explosive shells. He insisted on the use of field fortifications, and developed new innovations that would reduce the time of sieges. He adopted field glasses for observation and had a great interest in mapmaking.[12]

Maurice's innovations did not solve all the problems associated with the Spanish square. The pikeman's role was the same as before and the musketeers were still wed to the pike formation. In some ways, the new linear formation was not much more effective in defense than the system it replaced. The changes that Maurice brought about can be viewed as a transition between the earlier gunpowder era and the system adopted by Gustav Adolf. Gustav's modifications to Maurice's system basically lasted to the French Revolution, with minor modifications. Together, Maurice and Gustav's fundamental concept of linear formation and mobility lasted until the twentieth century.

The science involving fortifications and sieges was also transformed. The old medieval stone walls were quickly demolished by cannon firing iron ammunition. New fortifications capable of withstanding cannon fire were expensive and beyond the means of most small states.[13]

Geoffrey Parker mentions some other changes that took place in this period such as the emergence of military academies, the enactment of an embryonic form of "laws of war," and the proliferation of writings on the art of war.[14]

GUSTAV ADOLF'S REFORMS

It is easy to both overstate and understate the achievements of Gustav Adolf. There are examples of both extremes in the literature covering the period. It is true, as pointed out by Colonel Dupuy that many of Gustav's innovations were adopted from others and, furthermore, he was not the only one during the period who sought to improve the military system.[15] And Lynn Montross observes that *with few exceptions, Swedish military reforms owed in some measure to the experiments by others. . . . A talented organizer, Gustavus began where his predecessors left off, taking the best of their ideas and combining them with his own.*[16]

Maurice of Nassau and Gustav Adolf were not simply military theorists but military practitioners. However, it is hard to find anyone who so successfully bridged the gap between concept and practice or fitted the pieces together in an integrated system as did Gustav. Aside from Genghis Khan, Gustav Adolf is the only great captain who won fame on the battlefield using an instrument mainly of his own design.[17] Liddell Hart, who accords Gustav the title of "Father of Modern War," writes that *His outstanding achievement is in fact the tactical instrument that he forged, and the tactical "mechanism" through which this worked its triumphs.*[18]

Gustav's accomplishments were many. He created mobile field artillery, made combined arms operations possible, restored the role of cavalry, and developed the modern role of infantry. He was more than the author of the linear tactics of the eighteenth century—he laid the foundation for the infantry tactics of the twentieth century. He organized the first national army and created the first effective supply service, imposed a system of discipline, and laid the foundation of military law.[19]

Dupuy describes the army Gustav Adolf inherited thus:

At the time Gustavus Adolphus assumed the Swedish throne in 1611, the Swedish Army was in deplorable condition: poorly organized, under strength, short on pikes, musketeers equipped with the obsolete arquebus, and badly led. Administration was virtually nonexistent, recruitment at low ebb, morale poor . . .[20]

To this can be added Sweden's dire financial straits and a sense of weariness after nearly a century of almost continuous wars.

Gustav Adolf was not merely a copier or product improver; he introduced many changes of his own.[21] We shall now look at some of these, both refinements and those based on originality.

INFANTRY

The basic Swedish infantry tactical unit was the battalion or squadron consisting of 408 troops. This organization was still slightly pike heavy. There were 216 pikemen to 192 musketeers. Both pikemen and musketeers were arranged in three rectangular formations, each with a depth of six ranks. The difference was that all the pikemen were located in the center of the battalion formation with a frontage of 36 men while the musketeers were formed into two equal groups, one on each side of the pikemen. The frontage of each musketeer formation was 16 troops. Dupuy notes that an additional 96 musketeers were often attached to the battalion, performing out-posting, reconnaissance, etc. This formation enabled the battalions to deliver formidable firepower.[22]

While Lord Reay, a contemporary English observer, among others, has left diagrams, there was no standard formation for the brigades, which were tactical units. They were "task organized." Both size and formation depended

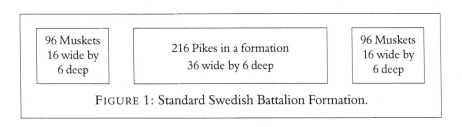

FIGURE 1: Standard Swedish Battalion Formation.

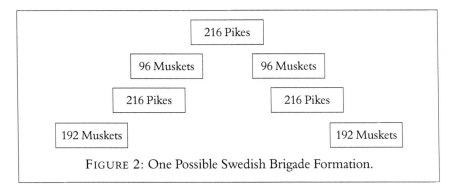

FIGURE 2: One Possible Swedish Brigade Formation.

on the battlefield, the enemy, strength of the battalions, and the experience of the troops. However, they usually consisted of between one full-size two-battalion regiment, and two reduced strength regiments. The numerical size usually varied between 1,000 and 2,000 men but this larger number strained the span of control.[23] The three-battalion brigade in Figure 2 had 1,224 troops. Two regimental guns were usually attached and cavalry was often found in the rear, between the lines of infantry.

Gustav Adolf also introduced "volley firing," since the inaccurate matchlocks and flintlocks were more effective when fired simultaneously. The volley fire was normally obtained by advancing the rear ranks of musketeers into the three-foot intervals between the musketeers in the front of them. This became the basis for European infantry tactics. According to a Scottish colonel, Robert Monro, who fought in the Swedish army as a mercenary for about six years, Gustav adopted a somewhat different method for delivering volley fire. According to Monro, Gustav had his first rank advance ten paces before the troops fired. The first rank then stopped in place to reload while the next rank passed through them to deliver its volley. This procedure was repeated for each rank. It had the advantage of always closing on the enemy and shortening the distance to the targets with each rank delivering increasingly accurate fire. Gustav had in effect changed the countermarch into an offensive operation.[24]

There is some conflict or confusion in the literature when it comes to the Swedish use of volley fire. Dupuy writes:

> *Further, the countermarch was so executed that the whole formation moved forward, and the fire was, in effect, a small-arms rolling barrage. During this movement, the musketeers were protected by the pikes while they reloaded. Later, Gustavus introduced the salve, or salvo, further increasing the firepower of his line. In the salvo, three ranks fired simultaneously. This made continuous fire impossible, but it proved effective just before a climatic charge by producing a volume of fire in a few minutes at close quarters that in the countermarch would have taken a half-hour or more.*[25]

I have found that the full salvo by three ranks of infantry was used sparingly. The musketeers would be rather helpless after delivering such a salvo since they all had to reload at the same time and offensive action by the pikemen to cover the infantry after a full salvo was problematic unless the second line of three ranks had closed up to the first.

Robert Frost writes that on the third day of the Mewe engagements, the first line of Swedish musketeers had fired a salvo at the Polish infantry when they were swept off the high ground by hussars before they could reload.[26] On the previous page he writes that the hussars, after driving the first Swedish line off the high ground were stopped by a salvo from a second line of Swedish infantry.

There are others who doubt that a full salvo was ever used. David Parrott contributed an article to Michael Roberts' book *Military Revolution Debate* and on page 35 of that book Parrott questions both the effectiveness of the salvo and whether it had ever been used. Frost recognizes Parrott's disagreement in a note.[27] In that note he labels Parrott's comment as unfounded and goes on to give an accurate description of a salvo: *The salvo was specifically designed for use against cavalry attack, where two salvos in quick succession by two lines each three ranks deep was all that the defenders had time to deliver.* The two lines of Swedish infantry at Mewe appear to have been more separated than was customary, and the two salvos were therefore not delivered in quick succession.

Gustav also made important changes in infantry weapons and equipment. Despite the fact that body armor was fast disappearing, the Swedish pikemen wore breastplates and greaves. A problem with the pike was that it was frequently severed by enemy cavalry using swords. To overcome this problem, Gustav sheathed the upper portion of the pike with a thin layer of iron. To compensate for the increased weight this caused, the pike was shortened from sixteen to eleven feet.

The arquebus was done away with and replaced by the matchlock musket. However, the earlier matchlock was also a heavy piece of equipment and required a fork rest to fire, adding to the weight a musketeer had to carry. In 1526, while engaged in his Polish campaigns, Swedish manufacturers invented a lighter musket with mechanical improvements permitting quicker loading. The heavy iron fork was also replaced by a thin double ended pike, known as a "Swedish feather." It had a dual purpose. In addition to serving as a rest for the musket, it was also useful as a palisade stake in presenting an obstacle for enemy cavalry. The consequent reduction in the weight that a musketeer had to carry allowed him to be armed with a saber. Both the saber and the Swedish feather gave the infantry some defense against cavalry attacks.[28]

By the end of the seventeenth century the flintlock had almost completely replaced the matchlock. The flintlock was generally less accurate and had a slower rate of fire than the improved matchlock. These were undoubtedly the reasons for the resistance by many practitioners to its adoption. However, the advantages were also great. First, it was less vulnerable to weather. Second, it removed the intrinsic and obvious danger of a lit match. Third, by the removal of the danger of accidents with lit matches, troops could be placed closer together, thus increasing the volume of fire delivered from a given space.[29] To that can be added another important advantage of the improved musket: its increased penetration; the ball could penetrate some of the body armor of the day.

The introduction of the bayonet also took place during the seventeenth century. The plug bayonet appeared first in France in 1647.[30] Forty years later the plug bayonet was replaced by the socket bayonet, where the bayonet is fastened to a socket on the musket barrel. By the first quarter of the eighteenth century the bayonet had replaced the pike.

The Swedes also standardized the caliber and the powder charge. Although the paper cartridge was apparently not a Swedish invention, they seem to have been the first to put it to full use as standard infantry equipment. The cartridge contained a carefully measured fixed charge with a one ounce ball attached. Each soldier carried fifteen cartridges in a cloth bandolier across his chest. When reloading all a soldier had to do was to bite off the end of the cartridge and push it into the musket with the ramrod. This saved many motions in reloading and represented a significant increase in firepower. In large measure due to constant training in the 1620s, the Swedish army improved reloading speed to the point where the six ranks of musketeers could maintain a continuous barrage.[31]

The Swedish battalion bore a clear resemblance to those of Maurice. However, without the attached musketeers, it was slightly smaller. Both organizations were primarily defensive in nature but could be used offensively if properly reinforced and supported. To acquire an offensive capability several battalions had to be combined into a brigade adequately supported by cavalry and artillery.

The weaknesses of the linear formation were that it was no longer able to adequately defend its own flanks and rear. This problem increased with progressively fewer ranks in order to maximize firepower to the front. Gustav Adolf's triangular and checkerboard brigade formation compensated for this weakness since the flank units could turn to present the enemy with a new front.

CAVALRY

The Swedish cavalry was manned by volunteers, and most were light cavalry. The Swedish horses were small but performed well against the bigger horses in the continental armies. By 1630 Gustav Adolf had a cavalry force of 8,000 native Swedes and Finns. A high morale was maintained by regular pay supplemented with bonuses in the form of land or rental income.[32]

Gustav realized, under the conditions then prevailing, that battles could not be won by firepower alone, and that he needed the shock power that only cavalry could provide. He discarded both the caracole and the customary deep cavalry formations.[33] He formed the cavalry in six ranks as he used for the infantry but later changed that to three ranks. Although he had done away with the caracole the riders still carried pistols, but only the first rank fired and the others used them for emergencies. The main weapon was the saber. Firepower support was provided by musketeer detachments deployed between the cavalry squadrons. After an initial salvo to disrupt the enemy line, the musketeers reloaded while the cavalry charged. The reloading exercise was primarily to be ready for a second charge or to cover a cavalry retreat. The light regimental artillery guns could also lend fire support if needed.

The Swedes, like other armies of the period, employed dragoons. In the case of the Swedes, these were basically mounted infantry armed with carbine and saber. They were useful for a variety of tasks such as quick raids, skirmishing, and foraging. Through the employment of small units in this manner, Gustav Adolf was able to concentrate the organization and training of his regular cavalry for shock tactics only. A company of cavalry consisted of 115 men and a cavalry regiment had an average strength of 800 to 1,000.[34]

ARTILLERY

Before Gustav Adolf's arrival on the scene, artillery was considered a specialty, and it was usually operated by civilian mercenaries. These were an unruly bunch that often showed utter contempt for military discipline. Gustav would not put up with this situation and formed the first military artillery company in 1623. By 1629 he had an artillery regiment consisting of six companies. He put this organization under the command of twenty-six-year-old Lennart Torstensson, undoubtedly the best artilleryman of his time. The artillery was thus established as a distinct branch of the army, manned almost entirely by Swedish soldiers.

Four of the six companies of artillery were true gun companies, one consisting of sappers, and the sixth of men, often called on during sieges, trained to handle special explosive devices. It was in weapons and the techniques of their use that set the Swedish artillery apart from that of other armies.

Gustav's objective was not only to simplify the guns but to do so with the goal of making the artillery arm a full and equal partner with the infantry and cavalry on the battlefield. To be that partner, the guns had to be at the right place when they were needed—in other words they had to be mobile. This meant reducing their weights.

Gustav started out by discarding the heavy 48-pounder. He retained the 24-pounders and 12-pounders. They were useful for siege operations and long-range bombardment. He exchanged the 8-pounders with very mobile and relatively quick-firing 3-pounders.[35]

Gustav first tackled the weight problem during the early period of the Polish campaigns. Improvements in the quality of gunpowder made it possible to equalize the pressure in the tube and reduce the thickness of the barrel. In the end, the Swedes had a field gun made that weighed only 90 pounds. It consisted of a copper tube (a metal the Swedes possessed in ample supply) reinforced by iron bands. It was also wrapped in ropes set in cement with a final layer of leather—hence the term "leather cannon." The tube was removable since it became exceedingly hot after a few rounds and had to be cooled. This innovation was soon removed from the arsenal as it proved too fragile and dangerous for field use.

Gustav Adolf continued his search for a light field piece. Metallurgic advances made it possible to develop a short cast iron gun without the sacrifice of safety as was the case with the "leather cannon." In 1624 Gustav had some of the old guns recast into new 3-pounders,[36] with a caliber of 2.6 inches, a length of 48 inches, and a weight of 400 pounds. With its carriage it weighed 625 pounds. Four men or one horse could move the new gun during battle. These guns became known as "regimental guns" since they were assigned to the regiments. It was the first regimental field piece in military history.[37]

The Swedes also developed the first packaged artillery cartridge for use with the regimental gun. It was a thin wooden case which held a prepared charge wired to the ball. The prepared charge increased accuracy and simplified loading. This led to a high rate of fire. The Swedish regimental gun could be fired eight times in the time it took musketeers to discharge six volleys.[38]

At first, one gun was assigned to each regiment. This was later increased to two.[39] The regimental guns changed the traditional role of the artillery and gave the Swedes an enormous advantage in battle, because for several years the Swedish army was the only army that possessed artillery pieces that could accompany the infantry into battle. The need for this type of firepower well forward has influenced all later tactical and organizational doctrines.

John Keegan appears to disparage Gustav Adolf's innovations in weapons and tactics, in sharp contrast to what others have written. For example, he is the only military historian I know who labeled the infantry guns ineffective when he writes that *in practice they did the enemy little harm.*[40] He appears to ignore the many battles from Breitenfeld onwards where these weapons had a devastating effect on thickly packed enemy ranks. Hans Delbruck writes that *the entire socio-political situation of Europe was transformed with the new military organization.*[41]

Gustav Adolf also turned artillery into an offensive tool. He wanted to concentrate maximum fire at the decisive point in a battle. The new regimental guns with their mobility allowed Gustav to achieve this aim. Up till then, the artillery had been positioned before the battle and remained in those positions for the duration, unable to move. The light regimental gun could be moved at will.

Not only was the quality of the Swedish artillery impressive, but so was the quantity. Parker points out that the Dutch army deployed only four field guns at the Battle of Turnhout in 1597 and only eight at the Battle of Nieupoort in 1600.[42] This stands out in sharp contrast to the 80 artillery pieces that Gustav brought with him to Germany in 1630.

When King Gustav appeared on the scene, the solid cast-iron projectile was still the artillery ammunition in use, but around 1580 there had been an improvement. Until then, the gunpowder in the hollow sphere was ignited separately from the propellant. It was ignited by a slow burning fuse before touching off the main charge. This meant that there was a serious problem if the main charge misfired. If the main iron ball was not removed in time, the whole gun could explode. This problem was overcome by a new type of fuse which was ignited by the propellant charge.[43]

An exploding shell, where a bursting charge filled half the container, was invented in the late sixteenth century. There were also experiments ongoing with time and percussion fuses but these ideas were too far ahead of the contemporary chemistry to become useful. The early hand grenade made its debut but its handling was a cumbersome and dangerous operation. It was ignited by a slow burning fuse and Montross writes that: *The soldier lighted the fuse and whirled the two-pound missile about his head to speed ignition before throwing. Accidents were frequent.*[44]

LOGISTICS

War in the patchwork of German states—some Protestant others Catholic—created a logistical problem. The question of food and ammunition became as important as the soldiers' pay. Commanders resorted to looting towns and villages, both for supplies and valuables, to make up the arrears of their soldiers' pay. Starving women and children became camp followers and their number often exceeded that of the armies. The Thirty Years' War *set up a tradition of looting as a legitimate operation in warfare.*[45]

Martin van Creveld defines logistics as *the practical art of moving armies and keeping them supplied.*[46] This is a good definition as long as it is realized that "moving" and "supplied" are broad terms that involve a myriad of separate elements and actions.

Downing writes that the system developed by the Swedes represented a change from the normal practices of the period and relied on large staffs, but seemed *little removed from plunder.*[47] The Swedes went about it in a very organized manner. Their quartermasters spread throughout Germany, inventoried the resources needed, and requisitioned them for their army's needs.

At least it was, in the beginning, done without the pillage and massacres that other armies resorted to in living off the land, especially the mercenaries. A functioning supply system also tended to shorten wars since the enemy commander could no longer hope that by waiting his opponent would run out of supplies.[48] Roberts writes that because the requisitions were usually spent in the same localities as they were made, the effects on the economy were not as injurious to the local populace as would appear at first sight. The long-term concern for future supplies from a particular region set the Swedish system apart from the practice of their opponents.[49] However one looks at it, it was part of the philosophy that "war should be made to pay for itself."

The alternative of letting soldiers forage for themselves often led to criminal behavior and desertions. In the case of Sweden's Baltic campaigns in the second half of the sixteenth century, they had to deal with mutinies by mercenaries not properly paid and fed. The establishment of national armies in the seventeenth century with logistical commands led to better disciplined troops, as they had an organization to rely on for critical needs.[50]

Logistic considerations always trump strategic and tactical ones. In succeeding chapters we will deal with several operations where logistical considerations prevailed over strategy. To plan a campaign without an adequate supply system is so full of risks that it should never be undertaken. Later in this book we will witness what happened to Karl XII when he drove deep into Russia without an adequate line of supply. Napoleon also had to learn this truism the hard way.

The only two powers in Europe to establish a national logistic apparatus for supplying their armies were France and Spain. When France entered the war after years on the sidelines, it constructed a supply system consisting of magazines and private contractors in the local regions. This blend of government and private enterprise worked well. The Holy Roman Empire built a road system to supply its armies. The two principal roads ran from Vienna to the lower Rhine and from northern Italy to the mouth of the Rhine.[51]

STAFFS

Military staffs have existed, in one form or another, throughout recorded history. At times they were primitive, composed mostly of informal group of specialists or trusted advisers relied on by the commander for advice. Like all other aspects of warfare, they evolved over time and became more sophisticated. As mentioned earlier, successful warfare is only possible when based on sound logistical preparation. We find that such preparations were present in the Roman Empire, but largely disappeared after its disintegration. It was not fully reestablished until Gustav Adolf revived it.[52]

Again we find that Gustav took an existing concept and improved it. The Swedish regimental staff consisted of a colonel, a lieutenant colonel, a major, a chief quartermaster, two chaplains, two judge advocates, surgeons, provost marshals, and a number of clerks.[53]

The staff at army headquarters mirrored that in the regiments except it was considerably larger and had added experts, such as a chief engineer and contractors. Both levels had a number of messengers.

Gustav was a meticulous planner. He would sit down with his staff and lay out various options, possible enemy reactions to those options, and logical Swedish counters to those reactions. These courses of action would then be assigned to various underlings to develop further. His council of officers acting as a general staff would then meet to discuss the various options, though the final decision lay with the king as commander-in-chief.

When a course of action was settled upon, it was reduced to a numbered document similar to the later five-paragraph field order. All unit commanders would become familiar with not only their own tasks but those of adjacent units. One person always present at these planning sessions was the quartermaster general. This shows Gustav Adolf's concern for proper logistic support.[54]

The troops received their provisions from magazines established along routes and kept filled through shipments from Sweden as well as enforced contributions from the countryside. A commissary staff distributed these supplies to a central location for pick-up and distribution by their counterparts at the regimental level. Local peddlers were licensed and encouraged to set up booths near the camps for the sale of small luxuries. The troops were sheltered in huts or tents in the fortified camps but as a rule they were mostly quartered in towns. A soldier could demand a bed, salt, vinegar, and a place to cook his meals from the host. All other demands were considered looting.

RECRUITING

Gustav set the rebuilding and reorganization of the army as his top priority when he inherited the throne after his father in 1611. The first decision he had to make was whether to base the new army on mercenary forces as his predecessors had done to a large extent, or to form a national army. His decision was to base his reorganization on a national conscription system, the first in Europe. Recruiting regions were established that were responsible for raising and maintaining units. Gustav and his advisors realized that the

mercenary element could not be done away with in view of the nation's manpower needs, and the end result was that the Swedish army had a national
nucleus supplemented by mercenaries.[55] Norway also adopted universal conscription in the middle of the seventeenth century.[56] Thus the two Scandinavian states became the earliest to resort to this method for raising armies.

The system used to raise troops in Sweden and Finland was called *indelingsverket* (apportionment system), and had actually begun during the latter
part of Karl IX's reign. After a rather bumpy start the system was modified
in the 1620s through a ratio provision discussed in the Introduction. Each
parish had to equip and feed one soldier for every ten males in the parish who
had earlier been subject to conscription. All males between the ages of fifteen
and sixty owed military duty, and the unlucky one out of ten was chosen by
drawing lots.[57] There were many exceptions as for nobles, for the clergy, for
men serving in the mining industries, and for the only surviving son of a
widow. *Bonde* (farmer) was the most frequently listed occupation, by far, in
the enrollment register.

Parker gives some statistics for the annual conscription by the government and the numbers are surprisingly low; ranging from 8,000 in 1629
to 13,500 in 1627. He also shows the disastrous impact the system had on a
typical community—that of Bygdeå. It is worth quoting directly some of
what he had to say:

> *The parish of Bygdeå in northern Sweden, for example, provided 230 young
> men for service in Poland and Germany between 1621 and 1639, and saw
> 215 of them die there, while a further five returned home crippled. Although
> the remainder—a mere ten men—were still in service in 1639, it is unlikely
> that any of them survived to see the war's end nine years later. Enlistment, in
> effect, had become a sentence of death: of the 27 Bygdeå conscripts of the year
> 1638, mustered on 6 July before being sent to Germany, all but one were
> dead within a year.*[58]

Mercenaries and contract soldiers had long constituted an important
source of manpower, although probably not as important as some have concluded.[59] They came from all over Europe: Switzerland, Germany, Ireland,
Albania, Italy, and Scotland, to mention a few. Scottish regiments had served
in Scandinavia since the 1560s in support of the Protestant cause, either in

the armies of Sweden or Denmark. Parker put their number as high as 25,000.[60] Conscription in occupied territories provided additional troops.[61]

Those coming from Scotland and Ireland had the problem of how to get to Sweden. Some of them came to the west coast of Sweden when there were no hostilities with Denmark. Alternative routes were north German ports or by crossing Norway. The latter route was not safe as they were to discover in 1612 when a force of about 300, under colonels George Sinclair and Alexander Ramsay, was ambushed and wiped out by a 500-man Norwegian peasant militia at Kringen near Otta, apparently in revenge for an earlier massacre of Norwegian conscripts.

TRAINING AND DISCIPLINE

The new Swedish military organization and weapons described above would have been useless without rigorous training and strict discipline. Recruits were given two weeks basic training after enrollment. Here they learned how to march to the beat of drums, how to load their muskets, and how to handle the pike. The troops were never idle. Maneuvers by units at various levels were held frequently.[62]

Discipline was harsh but fair, and when taken together with the provision of regular pay,[63] resulted in an army that behaved better than most in that period. It was noted earlier in this chapter that the regimental staff had a judge advocate officer as a permanent member. The reason for this arrangement dates back to 1621, during the siege of Riga, when Gustav Adolf issued his field regulations. Since they proved so influential in the behavior of Swedish troops, it is worth quoting what an expert on the military staff, General Hittle, has to say about this arrangement:

> *Under these regulations the commanding officer of the regiment was the president of the court, and as in our present system, the other members who heard the case were chosen from within the organization that convened the court. There was a clear delineation of authority between the provost marshal and the courts, for although the provosts could arrest an individual they were prohibited from inflicting capital punishment, except under very special circumstances.*
>
> *. . . in addition to the regimental court martial, there was to be a permanent general court martial, of which the royal marshal of Sweden was to be*

president and high military officers were to be members. The regimental courts had jurisdiction over thieving, insubordination, and all minor crimes, and the higher court took cognizance of treason and other major offenses.[64]

Every regimental commander was required to read the Articles of War (as the 1621 regulations came to be called) to his troops once a month. Men accused of serious infractions had the right to appeal the verdict of the court to the monarch. Punishment for infractions of these articles was severe, and Gustav's soldiers had a reputation for good behavior unusual for troops of the day.[65]

In addition to those rules listed in the previous section, I note some others mentioned by Montross:[66]

1. Theft, looting, cowardice and violence to women were punished by hanging.
2. Local thieves and harlots were drummed out of camp.
3. Minor culprits might be shackled or made to "ride the wooden horse" with a musket tied to each foot.
4. Prohibition against a rabble of camp followers. One imperial army of 30,000 fighting men is said to have been encumbered by 140,000 non-combatants—women, children and cripples which had been reduced to destitution by past devastations. The Swedish army permitted a man's wife and family to follow the regiment. The children attended regimental schools. This allowed the Swedes to reduce their baggage train substantially and thereby increase the mobility of the army.

The effects of all these reforms and procedures were the creation of the first truly national army of modern times, one that was also, with great consistency, victorious on the battlefields.

NOTES

1. Brian M. Downing, *The Military Revolution and Political Change: Origins of Democracy and Autocracy in Early Modern Europe* (Princeton, New Jersey: Princeton University Press), p. 65.
2. John Childs, "The Military Revolution I: The Transition to Modern Warfare" in *The*

Oxford Illustrated History of Modern War, edited by Charles Townsend. (New York: Oxford University Press, 1997), p. 19.

3. Roberts, *Gustavus Adolphus,* volume 2, pp. 41–43.

4. Hans Delbrück, *History of the Art of War: The Dawn of Modern Warfare.* Translated from the German by Walter J. Renfroe, Jr. (Lincoln, Nebraska: University of Nebraska Press, 1990) Volume 4, pp. 117–153.

5. Downing, *op. cit.*, pp. 68–69.

6. *Ibid*, p. 74.

7. Wilson, *The Thirty Years War*, pp. 139–145.

8. Trevor N. Dupuy, *The Evolution of Weapons and Warfare* (New York: The Bobbs-Merrill Company, Inc., 1980), pp. 131–132.

9. Childs, *op. cit.*, p. 24. Dupuy, *The Evolution of Weapons and Warfare, p. 132,* claims that the ranks were eventually reduced to five.

10. Childs, *op. cit.*, p. 24.

11. Dupuy, *The Evolution of Weapons and Warfare*, p. 133.

12. *Ibid*, p. 132.

13. Downing, *op. cit.*, p. 67.

14. Geoffrey Parker, *The Military Revolution: Military Innovation and the Rise of the West 1500–1800.* 2nd edition. (New York: Cambridge University Press, 1999), p. 2.

15. Dupuy, *The Evolution of Weapons and Warfare*, p. 138.

16. Lynn Montross, *War Through the Ages.* Third Edition. (New York: Harper & Row Publishers, 1960), p. 271.

17. Dupuy, *Gustavus Adolphus*, p. xv.

18. Liddell Hart, *Great Captains*, p. 151.

19. *Loc. cit.*

20. Dupuy, *The Evolution of Weapons and Warfare*, p. 133.

21. Montross, *op. cit.,* p. 269.

22. Dupuy, *The Evolution of Weapons and Warfare*, p. 134. Montross, *op. cit.*, pp. 270–271 claims that the ratio was four musketeers to three pikemen.

23. Montross, *op. cit.*, p. 271 has a formation diagram of a brigade of 2,016 men.

24 Parker, *The Military Revolution*, p. 23 and Roberts, *Gustavus Adolphus,* volume II, p. 258. See also Robert Monro, *Monro, His Expedition with the Worthy Scots Regiment Called Mac-Keys* (Whiteface, Montana: Kessinger, 1999—this is a reprint of the original).

25. Dupuy, *The Evolution of Weapons and Warfare*, p. 137.

26. Frost, *op. cit.*, pp. 104–105.

27. *Ibid*, note 6, pp. 128–129.

28. Montross, *op. cit.*, pp. 269–270.

29. Dupuy, *The Evolution of Weapons and Warfare*, pp. 130–131.

30. It is called a plug bayonet because it was driven into the barrel of the musket. Its great disadvantage was that the muskets became useless for firing after bayonets had been inserted in their barrel.

31. Montross, *op. cit.*, p. 270; Dupuy, *The Evolution of Weapons and Warfare*, p. 135; and

Parker, *The Military Revolution.*, p. 22.

32. Dupuy, *The Evolution of Weapons and Warfare*, p. 134.

33. The caracole was a cavalry tactic that called for the cavalry to approach the enemy at a trot until they were within pistol range, fire their pistols, and then wheel to the right and left to let the following ranks repeat the procedure.

34. Montross, *op. cit.*, p. 269.

35. Dupuy, *The Evolution of Weapons and Warfare*, pp. 135–136.

36. Montross, *op. cit.*, and John Keegan and Richard Holmes, *Soldiers: A History of Men in Battle* (New York: Viking Penguin, Inc., 1986) p. 107, refer to them as 4-pounders.

37. Parker, *The Military Revolution*, pp. 16–20.

38. Montross, *op. cit.*, p. 273.

39. Parker, *The Military Revolution*, p. 23 claims that each regiment was issued four guns.

40. John Keegan and Richard Holmes, *op. cit.*, p. 107.

41. Delbruck, *op. cit.*, volume 4, p. 223.

42. Parker, *The Military Revolution*, p. 23.

43. Montross, *op. cit.*, p. 272.

44. *Loc. cit.*

45. H. G. Wells, *The Outline of History*. Two volumes. (New York: Doubleday & Co., Inc., 1961), volume II, p. 652.

46. Martin van Creveld, *Supplying War: Logistics from Wallenstein to Patton*. 2nd edition. (New York: Cambridge University Press, 2004), p. 1.

47. Downing, *op. cit.*, p. 70.

48. Martin van Creveld, *Supplying War*, pp. 7–8.

49. Michael Roberts, *The Swedish Imperial Experience, 1560–1718* (Cambridge: Cambridge University Press, 1992), pp. 52–53.

50. Delbrück, *op. cit*, volume 4, pp. 64, 160.

51. Van Creveld, *Supplying War*, pp. 17–22.

52. James D. Hittle, *The Military Staff: Its History and Development*. Third edition. (Harrisburg, Pennsylvania: The Stackpole Company, 1961), p. 40. See also Wilson, *Thirty Years War.*, pp. 94–96.

53. Wilson, *Thirty Years War*, p. 94 also mentions there was a surgeon assigned to each company who doubled as a barber. It is also possible that each company had a designated provost marshal.

54. Peter Paret, *Makers of Modern Strategy: From Machiavelli to the Nuclear Age*. (Princeton, New Jersey: Princeton University Press, 1986) pp. 64–90.

55. Dupuy, *The Evolution of Weapons and Warfare*, p. 134.

56. Ersland and Holm, *op. cit.*, volume 1, pp. 164–165.

57. Montross, *op. cit.*, pp. 265–266.

58. Parker, *The Military Revolution*, p. 53. For additional information on *indelningsverket*, see Roberts, *Gustavus Adolphus*, volume II, pp. 207–211 and

59. Parker, *The Military Revolution*, p. 49.

60. *Loc. cit.*

61. Michael Howard, *War in European History*. Third edition. (New York: Oxford University Press, 2009). pp. 20–74.

62. Dupuy, *The Evolution of Weapons and Warfare*, p. 136.

63. Montross, *op. cit.*, p. 236. *As a poor agricultural country Sweden had an annual revenue of only 12,000,000 riks-dollars (a monetary unit equaling three and a half English shillings), of which five-sevenths had been set aside for the army. This sum supported a total establishment of about 40,000 troops. Subsidies from allies as well as payment from conquered districts footed a large part of the cost, so that within two years Sweden cut her military budget from five-sevenths to one-sixth of the national income.*

64. Hittle, *op. cit.*, pp. 41–42.

65. Martin van Creveld, *Command in War* (Cambridge, Massachusetts: Harvard University Press, 1985), pp. 1–6.

66. Montross, *op. cit.*, pp. 266–267.

3
Sweden Intervenes in the Thirty Years War

Sweden is in danger from the power of the Hapsburg; that is all, but it is enough. That power must be met, swiftly and strongly.
GUSTAV ADOLF TO THE SWEDISH
RIKSDAG (PARLIAMENT)

I n the last chapter we saw tremendous strides in military armaments, strategy, and tactics. This set the stage for the Swedish victories on the battlefield, which are covered in this and the next three chapters. We will also learn how the Swedes overcame the problems of recruitment and finances.

In the period leading up to Sweden's intervention in the Thirty Years War there were convoluted and confusing political/military activities both in and out of the Holy Roman Empire.[1] Space restrictions do not allow for coverage of the religious wars that broke out almost immediately after Martin Luther is reputed to have nailed his 95 Theses to the church door at Wittemberg Castle—an act that began a period of religious wars that ravaged the continent for over a hundred years. H.G. Wells notes that *at the close of the struggle all Germany was ruined and desolate* and that *Central Europe did not fully recover from these robberies and devastations for a century.*[2]

There are several good books dealing with this earlier period of religious wars and my recommendation is to read what Peter Wilson has written.[3] There are also other good books in English covering that period and they are easy to obtain through our library system.[4]

The period following Martin Luther witnessed the beginning of a series of wars that would ultimately divide the Catholic realm to a point beyond recovery. Religious conflicts also haunted France and Holland. All these conflicts, throughout much of Europe, from about 1550 to 1650 are often collectively referred to as the Religious Wars.

In no part of Europe did the idea of unified Christianity bring about more disastrous consequences than in Germany. The patchwork of sovereign principalities, duchies, and bishoprics that collectively made up most of Germany had little in common with the policies of the empire in Vienna. Most of the northern German dominions were smaller in size than many counties in our United States. The empire to which they belonged was mostly concerned with its southern holdings and the threat from the Turks. The German principalities had a western and Baltic affinity and a disposition to the Protestant teachings and indifference to the Turkish menace that preoccupied the Catholic Empire to which they belonged. The only lay prince of any importance on the side of the Catholics was Maximilian I of Bavaria (1573–1641).[5]

The Thirty Years War is traditionally dated from 1618 to 1648. By this time the religious factor had been supplanted by political motives. The first conflict began in Bohemia in 1618, a state that tolerated a variety of religious views. Emperor Mathias, who did not have a biological heir, wanted to assure an orderly transition during his lifetime by selecting Ferdinand of Styria, who had a Jesuit background, and who became king of Bohemia and Hungary in 1617. Ferdinand set about imposing strict Catholicism on his kingdoms. The Bohemians rose in revolt and offered the throne to Frederick V of the Palatinate (1596–1632), who accepted. This brought conflict between the Protestant Union and the Catholic League. The war was short, lasting less than two years, with the Catholics under Ferdinand and Field Marshal Johan Tzerclaes Count von Tilly (1559–1632) prevailing in the climatic Battle of White Mountain, near Prague, on 8 November 1620.

However, the killing did not stop. Those who did not accept Catholicism were persecuted for the next ten years. The Bohemian revolt, although local in nature, was the opening salvo in a series of wars that would last uninterrupted until 1648. As in most conflicts, the war was a mixture of politics and ideology. Recourse to religious argumentation was used to influence and propagandize the masses.

Gustav Adolf wrote that *all the wars of Europe are now blended into one*.[6]

When it was over, great areas of the continent were devastated and one third of the population of central Europe had died.[7]

The Protestant defeat at White Mountain led to the dissolution of the Protestant Union. Frederick V's holdings were confiscated and he was outlawed from the Empire. His territories in the Rhine Palatinate were given to Catholic nobles and the title of elector of the Palatinate was conferred on Duke Maximilian of Bavaria. However, in an effort to outflank the Dutch in their 80-year revolt, the Spaniards occupied the Palatinate.

The fighting did not cease in the Palatinate. The Protestant leadership was taken over by Count Ernst von Mansfeld (1580–1626) and Duke Christian of Brunswick (1599–1626). Most of the engagements against the Spanish were so minor that they were inconsequential. Eventually, both leaders withdrew and took up service with the Dutch. However, Christian became involved in Lower Saxony, and when he withdrew back to the Dutch frontier he was caught by Tilly and soundly defeated in the Battle of Stadtlohn, losing about 80 percent of his 15,000-strong army. Mansfeld and Christian would again appear on the scene after the Danish intervention.

INTERVENTION OF DENMARK

Kristian IV of Denmark watched the developments to the south of his realm with growing concern. Because he was the king of a Lutheran country, as well as the Duke of Holstein, a duchy within the Holy Roman Empire, he found himself in a peculiar situation. Kristian's objectives were first and foremost to extend Danish influence across the great trading rivers of the Elbe and Weser and, secondly, to secure territories for his younger sons.[8] These objectives had virtually nothing to do with religion.

Kristian IV had proven himself an excellent strategist in the Kalmar War (1611–1612), discussed in Chapter 1. This had given him an unwarranted military reputation because he was an uninspiring leader of men and lacked determination. He commanded huge personal resources since all the tolls from transit in and out of the Baltic ended up in the royal coffers rather than with the state. So did the huge ransom extorted from the Swedes. He was therefore probably the wealthiest monarch in Europe and as such well in position to finance a war on his own, or so he thought. In the Riksdag his planned war was as unpopular as it was with the Danish nobles.

A possible Danish intervention also posed problems for Emperor Ferdinand II. Kristian IV was the leader of the most powerful state in the north, and possessed a strong army and a navy rated the first in Europe. Coping with Kristian at the same time as he dealt with rebellious Protestants could be very problematic.[9]

Denmark intervened in June 1625 and the war was known in Denmark as the *Kejserkrig* (Emperor's War). England and Holland promised monetary support and volunteers. Both countries were worried by the northward expansion of the Empire. They were hoping that Denmark would succeed where Mansfeld and Duke Christian had failed.[10] King Kristian believed the time for intervention was right since his arch-rival Gustav Adolf was fully mired in his war in Poland.

The money promised was 30,000 pounds per month from the British and an additional 5,000 pounds from the Dutch, money which never materialized in the amounts promised. As far as troop support, Mansfeld, still in Holland, had 4,000 survivors. He was joined by another 2,000 Britons and 4,000 German, French, and Dutch recruits. Duke Christian of Brunswick recruited three cavalry regiments which marched together across northern Westphalia in October to join the Danes. Tilly, whose army had lost 8,000 troops to plague and hunger, was too weak to stop the reinforcements for the Danes.[11] In addition, Kristian pressured the Lower Saxon assembly to mobilize 12,000 men, though only 7,000 actually appeared.[12]

William Guthrie believes that the intention of Kristian IV in 1625 was first to gather allies in Germany, such as the peasants in Hesse-Cassel.[13] Wilson takes issue with this conclusion and points out that Kristian's activities were focused on Lower Saxony.[14]

Ferdinand II did not want a new war against an opponent which he rated more powerful than events were to prove. The other Hapsburgs in Spain urged Ferdinand to come to an understanding with Kristian IV in order to prevent a new war in the Empire. Ferdinand was willing to contemplate an agreement with the Danes, but before he was willing to carry it out Kristian had to withdraw. But Ferdinand also took military measures. He called upon Field Marshal Albrecht von Wallenstein (1583–1634) to raise a new army and take over the Empire's war effort. Wallenstein was one of the most respected, and feared, military leaders in Europe and he would be assisted by Johan Tilly, another very able field marshal.[15]

The war went nowhere in 1625, the year when the imperial forces were weakest, and Kristian IV must bear full responsibility for the laxity with which it was prosecuted. The movement of his forces across the Elbe west of Hamburg and on to the Weser had no visible military objectives. Tilly blocked his way for further movements by seizing the Weser crossings. Kristian appeared only to be trying to improve his position in preparation for negotiations with Tilly and Ferdinand. Wilson reports that Kristian kept contact with these two opponents by courier as soon as he began operations![16]

By 1626 Kristian IV's ineptitude had lost the opportunity to prevail in the war. He was now confronted by the two best generals in Europe with new manpower by which to prosecute the war against Denmark. Kristian tried to position his army so as to prevent a junction of the forces under Wallenstein and those under Tilly. In early 1626 he concentrated his main army of 20,000 troops at Wolfenbüttel. Wallenstein, with roughly the same number of troops as Kristian, was located at Halberstadt to the southeast while Tilly, with almost the same number, was located on the Weser, with the Hartz Mountains between them.

Kristian IV was finding the war more expensive than he had anticipated. Already in early 1626 he was, despite his wealth, running short of funds, and those promised by England and Holland were not being delivered as promised. When his funds began to run short he found it increasingly difficult to keep his authority over those who had joined him. His ratification of the Hague alliance in early 1626 only made peace with the Empire more difficult and it became obvious that a decision had to be sought on the battlefield.

Wallenstein was also concerned by the operations of Mansfeld, who had 12,000 men at Lauenburg on the Elbe and who was ready to turn Wallenstein's flank by invading Brandenburg. Mansfeld threatened the only permanent bridge between Magdeburg and Dresden, the capture of which would sever Wallenstein's supply line. He moved south, and with his arrival the defenders numbered 14,000. Mansfeld, with only 7,000 troops, was seriously outnumbered. However, he gambled on one final assault, was driven back, and then attacked from the flank by Wallenstein's troops. Mansfeld's cavalry fled and the infantry surrendered.

Facing the two best military leaders in the Empire, the war quickly went downhill for Kristian IV. Kristian knew nothing about the addition of Wallenstein's forces when the war began. Potential allies were busy with their own troubles: England was internally divided; France was in the midst of a civil war caused by a Huguenot revolt; and Brandenburg and Saxony did not want to disturb the relative peace that existed in eastern Germany. In 1627, France and Spain formed an alliance against England.

Kristian IV was forced to retreat. Tilly, having been reinforced by 8,000 troops dispatched by Wallenstein after the defeat of Mansfeld, faced the Danish army near the fortified town of Lutter in on 27 August 1626. The Danes were heavily outnumbered in infantry but had a slight advantage in cavalry. The battle was a bloody affair, particularly for the Danes. The Danish infantry was quickly swept aside, but the cavalry put up a more robust defense. The king was in the midst of the fighting and had his horse shot from under him. The cavalry put up a last ditch defense near the Lutter castle but after the main army had fled along with the king, they surrendered at nightfall. It is reported that 2,500 were captured and that the Danish dead numbered about 6,000.[17] Kristian IV lost about one half of his army.

Wallenstein laid siege to Stralsund in February 1628 but broke if off in July that year. Wallenstein turned his attention to Denmark and overran much of the Jutland peninsula. After a final Danish defeat in the Battle of Wolgast, both sides were ready to negotiate. Wallenstein feared a possible alliance between Denmark and Sweden and he could not knock Denmark out of the war without a fleet to cross to the islands. The war ended with the Treaty of Lübeck in 1629. Kristian IV was forced to agree to stop his support of the Protestants in the Empire.[18]

With the momentum on its side, the Catholic League urged Emperor Ferdinand to restore all Catholic lands lost in northern Germany, primarily church properties. This law of restitution meant for the Lutherans the loss of their lands in addition to their religious freedoms.[19]

Gustav Adolf viewed the beatings inflicted on Kristian IV by Wallenstein and Tilly with mixed feelings. Kristian IV was his arch-rival since the Kalmar War and a dissipation of Danish power was welcomed since it contributed to Swedish dominance of the Baltic. However, he also saw that the defeat of Denmark was likely to seriously weaken the power and resolve of the Protestant states and make it easier for the Empire to establish itself on the Baltic shores.

Gustav Adolf arranged a meeting with Kristian IV in 1629. The purpose was apparently an effort by Gustav to engineer an alliance with the defeated Danes. Wedgwood's account of this meeting is based on Oxenstierna's description found in his correspondence and in Swedish diplomatic history.[20] The meeting, which ended in a shouting match between the two Scandinavian monarchs, was unsuccessful. However, the possibility of an alliance between Denmark and Sweden alarmed Wallenstein. The terms extended to the Danes at Lübeck by the Empire were quickly amended to make them more favorable to Denmark.

REASONS FOR SWEDEN'S INTERVENTION

Historians still argue over the motives that led a country of less than 1,500,000 inhabitants to enter the Thirty Years War. As a schoolboy in Europe during and immediately after World War II, this author was taught that it was a just and glorious intervention to save Lutheranism. This romantic view persists even today. Günter Barudio describes Gustav as an idealistic champion of constitutional principles, of the rule of law.[21] He may have been that, but as Michael Roberts has pointed out, he also had autocratic ambitions, despite a laudable adherence in most cases to Swedish constitutional principles.[22] Furthermore, he did not demonstrate a great respect for the constitutional principles of the German principalities.

Gustav Adolf's motives are more down to earth than religion and constitutionalism. Even his own reasons given to the Riksdag makes this clear.

Sweden is in danger from the power of the Hapsburg; that is all, but it is enough. That power must be met, swiftly and strongly. The times are bad; the danger is great. It is no moment to ask whether the cost will not be far beyond what we can bear. The fight will be for . . . house and home, for Fatherland and Faith.[23]

Gustav also brought the issue of his decision to go to war to the council of ministers. He told them *I did not call you together because I have any doubt in my mind, but in order that you might enjoy the freedom of opposing me if you wished.*[24]

That the religious element is not totally lacking is demonstrated by the first quotation above, but religion and politics had become so intermingled that it is difficult to separate the two. Gustav Adolf had to keep in mind that his family had secured the throne of Sweden at the expense of the legitimate heir on mostly religious grounds. Suffice it to say that religion did not play an important part at the outset of the German war.

The Swedish king and his policy makers had come to the conclusion at the time of the Danish intervention that Sweden would not in the long run be able to stay out of the German conflicts.[25] The one cardinal principle in the foreign and economic policies of all Vasa kings was their drive to control the shores of the Baltic, thus making it a virtual Swedish lake. The presence of the Empire on that coast was intolerable within their overall concept of the future. While Spanish plans to create a fleet in the Baltic did not materialize, it was entirely possible that the Empire, with the assistance of the Hansa League would be able to do so.

The threat to these cardinal interests posed by the Empire was clear. There were also both financial and manpower reasons for selecting a forward strategy as pointed out by Michael Roberts.[26] Sweden had limited economic and human resources and the maintenance of a large military establishment was possible only as long as there were large-scale contributions in both areas from allies and conquered territories.

Wallenstein had besieged the seaport of Stralsund in 1628 when he was in the process of driving the Danes out of north Germany. The reason for Gustav Adolf staying in his Vistula base triangle during most of the early summer that year may well have been his desire to stay near his fleet in order to be able to quickly move to the assistance of Stralsund to keep it from being captured by Wallenstein.[27] The Swedes also sent a small force to bolster the Danish and Pomeranian garrison of Stralsund. This was the time that Gustav Adolf and Kristian IV had their stormy meeting mentioned above. Gustav threatened to enter the war if the siege was not ended, and this, together with a possible Danish-Swedish alliance, prompted Wallenstein to end the siege in July 1628.

FINANCING AND MANPOWER

The degree of urbanization in Sweden was still very limited. The country was essentially composed of farmers and peasants but progress was in motion. The Swedish armament industry had achieved a leading position in Europe in the years before the 1630s. The sales on the European arms market constituted a steady income, supplementing the export of iron and copper. Foreign expertise was brought in to modernize both the mining and gun manufacturing industries.[28]

Nevertheless, one problem that had continually haunted Sweden in its earlier wars, as seen in the previous chapters, was lack of funding. The heavy war debt to Denmark was finally paid in full in 1619, but left a bitter taste among the Swedes. The Swedish army and navy were undergoing expensive modernization that required extensive funds. How then could the Swedes hope to finance a much larger military enterprise against the Empire? Sweden was to field massive armies for its day, comprising over 175,000 troops, fighting against the combined forces of the Empire, Spain, and the Catholic League. The war effort also required the establishment of a substantial navy to protect the army lines of communication between Sweden and Germany. Gustav Adolf and his advisors were aware of these serious problems and the fact that the effort would quickly collapse without a steady and secure flow of funds, supplies, and troops to keep it alive.

Some things had changed to make the situation different from that in previous wars. The constitutional system now in place made the king a virtual partner with the Riksdag and he paid particular attention to keeping good relations with the parliamentarians, as we have seen, by keeping them informed of his plans. The system of raising domestic revenues had been improved along with recruiting efforts, both the responsibility of the Riksdag.

Roberts notes that efforts to increase domestic revenues prior to 1630 failed. Sufficient resources for a large modern army were simply not there.[29] He also notes that incomes from copper and silver actually fell prior to and during the war.[30]

However, for all practical purposes, Sweden controlled the Baltic trade. The country received substantial revenues from tolls levied in the ports of Estonia, Ingria, Livonia, and—as a result of the Truce of Altmark—from Brandenburg, Pomerania, Danzig, and East Prussian ports. The average annual Swedish receipts from the Baltic tolls between 1630 and 1635 were 580,000 riks-dollars and it increased every year in that period, reaching 812,000 riks-dollars in 1634.[31]

The normal state tax revenues could possibly support a permanent military establishment of 20,000 to 30,000 men. When the toll revenues are factored in, those numbers could probably be raised to about 50,000. However, it would not come near that required to support a military establishment in excess of 175,000 men. This is where Gustav Adolf's first principle of war— as Michael Roberts labels it—comes into play. That principle, expressed in a letter from Gustav to his chancellor in 1628, was that war should pay for itself.[32] In this principle, we find one of the keys to why Sweden was able to rise to the level of a great military power. It was based on making use of foreign resources, mainly German, to finance the war.

This principle also meant obtaining subsidies from other countries, mainly France and Holland. France financially supported the Swedish army throughout the war. The support began with 160,000 riks-dollars in 1632 and grew to annual payments averaging more than 400,000. It is ironic that a major Catholic power was the chief contributor to an army that was fighting the core of Catholic power. However, Cardinal Richelieu saw in this war an opportunity to weaken and humble both Spain and Austria, France's two greatest enemies, and would not let religion trump politics. The Dutch provided less than 100,000 riks-dollars in 1631 and 1632, but these were critical years as Sweden was actively seeking mercenaries to bolster its army.[33]

Coalitions were not available to defray the expenses in the early part of the war. Swedish efforts to create an anti-Hapsburg coalition before launching the intervention were fruitless. Most rulers, with the example of Denmark fresh in their minds, feeling that they would be set upon by the emperor's forces under Wallenstein and Tilly, were afraid to commit themselves openly.

The main source of both money and supplies for Sweden was in Germany. Enormous levies were imposed upon occupied territories, those of the enemy, or principalities and cities which bought their safety. The needs of the army were fully taken care of in this manner. Gustav Adolf dispatched highly skilled quartermasters to every region to determine what each of them could provide. They set up offices in various principalities and went about their task in a well organized manner. Michael Roberts writes that *the immediate impact of these procedures upon the Swedish Exchequer was startling: in 1630 the Swedish taxpayer had to find 2,800,000 silver daler for the German war; by 1633 the amount he had to contribute had dropped to 128,000.*[34] He goes on to make a statement more open to questioning:

> *A carefully devised and equitable applied system of 'contributions' was graded according to ability to pay; and since 'contributions' were paid in cash, and the money was usually spent in the area from which it was extracted, the system inflicted less damage on the economic life of Germany than might have been expected: indeed, it depended for its success upon the preservation of a reasonable measure of local prosperity.*[35]

The "contributions" did have a dramatic effect on the Swedish ability to wage a war that "paid for itself." Sven Lundkvist has estimated that after the Battle of Breitenfeld the annual German contributions to the Swedish army were ten to twelve times as large as Sweden's ordinary budget.[36] This is not to say that the Swedes did not pay anything. By the closing years of the war 35 percent of the Swedish budget still went to the military establishment as the homeland needed protection, the navy had to be provided for, and the forces in the Baltic provinces had to be paid.

It is equally obvious that Sweden could not have succeeded in the war by relying on its own manpower mobilization. It should not be surprising that the Swedes solved the manpower problem in a manner similar to that used for finances. Gustav Adolf fielded 175,000 troops in 1632. However, only 18 percent were Swedes, and even that figure declined before the end of the war. The overwhelming majority of troops were those provided by friendly principalities—allies if you will—and hired mercenaries.[37] Mercenary units of a defeated enemy often defected and joined the victor.

All this does not mean that Sweden did not sustain heavy losses. Their troops formed the core of the army and were exposed to heavy fighting. Swedish regiments were often composed of provincial levies and that meant that if such regiments suffered defeat or were badly mauled, the community from whence they came suffered staggering losses that left scars for generations.

PREPARATIONS AND LANDING

The Swedish Riksdag voted unanimously in 1629 to provide the funds thought necessary for a three years' war against the Empire. It was anticipated that the French would provide additional funds as promised by Cardinal Richelieu.

Gustav Adolf spent the winter of 1629–1630 in exhaustive preparations for war. A great amount of armament, ammunition, and equipment was needed. The industries, both government armories and private firms, were pushed to the limit to supply equipment. For example, it has been estimated that an infantry regiment of 576 muskets needed 3,000 pounds of gunpowder, 2,400 pounds of lead, and 3,400 pounds of match each and every month while campaigning.[38] The navy also needed to be strengthened by the addition of a number of warships and transports. Sweden also had to be protected against invasion as did the Baltic provinces.

It is difficult to fathom the gargantuan gamble taken by Gustav Adolf and his advisers. They were about to hurtle a nation of 1.3–1.5 million against the might of the Holy Roman Empire, the Catholic League, and Spain without any prospect of allies. They also had to consider the possibility that Poland, another Catholic state on their left flank, could intervene despite the Truce of Altmark. They could also not assume that Denmark would not make use of the opportunity on their right flank. This gamble shows an immense degree of self-confidence on the part of Gustav and his advisers in the new army they had shaped. Few could have anticipated that the Swedish landing at Usedom off Pomerania would forever change world history.

Sweden's conscription of 80,000 men since 1621 was already a serious drain on the country's population and economy. The lack of money is illustrated by the fact that the 4,000 cavalry in East Prussia refused to move until they received 16 months of pay owed them. Then the 43,000 Swedes and

Finns in the military in 1630 along with the 30,000 mercenaries had to be paid.[39]

Gustav and his advisers estimated that they would need 37,000 troops for the homeland and for protecting their possessions in the Baltic. They also figured that they would need 75,000 men to establish a bridgehead and break out of that bridgehead to secure the north German coastline. The plan was to launch the attack with 46,000 men but this had to be scaled back to 13,600 because of lack of transport. These 13,600 would be joined by the 5,000 Swedes in Stralsund. The Swedes had to resort to transporting a second wave of 7,000 which arrived in the summer, but even in November the size of the landing force was only 29,000, and a third of these were sick.[40]

Gustav Adolf crossed the Baltic in late June 1630, in a fleet of 76 ships equally divided between warships[41] and transports. Delayed by a storm, he did not land on an island in the Oder River estuary until 4 July 1630. His 13,900 men consisted of 92 companies of infantry and 116 squadrons of cavalry.[42] While the Swedish force was puny when compared to the imperial army, it was an elite force composed, to a great extent, of veterans from the Polish wars.

Some happenings in Germany as the Swedes were landing brought them some assistance. Emperor Ferdinand II called the German Electors to a meeting in Regensburg in early July. His purpose for doing so was to obtain their support for war against Holland to assist his ally Spain. He was rudely surprised at what happened next. First, some of the Protestant Electors—Brandenburg and Saxony—refused to attend. Second, the Catholic participants, led by Maximilian of Bavaria, were strongly opposed and refused to agree to war or even the use of German soil by Spanish troops in their war with the Dutch. They also demanded that the emperor dismiss Field Marshal Albrecht von Wallenstein, considered cruel and arrogant even by the Catholics. They also insisted that the army be sharply reduced in size since it cost the states large amounts of money to feed it. Ferdinand reluctantly agreed to these demands and dismissed Wallenstein and disbanded some army units. Consequently, arguably the best general in the empire was not in service when Gustav landed. The reduced imperial army was placed under the command of Elector Maximilian of Bavaria—now the second most powerful man in the Empire—and Field Marshal von Tilly.

The emperor was not as sympathetic to the demands of the Protestants.

The Elector of Saxony, John George (1586–1656), had sent a list of demands to the Regensburg meeting. He maintained that these demands were necessary for any peace in Germany. The main condition was the retraction of the 1629 Edict of Restitution which basically required that all church properties taken over by the Protestants be returned to the Catholic Church. Wallenstein and his troops were brutally enforcing the edict and even some Catholic princes were opposed to it. Ferdinand let it be known that he had no intention of revoking the edict and postponed any discussion of the subject to a future meeting. Instead of having a unifying effect, the Regensburg meeting revealed the considerable amount of unrest and disunity in the Empire.[43]

It was not unrealistic for Gustav Adolf to assume that the political infighting in the Empire would be of considerable benefit to his cause, but he was soon bitterly disappointed. In the words of Dupuy, *although the German Protestants had in the past begged him insistently for protection against the Emperor, now that he was on their shores, most of them cravenly hastened to assure Ferdinand of their support or their neutrality.*[44]

After having landed in Germany Gustav Adolf found himself alone. England was embroiled in internal problems and kept out of the war in Germany. The Netherlands was still at war with Spain and did not want to take on another enemy. Denmark had pledged neutrality and was alarmed by Sweden's growing power in the north. France, feeling abandoned by England, having Hapsburgs on three sides, and not ready for war, could provide no assistance except for subsidies. A mutual defense treaty was not concluded between France and Sweden until 1631.

THE ODER VALLEY, BRANDENBURG, AND POMERANIAN CAMPAIGNS

As he had in the last years of the Baltic war, Gustav's first order of business was to expand his bridgehead and establish a secure operational base for the arrival of supplies from Sweden. The immediate enemy, scattered in numerous garrisons in Pomerania and Mecklenburg, should not have been surprised by the Swedish landing. The preparations that had been going on for a year in Sweden could not have been hidden from spies and informants. Nevertheless, the imperial forces made no effort to contest the landing nor does it appear that they had made any preparations for dealing with such an eventuality.

The commander of imperial forces in this part of the country, General Torgauato Conti (1591–1636), withdrew with most of his forces seventy kilometers up the Oder River to the fortified towns of Gartz and Greifenhagen. Frederico, Duke of Savelli (1595–1649), Conti's deputy, retired with the rest of the forces to Anklam in Pomerania.[45]

Still in the process of establishing a secure operational and logistic base, Gustav Adolf secured Stettin, the capital of Pomerania. He sailed upriver to Stettin on 19 July with about 9,000 troops and debarked downriver from the city. The governor insisted that the Swedish troops withdraw but Gustav demanded to speak to Duke Bogislav XIV of Pomerania (1580–1637).

When the duke arrived, Gustav informed him that he would not tolerate Pomeranian neutrality. The Swedish troops were in the process of deploying into battle formation and Gustav informed Bogislav that if he did not agree the city would be taken by force. As more and more Swedish troops were disembarking, Duke Bogislav yielded to the Swedish demands and the city was occupied the next day. Bogislav was left as the titular ruler of Pomerania, but the Swedes were otherwise in full control. The agreement was spelled out in a treaty. A force of 3,000 Pomeranian troops commanded by Count Damitz took service with the Swedes and later distinguished themselves in battle.

Gustav Adolf issued a manifesto during his stay in Stettin spelling out the reasons for the Swedish invasion of Germany. It was very accusatory toward the emperor about all the unfriendly acts toward Sweden and the persecution of the Protestants. He pointedly left out any reference to the Catholic League as he was still hoping that some of them would come over to his side.[46]

By August, the Swedish army in Germany had grown to 25,000 men, had seized the lower Oder region without any losses, controlled Stralsund, and the Swedish navy had occupied the island of Rügen. In the view of the Swedish king the bridgehead was still too small. Imperial troops still held most of the coast in a semicircle around the bridgehead, preventing overland communication with both Stralsund and East Prussia.

The Swedes began extending the area under their control during August by capturing and fortifying a number of towns on both sides of the Oder River above Stettin. Gustav made another reckless personal reconnaissance of the imperial strong points at Gartz and Greifenhagen and decided they were too strong to be taken with the forces at his disposal. The reconnaissance party rode into an ambush and the king came very close to being captured.

Gustav decided to invade Mecklenburg to secure the ports of Rostock and Wismar. Leaving General Gustav Horn in command at Stettin, Gustav Adolf's plan was to capture these two cities from the sea in order to avoid the sizeable imperial forces between him and the land side of the ports. He sailed to Stralsund to wait for the troops which were to follow. They were delayed for three weeks by a storm and did not bring any heavy artillery.

The Swedish king had to be content with the capture of the nearby smaller ports of Damgarten and Ribnitz. Damgarten surrendered without a fight but Ribnitz held out until 26 September. He was planning to continue westward along the coast when he received intelligence indicating enemy activity at Demmin, a short distance south of Stralsund. General Horn had laid siege to Demmin and an imperial army was advancing to relieve the town. Gustav Adolf took 3,000 men and intercepted and scattered these imperial forces.

While Gustav was dispersing the imperial forces near Demmin, imperial troops from Gartz attacked Stettin on two occasions. They also tried to interfere with the Swedish siege of Kolberg. General Horn had no trouble repelling both efforts. Duke Savilli's forces did capture two small towns near Stralsund held by Swedes. After they were captured, the imperial forces massacred the garrisons. Word of this quickly spread in the Swedish army and the troops swore vengeance.

The Swedes received intelligence in December 1630 that the imperial garrison of Gartz had been reduced to less than 6,000 troops. It was also learned that there was a new commander of the fortress, Count Schaumburg, and that the imperial cavalry had been scattered in nearby villages because of the lack of feed for the horses. The garrison of Gartz was a constant threat to Stettin from the south. The accumulative intelligence and the fact that the enemy was not used to active winter campaigning convinced Gustav Adolf that this was a good time to remove the threat.

Gustav Adolf moved south on Christmas Eve 1630 with a force composed of 8,000 infantry, 6,000 cavalry, and both siege and field guns. A river flotilla carrying equipment for a floating bridge accompanied the army. The fortified town of Greifenhagen on the right bank of the Oder was an intermediate objective.

The imperial forces were totally surprised by this winter offensive. Nevertheless, Colonel di Capua, the commandant of Greifenhagen, put up a strong resistance. However, after the siege guns had battered down the city wall, Gustav personally led an assault through the breach. The Swedes were repelled twice but broke into the town on the third try. Colonel di Capua realized that the situation was hopeless and surrendered the town. The Swedish losses were minor.

Gustav continued his southward move toward the fort on the right bank of the Oder River that protected the bridge leading to Gartz. The garrison of the fort withdrew to the left bank of the river as soon as they saw the Swedish advanced guard, burning the bridge in the process. They did not know that the Swedes also had a force approaching Gartz on the left bank of the river. When the Swedish force on the left bank approached, accompanied by a river flotilla, Count Schaumburg threw his heavy guns into a marsh, set fire to the town, and fled into Brandenburg. The Swedes launched a cavalry pursuit, one detachment heading towards Küstrin, one towards Landsberg, and a third towards Warte with the intention of cutting off the imperial retreat at the bridges located in those towns. However, the Brandenburg commander at Küstrin refused passage over the Oder River to the Swedes. Gustav decided that he would, for the time being, respect his brother-in-law's neutrality. Count Schaumburg and the remnants of his troops eventually escaped to Frankfurt on Oder.

Except for a few small besieged garrisons, the imperial forces had been cleared from Pomerania. The winter campaign had been very disconcerting to the imperialists, conditioned to feel safe in their winter camps. They were not equipped for winter warfare. The Swedish troops, on the other hand wore fur-lined coats and boots, and had fur lined head cover and gloves. But an even greater advantage over the imperial troops was the skill and vigor of the Swedish commanders who had demonstrated a complete dominance in these early encounters.

The imperial commanders were beginning to get a taste of Gustav's abilities, a person who Tilly had derisively referred to as "the snow king who will quickly melt in the German sun." Emperor Ferdinand, when told about the Swedish invasion, is reported to have said, "So we have another small enemy, do we." He would also soon change his mind.

By the beginning of 1631 the Swedes had established a large and secure operational base along the lower Oder River and in Pomerania. Gustav Adolf still felt unable to advance deeper into Germany, however, because his routes were blocked by the two most important Protestant states in this part of the country, Brandenburg and Saxony. Both states were clinging to neutrality and would not let Swedish troops pass through their territories. In one way, their reluctance is understandable. They had recently witnessed the crushing defeat of Kristian IV of Denmark at the hands of Tilly and Wallenstein. They felt that the same fate might befall the Swedes and they would be left to face the consequent fury of the Empire while all the Swedes had to do was withdraw across the Baltic.

This left Gustav Adolf, after six months in Germany, with no allies if we disregard the "forced" alliance made with Duke Borislav. The Elector of Saxony, John George, called a meeting of all Protestant states in February 1631. The stated purpose of this meeting, which took place in Leipzig, was to coordinate policies for the upcoming negotiations with Emperor Ferdinand over the grievances caused by the Edict of Restitution. In a manifesto issued in April 1631 they took a strong stance against the edict and the taxes levied to support the armies of the Empire. The manifesto, signed by the Electors of Saxony, Brandenburg, and a number of other princes and free cities, warned the emperor of consequences beyond their control if their demands were not addressed, without specifying what these consequences might be. In order not to offend Ferdinand, no mention was made of the Swedish invasion, as if it did not exist. Plans were made for a Protestant defensive alliance, the Leipziger Bund, with an army of 40,000. It appears that this alliance was as much directed at the Swedes as it was at the Empire—a form of armed neutrality.[47]

Gustav Adolf sent an emissary to the Leipzig meeting. This emissary had instructions to stress Sweden's resolve to prosecute the war, with or without their help, until the rights of the German Protestants were fully secured. However, it became evident that John George and the other Protestant representatives were hoping to obtain concessions from the emperor without having to go to war.[48]

French contributions to the Swedish war effort had so far been only a promise. Richelieu had internal problems to cope with but the promised subsidies were finally pinned down in the Treaty of Bärwalde (which was actually an alliance between France and Sweden) on 23 January 1631. The French promised a subsidy of 200,000 thalers twice annually for the next five years—

the life of the treaty. For their part, the Swedes were obligated to maintain a force of 30,000 infantry and 6,000 cavalry in Germany. Gustav Adolf also promised not to make a separate peace for the next five years and not to disturb the domains of Maximilian of Bavaria, who had a secret alliance with France.[49]

The Swedish king insisted that the Treaty of Bärwalde be made public. Cardinal Richelieu would have preferred not to do this since it revealed the cardinal's dealings with a Protestant power. He finally agreed to the demand of the Swedish king. Gustav had wanted to have the treaty made public for two reasons. First, it showed that France and Sweden were equal, and one not doing the biddings of the other. Second, a provision of the treaty allowed any other state or principality to join. It was therefore an invitation to the Protestant principalities to rise in revolt against the Empire.[50]

Meanwhile, the battlefield was active. With his base area secured, Gustav Adolf continued his southward drive up the Oder River valley. First, he reduced the remaining imperial strongholds in Pomerania. The well-fortified town of Demmin, held by Duke Savelli, was the first to be attacked. Its garrison of 1,700 troops resisted the siege for two days before they surrendered. Savelli and his troops were permitted to retire with the honors of war. The same happened to Kolberg, which surrendered on 2 March after a five months' siege.[51]

Field Marshal Tilly finally moved into Pomerania and attacked the town of Neubrandenburg. The Swedish garrison gave a good account of themselves, but the town was taken by storm and the defenders were all killed. The town was thoroughly pillaged by the imperial troops. The Swedes had expected that Tilly's next target would be either Stettin or the besieged town of Greifswald, but instead he withdrew southward to Neuruppin. His plans were apparently to join Field Marshal Gottfried von Pappenheim who was besieging Magdeburg.

Gustav Adolf did not follow Tilly but decided to move against Frankfurt on the Oder in the hope that this would draw Tilly away from Magdeburg. The attack on Frankfurt was made by a very strong force and for the first time Gustav ignored his brother-in-law's declaration of neutrality by marching across Brandenburg territory from Schwedt. The Swedish army consisted of 14,000 troops with 200 pieces of artillery. The advance, which began on March 27, 1631, took place on both sides of the Oder River. The main force was on the left bank. As was done earlier, Gustav made use of the river for the transport of supplies, bridging equipment, and artillery. The Brandenburg garrison of Küstrin, seeing the size of the Swedish force, opted not to offer any resistance and allowed the Swedes to pass. They reached Frankfurt on the Oder on 2 April 1631.

While Gustav Adolf was planning to storm the city, he began siege operations as a means to deceive the defenders. The imperial garrison consisted of 6,000 troops, with several prominent commanders among them. The surprise assault by Swedish infantry took place on 3 April after a heavy bombardment by artillery directed against the walls and concentrated on selected city gates.

The Swedish infantry quickly crossed the moat, and using ladders and explosives penetrated or topped the walls in one determined assault. The defenders were unable to put up an organized defense and were systematically killed, with the Swedes calling out *"Neubrandeburg quarter,"* a reference to the earlier slaughter of the Swedish garrison of that town. The streets of Frankfurt were soon littered and obstructed by bodies. Count Schaumburg was among those killed. As a further revenge for the massacre at Neubrandenburg, the city was turned over to the soldiers to plunder for three hours, but with instructions that civilian lives were to be spared. The imperial losses were 2,700 (1,700 killed and 1,000 captured), with the rest of the garrison managing to escape.

The capture of Frankfurt on the Oder was followed by the capture of Landsberg. Its garrison of 4,000 surrendered after a short fight. The capture of Frankfort and Landsberg completed the Swedish security operations for their hold on Pomerania.

THE TRAGEDY OF MAGDEBURG

Meanwhile, there were dissensions in the imperial ranks. Wallenstein, no longer in the imperial service, refused to provide any supplies or shelter for Tilly's troops. He even threatened to join the Swedes.[52] It appeared that the 72-year-old Tilly was unsure about what to do after his earlier stab at Stettin. At the urgings of his cavalry commander, von Pappenheim, who was involved in the siege of Magdeburg, he decided to join his impetuous cavalry colleague. Magdeburg, a large and prosperous, largely Protestant city located on the Elbe River, had sought Swedish protection after twice refusing to let imperial forces enter. In fact, Magdeburg had rejected imperial authority and allied itself with Sweden as early as August 1630.

Tilly may have realized that it would be difficult for the Swedes to come to Magdeburg's assistance, since doing so would require the crossing of considerable hostile or neutral territory—particularly Brandenburg and Saxony. He may have calculated that a successful siege of Magdeburg would produce one of two results: If Gustav tried to cross Saxon territory without permission it could place that large state securely in the imperial camp. On the other hand, if Gustav did not undertake to violate Brandenburg and Saxon territories, there was a good chance that Magdeburg would fall now that the besieging force numbered at least 25,000. The failure of the Swedes to come to the aid of Magdeburg would prove their impotence in protecting their allies.

If these were his thoughts, they may well have worked except for the atrocious behavior of the besieging army. Gustav Adolf was in a dilemma. He knew that Magdeburg was in imminent danger but his hands were tied. In fact, the only thing Gustav was able to do was to send Colonel Dietrich von Falkenberg (1580–1631) to help organize the defense of the city.

To get to Magdeburg the Swedish army would have to cross Brandenburg and Saxony, and the electors of these two principalities maintained strict neutrality and refused free passage. That meant that the Swedes would have to fight for all the bridges across the intervening rivers and that would delay their relief attempt. Furthermore, he risked driving both Brandenburg and Saxony into the imperial camp, or at least keeping them from becoming valuable allies. Nevertheless, he issued an ultimatum to his brother-in-law, Elector George William of Brandenburg (1595–1640). Gustav told him that if he did not give up Spandau and Küstrin voluntarily, he would take them by force. This brought results. George William agreed to turn the two fortified towns over to the Swedes for the duration of the Magdeburg emergency.

Saxony was a different matter. Elector John George, with an army of 40,000, could not be treated in the same way as George William. John George refused Gustav's request to use the bridges at Dessau and Wittemberg. The Swedish relief army was forced to halt at the Havel River.

While Gustav Adolf watched helplessly from Brandenburg, the Magdeburg situation went from serious to grave. Colonel Falkenberg had only 2,000 men at his disposal to counter the 25,000 battle-hardened imperial troops.

Tilly and Pappenheim were exerting relentless pressure, and the outworks of the defenders were lost by the end of April 1631.[53]

Both Gustav Adolf and Tilly were anxious—Gustav for reaching some agreement with John George that would allow him to go to the aid of Magdeburg, and Tilly because he feared an alliance between Saxony and Sweden that would jeopardize his operations. His army was already running short of supplies. That explains the relentlessness with which the siege was being conducted. The imperial troops kept up a heavy bombardment of both the walls and the interior of the city. The morale of the inhabitants was also declining, and Catholics in the city informed Tilly about that condition as well as weak points in the defense works. Some of the defenders, knowing what usually happened to a city being stormed, also had begun to argue for surrender, and the city council appeared to have reached this point in mid-May. Tilly gave the city a final ultimatum: surrender or face destruction.[54]

The city council was debating this demand on the morning of 20 May while Tilly's messengers waited for an answer. This was the moment the imperial army launched its final attack. It is not clear how the attack took place in the middle of a peace parley. Some have blamed the treacherous behavior on Tilly, but others, with perhaps more logic, have put the blame at the feet of Pappenheim. The surprise was complete and Colonel Falkenberg was killed in the first onslaught. The defenders were killed or scattered and the imperial troops entered the city. The worst massacre of the Thirty Years War—which was full of massacres—began.

Magdeburg was given up to plunder after its seizure. The imperial soldiers had suffered from hunger and the winter weather during the six-plus months of the siege. They now exacted a horrendous retribution from the helpless inhabitants of Magdeburg. Hollway writes that the imperial officers vainly tried to control their men.[55] This is not likely. Captured towns were normally turned over to troops for a specific period of time for looting and pillaging, and commanders seldom or never interfered in the conduct of their troops during this period. In addition, as pointed out by Hollway, some of the captive women were brought to the imperial camp and this is unlikely to have happened except by the knowledge and approval of Pappenheim and/or Tilly. The story that they were brought to the camp to save them from the fires rings hollow.

The first chapters of Defoe's *Memoirs of a Cavalier*, with its vivid description of the massacre and burning of Magdeburg, was the first account to reach English readers. Wells writes that these chapters give the reader a far better idea of the warfare of this time than any formal history.[56]

During the pillage and plunder, fires sprung up almost simultaneously in various parts of the city. These blazes were whipped into a firestorm in the narrow streets with their wooden structures. The raging fires spared neither civilians nor soldiers, and it took three days before it burned itself out, leaving Magdeburg in charred ruins. Only the stone cathedral remained standing. Out of a population of 30,000, less than 5,000 survived the fires and the killing of the uncontrolled soldiery. The bodies of the victims were thrown into the Elbe River in order to prevent an outbreak of plague.

It has never been established how and why the fires started. It is unlikely that Tilly gave the order to destroy the city. He needed the considerable supplies stored there as well as the plunder from its wealth. However, he may have been indirectly responsible by giving the city over to a rabble of drunken soldiers to pillage and plunder.

Europe, particularly Germany, was horrified by the fate of Magdeburg's population. The impact of this event on Protestants can hardly be overestimated. The city had been a symbol of successful Protestant resistance to the Empire. Until the fall of Magdeburg, Emperor Ferdinand II could count on some loyalty from the Protestants, particularly the Lutherans, despite the Edict of Restitution. Now that fledging loyalty was lost as thousands of pamphlets appeared all over Germany accusing the emperor of having been seduced by the Jesuits who wanted to turn the Empire into an absolute monarchy like Spain.[57] The reaction was not limited to Germany. The Netherlands concluded a treaty with Gustav Adolf on May 31 which pledged subsidies for the Swedish army. While most of the Protestant principalities in Germany mobilized their armies in the wake of Magdeburg, they still continued the policy of neutrality.

Gustav Adolf expected Tilly to move against him, and he prepared to meet him near the Havel River. Since Gustav was criticized for failure to come to the aid of Magdeburg, he issued an angry statement putting the blame squarely on the Elector of Saxony for denying Swedish passage through his territory.

Gustav was still worried about not having a secure line of communication to his base in Pomerania through Brandenburg, and decided to immediately rectify that situation. He appeared in Berlin with a small force and aimed his artillery at the Elector's palace. Then he gave his brother-in-law George William a blunt ultimatum. George William signed an agreement with Gustav which turned over Spandau and Küstrin to the Swedes for the duration of the war. His brother-in-law also promised to pay a subsidy of 30,000 thalers per month. The agreement was sealed with a family feast.[58]

Tilly did not move against the Swedes as Gustav had anticipated, but remained in the vicinity of Magdeburg. This gave Gustav an opportunity to further strengthen his position in Brandenburg and Pomerania, and several towns on the lower Elbe and Havel were fortified. Gustav meanwhile sent General Åke Tott against Greifswald, the only remaining imperial position in Pomerania. General Tott captured that place on 25 June after a very short siege. Tott was promoted to field marshal and entrusted with the conquest of Mecklenburg, and by midsummer he had accomplished his task except for the capture of Rostock, Wismar, and Domitz, which he blockaded. Gustav reinstated the Duke of Mecklenburg who had earlier been evicted by the emperor.

NOTES

1. I will refer to the Holy Roman Empire as "The Empire" and troops of the Empire as "imperial" or "imperialist."

2. Wells, *op. cit.*, volume II, p. 652.

3. Wilson, *Thirty Years War.*, pp. 197–423.

4. Richard S. Dunn, *The Age of Religious Wars, 1559–1715.* Second Edition. (New York: W. W. Norton & Company, 1979); Geoffrey Parker, *Europe in Crisis 1598–1648.* Second Edition. (Malden, Massachusetts: Blackwell Publishers, 2001).

5. Samuel Rawson Gardiner, *The Thirty Years War 1618–1648* (New York: Scribner, Armstrong & Co., 1874). Kindle edition, p. 15.

6. As quoted in Anthony Pagden, *Worlds at War: the 2,500-year Struggle Between East and West* (New York: Random House, 2008), p. 305.

7. *Loc. cit.*

8. Wilson, *Thirty Years War*, p. 387.

9. Fletcher Pratt, *The Battles That Changed History.* Originally published by Doubleday in 1956. (Minneola, New York: Dover Publications, Inc., 2000), p. 176.

10. Wilson, *Thirty Years War.* p. 385.

11. *Ibid*, p. 391.

12. Paul Douglas Lockhart, *Denmark in the Thirty Years War, 1618–1648* (Selinsgrove: Susquehanna University Press, 1996), pp. 108–141.
13. William P. Guthrie, *Battles of the Thirty Years War: From the Battle of Wittstock to the Treaty of Westphalia*. e-Book Edition. (Westport, Connecticut: Greenwood Press, 2003), p. 119.
14. Wilson, *Thirty Years War*, p. 387.
15. Dupuy, *Gustav Adolphus*, p. 47.
16. Wilson, *Thirty Years War*, p. 390.
17. C. V. Wedgwood, *The Thirty Years War* (New York: The New York Review of Books, 2005)—Originally published in 1938, p. 205.
18. Paul Douglas Lockhart, *Denmark 1513–1660: The Rise and Decline of a Renaissance Monarchy* (London: Oxford University Press, 2007) p. 170.
19. For a comprehensive discussion of the law of restitution, see Wilson, *Thirty Years War*, pp. 446–454.
20. Wedgwood, *op. cit.*, 243.
21. G. Barudio, *Gustav Adolf der Grosse* (Frankfurt am Main: S. Fischer, 1982).
22. Roberts, *Gustav Adolphus*, pp. 26–28.
23. As quoted by Montross, *op. cit.*, p. 265.
24. As quoted in *Ibid*, pp. 267–268.
25. Sven Lundkvist, "Die schwedischen Kriegs- und Friedensziele 1632–1648" in Repgen, editor. *Krieg und Politik: Europäische Probleme und Perspktiven* (Munich: 1988), p. 223.
26. Michael Roberts, *The Swedish Imperial Experience* (Cambridge, 1979), pp. 28–36.
27. Dupuy, *Gustav Adolphus*, p. 47.
28. Ronald G. Asch, *The Thirty Years War: The Holy Roman Empire and Europe, 1618–48.* (New York: St. Martin's Press, 1997), p. 101.
29. Roberts, *Gustavus Adolphus*, Volume 2, pp. 43–44.
30. Ibid, volume 2, pp 80–104.
31. *Ibid,* volume 2, p. 84.
32. Roberts, *The Swedish Imperial Experience*, 1992 Edition, p. 52.
33. See Geoffrey Parker, editor, *The Thirty Years War*, (New York: Routledge, 1997) pp. 124–125 and Günter Barudio, *Der Teutsche Krieg*, (Frankfurt am Main: S. Fischer, 1985).
34. Roberts, *The Swedish Imperial Experience*, 1992 edition, p. 53.
35. *Ibid,* pp. 52–53.
36. As reported by Roberts, in *ibid*, p. 53.
37. *Ibid*, p. 44.
38. Montross, *op. cit.*, pp. 268–269.
39. Wilson, *Thirty Years War*, p. 459.
40. *Loc. cit.*
41. The Swedish Royal Navy consisted of 54 vessels, with the 32-gun *Mercury* as flagship,

42. Montross, *op. cit.,* p. 169.

43. Dupuy, *Gustavus Adolphus*, pp. 71–72 and Wilson, *Thirty Years War*, pp. 454–458.

44. Dupuy, *Gustavus Adolphus*, p. 73.

45. *Ibid*, p. 75.

46. Parker, *The Thirty Years' War*, p. 109.

47. Asch, *op. cit.*, p. 105 and Parker, *The Thirty Years' War*, pp. 116–118.

48. Parker, *The Thirty Years' War*, pp. 106–107.

49. Dupuy, *Gustavus Adolphus*, pp. 73–74; Asch, *op. cit.*, p. 105; and Parker, *The Thirty Years' War*, pp. 111–112.

50. Wedgwood, *op. cit.*, pp. 268–269.

51. Dupuy, *Gustavus Adolphus*, pp. 84–85.

52. Don Hollway, "Triumph of Flexible Firepower" in *Military History*, February 1996, p. 40.

53. Dupuy, *Gustavus Adolphus*, pp. 88–89.

54. Hollway, *op. cit.*, p. 41.

55. *Ibid,* p. 39.

56. Daniel Defoe, *Memoirs of a Cavalier: A military Journal of the Wars in Germany, and the Wars in England. From the Year 1632 to the Year 1648.* Edited with Introduction and Notes by Elizabeth O'Neill, 1922. Kindle Edition. Also Wells, *op. cit.* volume II, p. 652.

57. Asch, *op. cit.*, p. 106.

58. Dupuy, *Gustavus Adolphus*, p. 91.

4

The Breitenfeld and Rhine Campaigns

*Means must be devised to check this imperious
Visigoth, since his success will be fatal to
France as to the Empire.*

CARDINAL RICHELIEU

START OF THE CAMPAIGNS

By early summer 1631, the Swedes controlled northeastern Germany—Pomerania, Mecklenburg, and Brandenburg. With his base and his line of communication secured, Gustav Adolf advanced down the Havel River to the Elbe with an army of about 7,000 infantry and 3,000 cavalry. The river being low due to an exceptionally dry summer, the Swedish army managed to ford it between the imperial positions of Werben and Burg. The surprised imperial garrison surrendered Tangermünde on 2 July 1631 after little opposition.

The strategic situation changed with the capture of Tangermünde. The Swedes were across the Elbe in strength and the imperial forces withdrew their outposts on the eastern bank. A rich farming area sorely needed was available to Gustav Adolf's troops. The Swedes had now outrun the maps they had brought from Sweden, and this shows that their penetration of the country was quicker than had been expected.[1]

Gustav Adolf was in the process of concentrating his forces, and since he found Tangermünde unsuitable for such an assembly, he decided to move north to Werben, on the western bank of the Elbe at the confluence of that river with the Havel. This place was heavily fortified and a floating bridge (boat-bridge) connected the camp to the Elbe's eastern bank. The location, at the confluence of the Havel and Elbe rivers, placed Gustav Adolf in an excellent strategic position since he could strike out in several directions. The drawback was the single bridge that would have to be used in case of a withdrawal. Gustav Adolf also built two small forts on the right bank of the river to serve as a bridgehead against unforeseen contingencies.

On the eve of his first campaign deep inside Germany it is time to update the description of this unusual military leader. It had become obvious that Gustav Adolf was adored by his men, and this was to be demonstrated in the campaigns to follow. He shared with them the dangers and hardships in campaigns and led from the front in battle, recklessly at times. By the time he began his campaigns in Germany he was already recognized as one of the three leading military commanders of the time, along with Field Marshals Wallenstein and Tilly. As already noted, he is the only great captain in history, other than Genghis Khan, who created the military system he brought to war. Both the man and his system were about to be tested.

Gustav did not wear armor since it was hurtful to a wound he had received at Dirschau during the Polish campaigns. His example was followed by his musketeers who used only a pot helmet. Many infantry soldiers were beginning to question the usefulness of armor because, as more effective firearms were developed, they produced more serious wounds than the medical personnel of the time were used to handling. The reduction of weight also made the infantryman more mobile. Most pikemen and heavy cavalrymen, however, continued to wear body protection.

The Swedish king was always visible to his men and in the thick of the actions. Montross writes: *No more Homeric figure has ever emerged from the pages of military history. The blond and burly king was to them* [his men] *a symbol not only of the cause and faith but also of a stirring national adventure.*[2]

THE BATTLE OF WERBEN

While Gustav Adolf was establishing himself at the confluence of the Havel and Elbe, Field Marshal Tilly had moved into Hesse-Cassel. One of Gustav's objectives in moving to Werben was to keep Tilly away from that principality. Tilly stayed in Hesse-Cassel, provisioning his troops and trying to convince the landgrave to join the imperial cause. The landgrave, however, entered into an alliance with Gustav Adolf instead.

Tilly received a message from Field Marshal Pappenheim requesting assistance in defending Magdeburg against a possible advance by the Swedish army. The combined imperial army of 27,000 men positioned itself at Wolmirstädt, north of Magdeburg, awaiting developments. On 27 July 1631, Tilly sent three cavalry regiments on a reconnaissance towards Werben.

Although Gustav had only 16,000 men in Werben, he took quick action to counter Tilly's cavalry thrust.[3] On 1 August 1631 Gustav personally led a force of 4,000 Swedish cavalry in a surprise attack on the imperial cavalry detachments at Burgstall and Angeren. The imperial cavalry were scattered with heavy losses, including all their baggage. Gustav, as usual, exposed himself recklessly, and narrowly escaped death or capture.

From captured prisoners the Swedes gained important information for their future operations. They had worried that Tilly might drive past Werben into Mecklenburg, but the information received confirmed that he intended to attack Werben.

Tilly was reportedly enraged by this cavalry setback at the hands of the Swedes.[4] He immediately moved against Werben with a force of 15,000 infantry and 7,000 cavalry. Tilly was anxious for battle but the sight of the Swedish defenses cooled his desires. He had expected to catch the Swedes in halfway prepared positions, but instead found they were formidable. The Swedish habit of immediately preparing defensive positions whenever they stopped had paid off.

When he arrived at the Swedish fortified camp, Tilly opened fire with his sixteen heavy guns, and the Swedish artillery immediately replied. The fighting on the first day was limited to sorties and heavy skirmishing outside the Swedish perimeter.

The artillery duel and skirmishing continued on the second day. Then Tilly received intelligence to the effect that on that day a German unit in a sector of the enemy perimeter would mutiny and spike[5] all the Swedish guns in that sector. While Tilly was suspicious about the veracity of his informant, he had no way of confirming it and decided it was not something he could ignore.

Tilly launched a full-scale assault on the Swedish entrenchments at the time indicated by the intelligence, but it was met by concentrated and accurate fire from Swedish artillery and musketeers. The imperial attack was repulsed with heavy losses. As the imperial infantry withdrew, they were struck in the flank by the Swedish cavalry under Colonel Wolfgang Henrik von Baudissin (1597–1646). This scattered the imperial infantry and they fled the field. Tilly's losses were estimated at about 6,000 killed and wounded and many troops deserted after the debacle.[6]

It was in Gustav Adolf's interest to keep Tilly at Werben because the Swedish king expected significant reinforcements within a few days; but for the moment, Tilly withdrew to Tangermünde. While this battle and its results are confirmed in virtually all sources, the German military historian Hans Delbruck fails to mention it.[7]

Werben, and what followed, also had important political implications. The Swedish king's advisers—and the king himself—had become disillusioned and cynical by the behavior of the German Protestant princes. One of his advisers, Lars Grubbe, recommended that the Swedes establish a forward defense line along the Elbe and then withdraw to Sweden.[8] Gustav's own mental reservations are illustrated by what he told his council on 15 July 1631, that the Protestants in Germany "are no further disposed towards us than that they may be maintained by us against the Emperor, and that they may put themselves under the protection of our arms for the recovery of their freedom; after which they will be ready, one and all, to drive us away with violence and ingratitude."[9]

Sweden's only enthusiastic supporters were Philip Reinhold von Solms (1593–1635) and Bernhard of Weimar (1604–1639). Bernhard was actually present at Werben and distinguished himself in the fighting and was given a Swedish command. He remained loyal to the king until the latter's death.

Tilly was compelled to give up his plans against Hesse or making another move against Werben. The small force he had left to keep an eye on things in Hesse was quickly dispersed by the forces of Landgrave William V (1602–1637) of Hesse-Cassel. William V had now irrevocably committed himself, and an alliance was concluded between Sweden and Hesse-Cassel at Werben in August 1631.[10]

IMPERIAL CAPTURE OF LEIPZIG

Tilly had in the meantime received orders from Emperor Ferdinand to move against Saxony and to force Elector John George to pledge allegiance to the emperor and disband his army. So far Saxony had escaped war damage, and Tilly knew that he would be able to find supplies for his army in that area.

Elector John George kept up his vacillation to the very last, even after receiving an ultimatum from Tilly when the latter reached the Saxon border. John George refrained from an immediate answer, probably hoping to gain better terms from Gustav Adolf. Tilly did not procrastinate after finally receiving a negative answer from the elector. He had received reinforcements bringing his field strength to 36,000. He needed supplies for this larger force and without any further ceremony he moved into Saxony.

This action on the part of Tilly finally energized Elector John George. He contacted Gustav Adolf and asked for help. Negotiations began immediately as the imperial forces began plundering and ravaging the territory. They had captured Halle and Merseburg, and on 8 September Tilly was approaching Leipzig. After his demands for supplies were refused he began siege operations while devastating the surrounding countryside.

A treaty of alliance was signed between Gustav and the elector on 11 September 1631. The Swedes undertook to provide protection for Saxony, and in return the elector agreed to place his army under Gustav Adolf's command, give the Swedish army one month's pay, furnish it shelter and food, and make no separate peace with the Empire.

Delbruck writes that Tilly was eager for battle; but he implies that Gustav Adolf showed timidity and reluctance to meet Tilly in a decisive showdown, even after his alliance with John George, and therefore, in Delbruck's opinion, showed little strategic foresight.[11] While Gustav showed personal recklessness in battle, he was a careful and prudent planner. He was not at all sure about the steadfastness of his new allies, despite their splendid attire.[12]

This may have influenced his initial plan after linking up with the Saxons at Düben, 40 kilometers north of Leipzig. He may also have wanted to feel out John George. Gustav suggested to Elector John George when the two met on 15 September that they maneuver around Leipzig to wear down the imperial forces before a general engagement.[13] It may also have been a way to shift the blame for a setback on the Electors of Brandenburg and Saxony.

John George, anxious to relieve Leipzig and spare Saxony from devastation, insisted on bringing Tilly to battle. He was supported by William, the Elector of Brandenburg. Gustav was apparently pleased by the display of offensive spirit and determination from the electors, and agreed.

The very next day, 16 September, the Swedes and their new allies marched toward Leipzig to force Tilly to give battle. However, the garrison of Leipzig, apparently unaware that help was on its way, surrendered to the imperial forces on the same day as Gustav and his army were approaching. The imperial troops had taken an enormous amount of plunder in Leipzig and now, with the Swedes and their allies approaching, they had to stop their looting.[14]

There are also no solid indications that Tilly was adverse to a showdown with the Swedes. There was near parity in the forces involved, and Tilly may have shared Gustav's opinion on the steadfastness of the Saxon army. While no reinforcements were available for the Swedes, there were significant forces on the way to join Tilly from south Germany. One corps, under General Johan Aldringen (Field Marshal in 1632) had already reached the vicinity of Jena and could reach Tilly within a few days. This army corps was reportedly 6,000 men strong. Tilly could have taken up a position behind the Elster and waited for Aldringen—the combined force would have given him considerable superiority.[15]

Delbruck, in note 11, page 216, volume IV, refers to Walter Opitz' contention that—in case the Swedes refused battle—Tilly wanted to move from Leipzig to the Elbe to gain a crossing and have Field Marshal Tiefenbach join him from Silesia. After the juncture of the two forces, Pappenheim was to drive into Mecklenburg, in the rear of the Swedish army.[16]

Tilly's subordinates, particularly Pappenheim, were clamoring for a showdown with the Swedes. Pappenheim reportedly considered Tilly, at age seventy-two, too old and cautious to face the Swedes in battle. Pappenheim is alleged to have gone as far as believing that Tilly was almost senile.[17] Then there probably was the enthusiasm of the imperial troops and subordinate commanders. They were accustomed to victory and fully expected Tilly to deliver one.[18]

Several authors repeat the story that Pappenheim forced a general engagement by undertaking a reconnaissance in force on 16 September. He is alleged to have sent back a report that he was heavily engaged with Swedish forces and requested assistance. Tilly decided to go to Pappenheim's rescue. This engagement probably never took place since there is no mention of it in the very detailed Swedish records. There is still the possibility that Pappenheim fabricated the whole report about an engagement. From most accounts, Tilly was resolved to fight without such drama by Pappenheim.[19] When moving out he left a garrison of about 1,000 to hold the city of Leipzig.

BATTLE OF BREITENFELD

Both sides converged on a relatively broad rolling plain north of Leipzig, stretching for miles. It was an ideal battleground for the large armies of that period, with no obstacles in the form of rivers or woods. This type of terrain also ruled out the element of surprise.

It was Tilly who selected the actual place of battle. It was located about seven kilometers north of Leipzig and straddled the road from Düben to Leipzig. He positioned his forces facing generally to the north on a gently sloping ridge between the villages of Breitenfeld and Seehausen. From here, the long-range imperial artillery could dominate the nearby plain, particularly the marshy Lober stream about two kilometers below the crest of the ridge. Tilly undoubtedly expected that the enemy formation would become a bit disorganized in crossing the marsh and stream under artillery bombardment. They would also have to fight with their backs against the stream after crossing it.

There are several differences in the sources when it comes to this savage engagement. This is to be expected in most cases, but it is nevertheless surprising considering that this is one of the decisive battles in world history. Some of these discrepancies will be noted as we go along.

STRENGTH OF THE OPPOSING SIDES

The size of the Swedish army is variously reported as 13,000[20] to 26,800.[21] The Saxons are reported as ranging in numbers from 12,000[22] to 18,000. The imperial and Catholic League forces are estimated at from 36,000 to 40,000. The writer who gives the largest total for the allied (Swedes and Saxons) in the battle is Fuller who places their total at 47,000.[23] The sources are in general agreement that Tilly had a numerical superiority of 2,000 to 3,000 in cavalry. Most sources fail to give the strength of the opposing artillery but Liddell Hart gives the Swedes a superiority of about 100 tubes versus 36 for the imperial forces. Parker notes that the imperial army was supported by 27 field guns while the Swedes and their Saxon allies had 51 heavy guns and every regiment each had their field guns.[24] Delbruck writes that the allies had 75 artillery pieces to 26 for the imperialists. Liddell Hart, Parker, and Delbruck are probably close to the actual number when the regimental guns are counted.

ORDER OF BATTLE

Gustav Adolf and his army approached the imperial position from the north along the Düben road. They observed the imperial forces in a battle formation that stretched almost 4 kilometers from flank to flank.

The two armies must have presented a spectacular, if mixed, sight. The imperial army and the Saxons were arrayed in impressive uniforms, while the Swedes were simply dressed in home-spun cloth. Furthermore, the Swedes had soiled clothing as they had slept in the open field the night before the battle and looked in the words of Colonel Monro *like kitchen-servants, with their uncleanly Rags*.[25]

Tilly's original disposition of his forces has been one of the most controversial aspects of the battle. Historians have differed on whether Tilly deployed his forces in one or two lines. Two lines was the customary way to deploy, and Liddell Hart believes that this practice was also followed by Tilly at Breitenfeld.[26] The infantry was formed into the usual "Spanish squares" but the exact number of squares is also controversial, the range being from thirteen to eighteen, including a reserve in the rear.[27] The squares varied in size from 1,500 to 2,000 men; most likely most of them were nearer to 1,500 based on the number of troops taking part. The line of troops had open flanks; that is, they were not anchored on some natural obstacles such as creeks or woods. The squares of pikemen were protected, as customary, by detachments of musketeers at the corners. (The Swedes did the opposite, using pikemen to protect their musketeers.) The depth of the infantry squares, with their own flank protection, actually made anchored flanks unnecessary. The 1,500-man squares are believed to have been 30 deep and 50 wide.[28]

The imperial artillery was posted in front of the infantry squares. The heavy pieces were positioned on the ridge, in front of the right wing.[29] The lighter artillery, perhaps some 20 guns, were in front of the center.[30] About 5,000 imperial cuirassiers, the famous Schwartzreiters, were on the imperial left flank under the command of Pappenheim. Generals Fürstenburg and Isolani commanded the cavalry on the imperial right, with 3,100 Catholic League troopers and 900 Croats. The heavy cavalry was also ranged in masses of about 1,000 each and with a depth of ten ranks. The few light cavalry units were distributed between the infantry squares. The 7,000 imperial troops under Fürstenburg had just arrived and were still tired, but morale was high as *the men had an invincible courage, believing they would be victorious*.[31] These

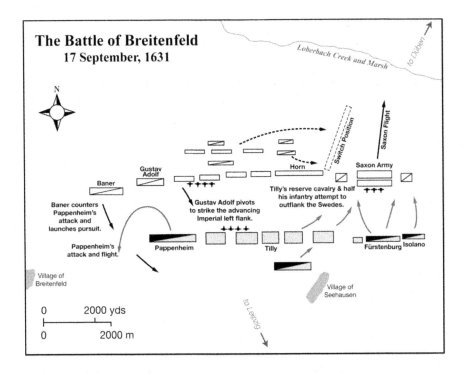

The Battle of Breitenfeld
17 September, 1631

Loberbach Creek and Marsh

to Düben

N

Switch Position

Saxon Flight

Gustav
Adolf

Baner

Horn

Saxon Army

Tilly's reserve cavalry & half
his infantry attempt to
outflank the Swedes.

Baner counters
Pappenheim's
attack and
launches pursuit.

Gustav Adolf pivots
to strike the advancing
Imperial left flank.

Pappenheim's
attack and flight.

Pappenheim

Tilly

Fürstenburg

Isolano

Village of
Breitenfeld

Village of
Seehausen

to Leipzig

| 0 | 2000 yds |
| 0 | 2000 m |

formations and their deployment had enabled the Hapsburgs to conquer half of the known world.

The Swedes and Saxons had camped about eight kilometers to the north of Breitenfeld on the evening of 16 September.[32] Gustav Adolf spent most of the night in a war council with his commanders and allies while his troops slept in the open field. Gustav had the drums beat assembly at first crack of dawn. The Swedes skipped breakfast, and after a short prayer the allies began moving south along the Dürben road in the direction of Leipzig and Tilly's campfires. They advanced in a line which was about five kilometers long. They were marching with the sun and wind in their eyes. The day turned out to be unusually hot and the wind was strong, out of the south or southwest.

The general battle dispositions had been agreed to during the war council. Gustav Adolf decided to place the Saxon army on his far left, separated from the Swedes. Gustav had doubts about the quality of his allies. They had trained only since April and were not organized along the lines of the battle-hardened Swedish veterans. These concerns undoubtedly influenced his battle dispositions.

An important factor—very familiar to those who have seen combat, and backed by voluminous research—is the value of comradeship in the will to fight. Troops "who have developed a sense of loyalty to each other are likely to fight with great commitment to one another and make personal sacrifices."[33]

This factor makes it important to place troops who know each other in proximity of one another for greater strength under pressure. A unit will gladly carry the brunt of a struggle to rescue its comrades. Not to do so would earn them the contempt of their comrades and fill them with shame and remorse. Years of campaigning had convinced Gustav that this factor was valuable, and it undoubtedly played a central role in the location he selected for the Saxon army.

The terrain was so clear of obstructions that the army marched in full battle array while still far away from Tilly's positions. When the two armies came within sight of each other the allies apparently moved to the right in order to deprive the enemy of some of the advantages of the sun and wind.[34] I have found no evidence of any unplanned movement to the right. The allied army had to leave the Dürben-Leipzig road by angling to the right in order to reach the imperial positions that were located to the right of that road.

What may have given rise to the conclusion that the allied army had shifted to the right was the fact that when the deployment was completed, the Swedish right extended beyond the imperial left. The fact that the mass of Tilly's army was not located in the center of his line but to the right of center also contributed to the conclusion that the Swedes had shifted to the right. The more open Swedish formations, the quarter mile gap Gustav intentionally left between the Swedish left and Saxon right, and the slight numerical superiority of the allies also meant that their battle line was considerably longer and therefore extended past the imperial left.

Since it may be helpful to the reader at this point, I have repeated a few passages from Peter Wilson's translation from Philipp Bogislaw von Chemnitz, who lived at the time of the battle:[35]

The King of Sweden deployed his men in two lines, each of a body mainly of infantry, flanked by two detachments of cavalry. . . . Between the cavalry regiments, particularly in the first line, the king had placed a good number of detached musketeers, partly from General Johan Banér's Regiment that was entirely musketeers, and partly from the strongest regiments. The weak infantry regiments were amalgamated in the center to make stronger brigades and the first line consisted of four infantry brigades. . . . In the second line there were three brigades . . . The great cannons were moved in front of the centre [and] each brigade had its own regimental pieces for its own defence, each pulled by one horse, or moved by two or three men if necessary, that could be turned and fired very quickly.

The allies broke into columns in order to ford the Lober stream. It took several hours to cross a marshy stream, which was more of an obstacle in the 17th century than today, and arrive within cannon shot of the imperial line. Tilly could have attacked while the allies were still crossing the stream but did not.

The allied armies redeployed into line in front of the imperial positions under enemy long-range artillery fire. The Düben-Leipzig road formed a natural boundary between the Saxons and the Swedes.

The Swedish center, commanded by Gustav, consisted of four mutually supporting infantry brigades in the first line with a cavalry and Scottish infantry regiment as a local reserve behind it. Behind this local reserve was a second line of three infantry brigades, again arranged to be mutually supporting, and behind that there were two cavalry regiments in general reserve.

The Swedish right wing was commanded by General Johan Banér (promoted to Field Marshal in 1634). He was also Gustav's second in command. Banér had five cavalry regiments in his first line with four companies of musketeers in the intervals between the cavalry regiments. There was one cavalry regiment in local reserve behind the first and second lines. The second line consisted of four cavalry regiments. Both the cavalry and musketeers were formed in squares six ranks deep.

The Swedish left wing was under the command of Field Marshal Gustav Horn. This flank was much weaker than the right. Horn's first line consisted of three cavalry regiments with two companies of musketeers in the intervals. His second line consisted of two cavalry regiments. It may have been that Gustav Adolf had foreseen that problems would develop on the left wing near where the Saxon army was positioned.

The Saxon army, a quarter of a mile to Horn's left, was commanded by Field Marshal Hans Georg von Arnim from Brandenburg, Gustav Adolf's opponent during his Polish campaign in 1629. How the Saxon army was organized for battle is not known, but it can be safely assumed that it was formed in the traditional manner with infantry in the center and cavalry on the wings.

The Swedish regimental artillery was positioned in front of their respective units. The reserve artillery, under General Lennart Torstensson, moved forward in front of the Swedish center, prepared to go into action when the battle started.

THE BATTLE

The Swedes and Saxons emerged from the Lober in the midst of a thick cloud of smoke from the imperial artillery and dust whipped up by the wind across the Breitenfeld plain. A steady stream of heavy cannon balls poured through the dust cloud from the imperial artillery on slightly higher ground and with the wind and sun at its back.[36] It was not until almost midday that the Swedish artillery, in front of their infantry, began to reply to the imperial guns. The Swedish guns were able to fire three times as fast as the imperial ones. This artillery duel lasted about two and a half hours. The imperial infantry got the worst of the exchange because their heavy phalanx-like formations were virtually impossible to miss and the effect was often disastrous in their closely packed ranks. The more open Swedish formations were more difficult to hit, but the crowded Saxon ranks took a beating. Hollway writes that Gustav Adolf shifted his entire line to the right in order to avoid the dust and smoke.[37] I have found no convincing evidence that this alleged shift took place.

After enduring the pounding by the quick-firing Swedish artillery for over two hours, Pappenheim on the imperial left had had enough. Without waiting for orders from Tilly, he launched an attack on the Swedish lines. In a sweep well to the west so as to avoid Swedish musket fire, he led his 5,000 black cuirassiers in a thunderous charge against the flank of the Swedish right wing. Tilly was dismayed at seeing this impetuous action on the part of his subordinate, but there was nothing he could do.

In accordance with accepted cavalry tactics, the German heavy cavalry on their large mounts trotted towards the Swedish line. As they came within range of the waiting Swedes—about 30 meters—the cavalrymen in the front rank fired their pistols, then wheeled to both sides to let the next rank fire.

This process, known as the caracole, was repeated by each rank. Gustav's combat groups of musketeers and horsemen had been drilled for such an emergency. They wheeled around so that the second line stood at right angles with the first. While the Swedish regimental guns poured a hail of death into Pappenheim's squadrons, the musketeers stepped forward, knelt, fired, and reloaded while the next rank stepped forward to do their business.

The musket fire inflicted huge losses on the German cavalry. The Swedish cavalry remained in place until the musketeers completed their work, and then joined in under the cover of the light artillery and muskets, then fell back. Seven times the German heavy cavalry charged the Swedish flank. The Swedish combined arms teams performed their tasks with lightning speed and effectiveness. Montross writes that, *Pappenheim, the scarred veteran of a hundred charges, endured the worst half hour of his life as his men dashed themselves to pieces against this flexible human redoubt.*[38]

Things were approaching a climax on the Swedish right wing. When Pappenheim's seventh attempt shattered against still unbroken formations, General Banér ordered the reserve regiment and the Swedish light cavalry to charge the flank of the imperial cavalry. Pappenheim's feared Black Cuirassiers were thrown into complete disorder and suffered overwhelming losses. Most of the survivors fled, pursued by the Swedish light cavalry. Then Banér personally led the cavalry regiments of the Swedish right wing forward in a crushing charge that utterly destroyed the left wing of the imperial army. The Swedes swept over the remaining imperial cavalry and rode down an infantry regiment that Tilly had sent to support Pappenheim.

Critical events were meanwhile taking place on the Swedish left wing. General Fürstenburg, seeing Pappenheim's charge on the other side of the field, may have concluded that a signal had been given for a general assault. He launched his cavalry against the Saxon army, sending General Isolani's Croats to sweep around its flank. Within a short half hour the whole Saxon army was in full and disorderly flight, leaving the left flank of the Swedish army exposed.[39] Elector John George fled with his troops and is alleged not to have stopped his flight until he was 24 kilometers from the battlefield.[40] His fleeing troops stopped only long enough to plunder the Swedish supply train. The Saxons lost about 1,000 men, mainly during the initial artillery duel and imperial pursuit. Only two Saxon cavalry regiments of experienced soldiers remained on the battlefield to join Field Marshal Horn.[41]

Visibility was becoming very difficult as a result of the gunsmoke and dust stirred up by thousands of feet and hoofs. General Fürstenburg was beginning to lose control of his cavalry, which was engaged in pursuing the fleeing Saxons as well as in plundering their abandoned baggage. Fürstenburg reached the abandoned Saxon positions about 1530 hours after outrunning his infantry—which had been sent forward in a piecemeal fashion. The lack of follow-up gave Field Marshal Horn the time to form a front at a right angle to the rest of the army and this line was reinforced by infantry from the second line of the center as well as reinforcements sent by Gustav Adolf. In this formation, Horn was easily able to disperse the troops Fürstenburg was able to gather.[42]

With the sudden departure of the Saxon army, the imperials enjoyed a decisive numerical advantage, perhaps by more than three to two. Things looked bleak for the Swedes as it appeared that the fortunes of war had turned against them. In a somewhat misleading statement, Delbruck describes the situation after the flight of the Saxons as *the Swedish army was enveloped simultaneously on both flanks.*[43] Achieving a double envelopment had been both the dream and nightmare of commanders since the Battle of Cannae. It would have been more correct for Delbruck to state that the imperial army tried to envelop both flanks, attempts that failed rather miserably.

Up to now, in the words of Liddell Hart, it had been a *soldiers' battle* with neither of the two supreme commanders controlling the action.[44] This was about to change. For Gustav, his subordinates had the battle well in hand. Tilly, seeing the Saxons fleeing, saw a chance to regain control of the action, despite the disaster to his left wing, and deliver a decisive blow against the Swedes. He ordered the right half of his "Spanish squares" to move obliquely opposite the exposed Swedish left flank, already overlapped after the flight of the Saxons. The captured Saxon guns were turned by imperial troops to fire down the line of Swedish troops. Liddell Hart saw Tilly's maneuver as perhaps the origin of Frederick the Great's famous *oblique order* of attack.[45]

It speaks to the discipline of the imperials that they were able to turn their massive squares around to perform this maneuver; but the going was slow. Their move and attack became disorganized and the hoped-for shock action never took place. Tilly's remaining infantry squares remained in position on the ridge, and in effect became the left flank of the imperial army.

Gustav Adolf may have been disappointed by the flight of the Saxons but he was surely not surprised. His deployment had been made with this possibility in mind. He was also not disappointed in the actions of his subordinates or well-trained troops in this crisis. To help Field Marshal Horn, two regiments of the general reserve were placed under his command, and Horn quickly turned his entire command to the left. This operation was covered by detachments of musketeers sent to hold the gullies parallel to the Düben-Leipzig road.

As the massive and ponderous imperial squares, supported by cavalry, trudged up to the Swedish left flank they found themselves facing a strong and well organized defensive position. This position consisted primarily of a line of musketeers supported by the feared quick firing regimental guns.

Having assured himself that the left wing was thus secure, Gustav rode quickly to his right flank. General Banér was ordered to charge the left flank of the massive squares attacking Horn's forces with whatever cavalry he could spare from the right flank.

A gap had developed in the imperial center when the right "Spanish squares" were ordered by Tilly to move obliquely against the Swedish left flank. With Horn holding along the Düben-Leipzig road and Banér's cavalry charge causing consternation in the massive squares facing Horn, the time had come for Gustav Adolf to administer a decisive blow against the imperial army from which it could not recover.

Placing himself at the head of four crack cavalry regiments—East Goth, West Goth, Småland, and Finland—he led a devastating full-speed charge at the flank of the imperial artillery and the massive squares left there when Tilly moved half of them against the Swedish left.[46] The imperial artillery was immobile as the 30 horses required to move each gun had been sent to the rear at the start of the battle. The Swedish cavalry swept over the gun positions killing all gunners who had not already fled. The captured guns were then turned against the imperial infantry masses still deployed on the ridge, resulting in a deadly crossfire from their own guns and those of Torstensson's reserve artillery. The artillery balls tore bloody pathways in the imperial lines as the Swedish musketeers and cavalry closed to complete the work of destruction. The imperial left wing was quickly reduced to a mass of confused and stumbling survivors.

A short time earlier, Tilly, who had been in process of achieving a perfect double envelopment, had now—in much less than two hours—found that his own situation had become desperate. His left flank troops were slowly being ground to pieces and his right flank had failed to make any progress against Field Marshal Horn's positions. Tilly was rapidly losing control of the battle.

Seeing the disorder in the imperial lines, Gustav Adolf now ordered the second and final blow against his opponent. In an amazing move he pivoted his whole center and right wing ninety degrees to their left. The Swedish center swept over the ridge, pushing the disintegrating imperial right wing before them. This move also served to cut the imperial army off from retiring on Leipzig.[47]

The left wing of Tilly's army was completely shattered, the Swedish cavalry repeatedly charging the milling masses of what had been the "Spanish squares," and the Swedish artillery as well as their own captured guns were, between the cavalry charges, creating gaping holes in the infantry masses. The infantry squares were quickly disintegrating. Tilly's army had become a mass of fleeing fugitives, and *as dusk fell over the field the Swedes rode into the milling fugitives to inflict "Magdeburg quarter."*[48]

How Tilly escaped from the battlefield is not certain. He had been wounded at least three times during the battle and barely evaded capture on one occasion. The wounds were not fatal. Delbruck speculates that he fled with the remnants of Fürstenburg's cavalry which had tried to strike Field Marshal Horn's wing from behind and were cut down in the process. He also has Tilly withdrawing toward Halle while other writers have him making an overnight stop in Leipzig before realizing that the city could not be held.[49] Haythornthwaite, on the other hand, writes that Tilly escaped with the survivors of the four regiments which made a last stand in the woods behind the original positions.[50] This is perhaps a more logical explanation of Tilly's escape than that provided by Delbruck, but we just don't know.

After an apparent short overnight stop in Leipzig, Tilly fled to Halle and from there to Halberstadt. This is where he joined with Pappenheim and they set about collecting the remnants of the once proud army. From Haberstadt the retreat continued to the Weser.

Not everyone describes the end as a total rout. Wilson writes that the *battered infantry retreated in good order to make a last stand at a wood behind their original positions.*[51] The 600 survivors of the veteran Belgian infantry regiments in those woods apparently did make their escape in relatively good order.

Pappenheim also managed to assemble some of his fleeing survivors and tried to join Tilly. One "Spanish square" on the right wing of the imperial army that had not taken part in the fighting after the flight of the Saxons, also headed in the direction of Leipzig without having been severely battered. Aside from these isolated exceptions, the imperial withdrawal cannot be described as orderly. Tilly's army had, in effect, been destroyed, and the casualty figures support this contention. Liddell Hart writes that the evening of September 17, 1631 saw *the long invincible Imperial army, under the iron heel of which all Germany had lain prone in ruin or terror, scattered to the winds, not merely defeated but destroyed for all practical purposes of resistance.*[52]

THE HUMAN COST

The Battle of Breitenfeld was the major turning point in the Thirty Years War. It was also the first great battle of modern times; it was a watershed. It was the first real contest between the old Spanish method of assembling and deploying troops in cumbersome masses intended to crush all resistance by sheer weight, and the mobile, flexible, and hard-hitting organization and tactics of Gustav Adolf. It was a victory of maneuver, vastly increased firepower, and excellent cooperation of the combined arms teams.

Wilson notes that later commentators have regarded what happened at Breitenfeld as the inevitable outcome of an allegedly superior military system.[53] By later commentators he is apparently referring to Geoffrey Parker as one who appears to credit all the success to the military system.[54] While what Parker writes is true, it fails to tell the whole story. A weapon or a system is only as good as the person wielding it. If it had not been for Gustav Adolf and his immediate subordinates employing the system they had created in an almost flawless manner, their quick and decisive actions while under great stress, and the iron discipline of the Swedish troops, the battle could well have ended with a different outcome.

The completeness of the Swedish victory is well illustrated by the casualties suffered by both sides. It was, as noted by Liddell Hart, a victory of dramatic decisiveness. Over 7,000 imperial soldiers were dead on the field. About 6,000 were captured on the battlefield—some wounded—while an additional 3,000 were captured by 19 September. The number of wounded among the imperial forces is not known but those who straggled away from the battlefield were set upon by Saxon peasants and butchered by the hundreds in revenge for their earlier pillaging.[55] The imperial army lost all its artillery, its entire baggage train, and the imperial field treasury. The vast majority of those captured entered Swedish service. In this manner, the Swedes, who had sustained 2,100 casualties in killed and wounded, ended up with a larger army after the battle than before. One hundred twenty enemy standards were captured and sent back to decorate the Riddarholm Church in Stockholm.[56]

The Swedes did not launch a determined and sustained pursuit of the defeated enemy. Failure to launch one immediately may have had something to do with the element of fatigue. However, failure to aggressively follow Tilly later can only be labeled a mistake. The Swedes may have felt that the destruction of the imperial army was so complete that a vigorous pursuit was not necessary. The facts appear to support this conclusion since Tilly could rally only 600 survivors and Pappenheim 1,400 after the battle. However, it was important to complete the destruction. Tilly and Pappenheim were able to gather 13,000 men while at Haberstadt, and this could serve as an important nucleus for a future build-up.

A sheepish John George showed up at the Swedish headquarters the day after the Battle of Breitenfeld to apologize for the conduct of his army. He assured Gustav that the army was being reorganized and would soon join the Swedes. Gustav treated the Saxon elector with dignity and kindness, giving the Saxons the honor of re-occupying Leipzig.[57]

Gustav proceeded to Merceburg with a force of 1,500 cavalry. That town was taken on 19 September and from there he proceeded to Halle, which fell on 21 September. He thereafter returned to his army near Leipzig to plan for further action.

AFTERMATH OF THE BATTLE

In both military and historical aspects, Breitenfeld ranks as one of history's most decisive battles. It was the first major Protestant victory in a long war full of defeats, and it immediately resulted in transforming the military and political situation.[58]

Breitenfeld's military importance lies in the fact that it was the first great contest between the old military system and the new one, based on Gustav's military theories of open flexible formations and firepower. His leadership and tactical skills were considerable. A new era of warfare had dawned, and henceforward Gustav Adolf became the schoolmaster for every thoughtful military leader. Breitenfeld was of sufficient importance alone by making Gustav Adolf one of the great captains of history.[59]

In political terms Breitenfeld stopped forever the previously irresistible drive by the Empire to turn all of Germany into a Catholic province. It demonstrated to the still vacillating princes that there was a bright new star in the heavens by the name of Gustav Adolf, and served to convince them that they needed to hitch themselves to this star. To the masses, Gustav became the rescuer and protector of the Protestant cause. Several writers attest to the fact that Vienna was *struck dumb with fright* when news arrived about what had happened at Breitenfeld.[60] This defeat came about the same time as an entire Spanish fleet set to land an army in Holland was destroyed. This became the turning point in the Dutch war of liberation.

STRATEGY AFTER BREITENFELD

I have always been baffled by Gustav Adolf's seeming inactivity immediately after the Battle of Breitenfeld. That battle took place on September 17 and the reason given for a failure to immediately pursue and destroy the imperial army is that the troops were too tired. Troops flushed with victory and seeing the possibility of a final defeat of their hated enemy can do extraordinary things. Instead, Gustav lingered around Leipzig for almost two weeks.

What to do next became the main subject of a war council held by Gustav Adolf after his return from the capture of Halle. Gustav Adolf's strategic options included pursuing and destroying the enemy before they could recover from the shock of the Breitenfeld defeat. Another option was to move to the Rhine and take control of a region rich in resources for his army. Finally, he could march directly on Vienna. Whatever option he selected needed the wholehearted support of his German allies. To obtain that support the Swedish king held his high-level war council in Halle.

Of these three options, Gustav Adolf selected the one that was least decisive. To me, the Swedish king allowed himself to take his eyes of the ball— the destruction of the enemy army. The military historian Lynn Montross observes that *Like Hannibal after Cannae, Gustav had placed himself in a position to choose between an assault on the head or the limbs of a reeling enemy. And like the Carthaginian, he took the less dramatic of the alternatives . . .*[61] The alternative chosen allowed his able opponent Field Marshal Tilly to escape and rebuild his forces. It also allowed the recalled Field Marshal Wallenstein to begin assembling a new army.

Gustav Adolf's Saxon and Brandenburg allies as well as most of his military commanders wanted to head straight for Vienna. Oxenstierna, his Chancellor, was one of the strongest advocates of this option, although he was not present at the war council. Gustav—impetuous in battle but a careful strategic planner—felt that a direct thrust at Vienna was premature and he decided to move to the Rhine. In this way he would be able to base himself in the Protestant Palatinate and easily supply his army from the fertile surrounding territories.

Gustav has been criticized for this decision, especially by Oxenstierna at the time, who maintained, after the king's death, that doing so would have quickly turned the Thirty Years War into a Fifteen Years War. Many historians have criticized Gustav Adolf for his failure to advance on Vienna and end the war while the imperial leadership was still demoralized and paralyzed by the disaster at Breitenfeld. One military historian notes that *never again did the imperial power appear so shaken, or its seat so defenseless, as on the morrow of Breitenfeld.*[62]

We have to remember, however, that the Empire was a formless entity with no real center of gravity. The emperor could simply have fled to another part of his empire to carry on the war, and Vienna would thereby lose its military and political importance. Fuller addresses this issue:[63]

> . . . *the road which ran to Vienna was bad; it passed through the forests of the Erzgebirge and the devastated lands of Bohemia, and winter was near. Secondly, Vienna was not the capital of a united nation, but the residence of a shadow emperor . . . Thirdly, Gustavus, hundreds of miles from his base, could not afford to risk a rising behind him; the loyalty of the Electors of Brandenburg and Saxony was suspect and Bavaria would hug his flank. . . .*

These were undoubtedly Gustav's concerns, particularly the loyalty and military reliability of his Saxon ally. In fact, later Wallenstein twice pried him loose from southern Germany by threatening his lines of communications and the loyalty of his allies. The Swedes also needed the fertile lands along the Rhine to feed their army—the Catholic areas of Würzburg, Cologne, Mainz, Worms, Bamberg and Spires. The resources of this area would thus also be denied to the Empire. The Swedes would thereby sever the imperial link between Italy and their forces in the Netherlands.

Gustav Adolf's decision has much in common with the decision of Alexander the Great after the Battle of Issus. Instead of giving in to the temptation to strike at the heart of the Persian Empire, Alexander deferred that drive until after he had secured his base area and lines of communications.

Having decided on a course of action, the Swedish army headed west to the Rhine while the reorganized Saxon army invaded Silesia and Bohemia. By winter Sweden and her allies controlled most of the Empire north of a line from Mannheim to Prague.

The Swedes occupied Würzburg on 16 October. From there they pushed on to Frankfurt on Main and then to Mainz, which surrendered on 22 December after a token two–day siege. He occupied both banks of the river Rhine, and that alarmed his ally France and led Richelieu to make the statement found at the beginning of this chapter.[64] Richelieu was alarmed by Gustav's formation of a Protestant league that could be as dangerous to France as it was to the Empire. Richelieu wanted the imperial power contained, not destroyed.

Moving into this area may also have been part of his plan to make "war pay for itself." Pomerania, Mecklenburg, Brandenburg, Saxony, and Magdeburg were already paying considerable sums for the maintenance of the Swedish army in Germany. Würzburg was ordered to pay 150,000 thalers in October 1631 and this was followed by 200,000 thalers only nine months later. Mainz was given a deadline of twelve days to come up with 80,000 in December 1631. Cologne and Trier were ordered to pay 40,000 per month into the Swedish treasury to prevent a Swedish invasion. The region along the Rhine River as far as the Neckar River had a 45,000 thalers tax per month levied on it. The "contribution" system was a beacon for corruption. Colonel Baudissin was suspected of keeping for himself 50,000 thalers of the money collected from Thuringia in late 1631. A Swedish commissioner accepted a bribe of 6,000 thalers for a significant reduction in the original demands on Würzburg.[65]

In the meantime, Tilly was able to rebuild his army to almost 38,000 men within less than two months after the Breitenfeld debacle by calling in garrisons from the northwest part of Germany. It appears to have been the field marshal's intention to go to the rescue of Würzburg but he was too late to do anything about that situation. He then turned towards Nuremberg and laid siege to that city. When Gustav Adolf turned in his direction with 26,000 troops, Tilly raised the siege and withdrew to take up positions on the Danube near Donauwörth to shield Bavaria from the Swedes. The Swedes returned to the Rhine.

The quick buildup of imperial forces reinforces my belief that Gustav Adolf should have gone after Tilly, Pappenheim, and Maximilian of Bavaria in the immediate aftermath of Breitenfeld. He had ample reasons to break his promise to the French not to molest Bavaria since his promise was based on the condition that Bavaria not take any hostile action against him. Maximilian had shown hostility by harboring Tilly and Pappenheim.

Instead of moving immediately against Tilly in Bavaria, Gustav spent the winter in Mainz dealing primarily with political and administrative matters. For unfriendly occupied territories that did not join the Swedes, a "government-general" was established at Frankfurt on Main under Oxenstierna. It was responsible for collecting funds and supplies for 120,000 troops in preparation for the next campaign.

The political/military league Gustav Adolf envisioned was one under his direction to guarantee Sweden's long-term security, and the treaties made with his Protestant allies contained a clause acknowledging the existence of a Swedish protectorate to remain even after the fighting ended. Pomerania was expected to become Swedish territory.

However, the Swedish army did not remain idle in the period between the Battle of Breitenfeld and the 1632 campaign. An energetic recruiting campaign was carried out to bring the strength of the army to the planned 150,000 level. General Banér (not promoted to field marshal until 1634) was sent to the middle Elbe south of Magdeburg, while Field Marshal Tott was given the mission of consolidating the lower Elbe region. Forces were also moved from East Prussia to strengthen the Pomeranian garrisons.

Within three months of the Breitenfeld victory, the Swedes had subdued all of the Rhineland, formed alliances, forced all the Catholic principalities along the Rhine to declare neutrality, and defeated and driven the Spanish troops that intervened back to Holland.

NOTES

1. Roberts, *Gustavus Adolphus*, volume 2, p. 518.
2. Montross, *op. cit.*, p. 268.
3. This is the figure given by Dupuy, *Gustavus Adolphus*, p. 92 and is probably fairly accurate. Roberts, *Gustavus Adolphus*, volume 2, p. 519 gives the figures as 15,000 troops, including 6,000 cavalry and 150 pieces of artillery. Reinforcements which would bring the strength to 24,000 were on their way.
4. Dupuy, *Gustavus Adolphus*, p. 92.
5. Spikes driven into the powder touchhole of cannon rendered the guns useless.
6. Charles Francis Atkinson, *Thirty Years War* (London: Encyclopaedia Britannica, 1911). Kindle Edition, p. 24.
7. See for example, Roberts, *Gustavus Adolphus*, volume 2, pp. 520–521; Thomas Harbottle, *Dictionary of Battles*. Revised and Updated by George Bruce (New York: Stein and Day, 1971), p, 302; Richard Ernest Dupuy and Trevor N. Dupuy, *The Encyclopedia of Military History from 3500 B.C. to the Present* (New York: Franklin Watts, Inc., 1969), p. 537; and Delbruck, *op. cit.*, volume IV, chapters V and VI.
8. Roberts, *Gustavus Adolphus*, volume 2, p. 521.
9. *Ibid,* p. 522, quoting Swedish archives.
10. *Ibid*, p. 526.
11. Delbruck, *op. cit.*, volume IV, pp. 202–203.
12. Roberts, *Gustav Adolphus*, volume II, p. 534, note 1.
13. Dupuy, *Gustavus Adolphus*, p. 95 and Delbruck, *op. cit.*, volume IV, p. 203.
14. Paul K. Davis, *100 Decisive Battles from Ancient times to the Present: The World's Major Battles and How They Shaped History.* (New York: Oxford University Press, 2001), p. 210.
15. Delbruck, *op. cit.*, volume IV, p. 203.
16. Walter Opitz, *Die Schlacht Bei Breitenfeld Am 17 September 1631.* Originally published in 1892. This is a facsimile reprint of the original. (Whitefish, Montana: Kessinger Publishing, LLC, 2010), p. 76.
17. Joseph Cummins, *History's Greatest Wars: The Epic Conflicts that Shaped the Modern World* (Beverly, Massachusetts: Fair Winds Press, 2009), p. 121.
18. See Haythornthweite, *op. cit.*, p. 37 and Liddell Hart, *Great Captains*, p. 128.
19. For example, Guthrie, *op. cit.* p. 23 and Haythornthwaite, *op. cit*, p. 37, repeat the old story that Tilly was reluctant, but was forced into battle by Pappenheim who was convinced the Saxons were rabble and the Swedes weak. Wilson, *The Thirty Years War*, p. 473 and note 32, p. 892, maintains that Tilly was eager for battle and refers to his correspondence with Maximilian of Bavaria.
20. Davis, *op. cit.*, p, 210. I assume the figure is a misprint for 23,000.
21. Dupuy, *Gustavus Adolphus*, p. 96. His figures are basically in agreement with those provided by Roberts, *Gustavus Adolphus*, volume 2, p. 535 as well as those given by Montross, *op. cit.*, p. 275.

22. Pratt, *op. cit.*, p. 183.
23. J. F. C. Fuller, *Military History of the Western World*, volume II (New York: Da Capo Press, 1999 [originally published in 1955]), p. 58.
24. Parker, *The Military Revolution*, p. 23.
25. Monro, *Expedition*, p. 189.
26. Liddell Hart, *Great Captains*, p. 127.
27. Dupuy, *Gustavus Adolphus*, p. 96, writes that the imperial forces had no reserve. I believe he is mistaken as will be shown later.
28. Parker, *The Military Revolution*, p. 24.
29. Cummins, *op. cit.*, p. 122 has the imperial artillery behind the center and wings. I don't see how this was possible. The gunners had to be able to see their targets and could not do so from behind the massed infantry. He also writes that the artillery duel lasted five hours while other sources state that it lasted 2 to 2 ½ hours.
30. Dupuy, *Gustavus Adolphus*, p. 97.
31. Wilson, *The Thirty Years War*, p. 473, quoting Jurgen Ackermann, *Jurgen Ackermann, Kapitan Beim Regiment Alt-Pappenheim, 1631* (German 1895 Edition p. 18). This antiquarian book is available in facsimile reprint by Kessinger Publishing, LTC, Whiteface, Montana, 2009.
32. Fuller, *op. cit.*, p. 59, claims that the Swedes bivouacked only one mile from the imperial battle position but this is obviously not so based on other sources.
33. Frank Tallett, *War and Society in Early-Modern Europe 1495–1715.* (New York: Routledge, 2001), p. 49.
34. Delbruck, *op. cit.*, volume IV, p. 204.
35. Peter H. Wilson, *The Thirty Years War: A Sourcebook* (New York: Palgrave Macmillan, 2010) pp. 231–233, quoting from Philipp Bogislaw von Chemnitz, *Königlich Schwedischer in Teutschland geführter Krieg*, (Stettin 1648 in 4 volumes; Stockholm, 1653; New Swedish edition published in 1855–1859 in six volumes), 1 part 3, p. 32.
36. Hollway, *op. cit.*, p. 42.
37. *Loc. cit.*
38. Montross, *op. cit.*, p. 277.
39. Liddell Hart, *Great Captains*, p. 132.
40. Cummins, *History's Greatest Wars*, p. 122.
41. Wilson, *The Thirty Years War*, p. 475.
42. *Loc. cit.*
43. Delbruck, *op. cit.*, volume IV, p. 205.
44. Liddell Hart, *Great Captains*, p. 132.
45. *Loc. cit.*
46. Pratt, *op. cit.*, p., 184.
47. Dupuy, *Gustavus Adolphus*, p. 103.
48. Montross, *op. cit.*, p. 277.
49. Delbruck, *op. cit.*, volume IV, p. 207.
50. Haythornthweite, *op. cit.*, p. 40.

51. Wilson, *The Thirty Years War*, p. 475.
52. Liddell Hart, *Great Captains*, p. 134.
53. Wilson, The Thirty Years War, p. 476.
54. Parker, *The Military Revolution* (1999 reprint of the 1996 edition), p. 23.
55. Cummins, *History's Greatest Wars.*, p. 123.
56. Generalstaben, *Sveriges Krig 1611–1632*, volume IV (Stockholm, 1937), pp. 472–486.
57. Dupuy, *Gustav Adolphus*, p. 104.
58. Montross, *op. cit.*, p. 278 and Parker, *Europe in Crisis*, p. 162.
59. Haythornthweite, *op. cit.*, p. 40.
60. See, for example, Liddell Hart, *Great Captains*, p. p. 135 and Montross, *op. cit.*, p. 279. Liddell Hart writes that *Bohemian forests were laid low to block the road, the walls of cities hundreds of miles from the battlefield were kept manned.*
61. Montross, *op. cit.,* p. 279.
62. It is ironic that this comment is by Sir Basil H. Liddell Hart, the advocate of the *strategy of the indirect approach.*
63. Fuller, *op. cit.*, volume II, p. 65.
64. *Loc. cit.*
65. Wilson, *The Thirty Years War*, pp. 482–483.

5
The Tortured Road
to Lützen

The Swedes came as if they had flown.
WALLENSTEIN

START OF THE 1632 CAMPAIGN

By the time Gustav Adolf went into winter quarters at Mainz in late 1631 he had made himself master of most of Germany and was the most powerful man in Europe. His accomplishments since July 1630 are nothing short of amazing. The small Swedish expeditionary force had, in eighteen months, swollen into an army of 108,000 and there were plans to nearly double this number in 1632, at very little expense to the Swedish treasury. At the end of 1631, less than 25 percent of these forces, stationed throughout the conquered territories, were Swedish.

The force disposition was one important strategic weakness in Sweden's position in Germany. Their forces, while impressive, were spread too thin. While the sources give slightly different numbers and locations, Gustav Adolf had perhaps 20,000 men under his direct command at Mainz. Field Marshal Horn had another army about the same size on the Main. General Banér held Magdeburg with 13,000 troops and Field Marshal Tott had another 20,000 in Lower Saxony, and there were 17,000 troops in Mecklenburg. The remaining troops were scattered in many garrisons throughout the occupied territories.[1] This was essentially a defensive disposition where none of the detachments had sufficient striking power for offensive operations. Gustav tried to control and direct these forces by couriers and this was neither effective nor appreciated.

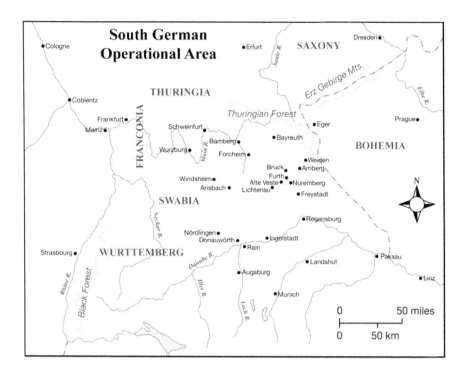

There were logical reasons for some of these dispositions of forces, but it was nevertheless a distinct weakness. First, logistics dictated that the forces be spread out in order to feed men and animals, as no single location could sustain the burden of very large armies. Second, some of the dispositions were dictated by political necessity. A number of allies were not trusted, and keeping forces in those areas gave some insurance that they remained loyal. Third, many principalities that had sided with the Swedes needed protection. Failure to provide such protection would make them easy targets for imperial forces.

However, these dispositions were invitations for the enemy to strike at any of the smaller Swedish forces with very little risk. It reinforces my earlier views that Gustav Adolf should have gone after Tilly, Pappenheim, and Maximilian of Bavaria immediately after Breitenfeld.

The Thirty Years War entered its most destructive phase in 1632 as each side had armies of around 100,000 men in the field. The campaign also marked the high point of Swedish success and power in Germany. The campaigns of 1632 were very intense as the Swedes sought to consolidate their conquests. The scope of the conflict had increased, as can be learned from the dispersed location of the major engagements. The year was marked by five major battles (Bamberg, Lech, Steinau, Alte Veste and Lützen) and numerous smaller engagements. This was a pattern that would persist until the end of the war.

Tilly's forces were disorganized and demoralized after Breitenfeld. Many soldiers had lost confidence in their commander and disliked serving under him. The number of troops available to Tilly fell further with the onset of winter and many died from the plague brought north by units from Italy. It was not until late winter that new troops were recruited, but most were untrained.

Pappenheim, as always, was very active, and the Swedes were impressed by his mobility and energy. In a lightning stroke in January 1632 he rescued the 3,500 imperial troops holding out in Magdeburg. After blowing up the fortifications he made his escape in the fog to Wolfenbüttel. In March he surprised the Swedes and Hessians at Höxter and evacuated the garrison at Stade. In the words of Peter Wilson, *he spent the summer running rings around his opponents who failed to combine against his troops.*[2]

The rebuilding of the imperial army during the winter and spring proceeded more rapidly than one would have expected after the debacles of 1631. There were a great number of unemployed men throughout Germany and many of these flocked to the army. The forces of the Catholic League now basically consisted of Bavarian troops defending their lands with a few scatterings in Westphalia and in the eastern part of Germany.[3]

Great changes had taken place in weapons and especially tactics—illustrating just how fast military technology spreads. The imperial military leaders had learned a valuable lesson from the fighting the previous year. They had, for the most part, discarded the massive "Spanish squares" and come up with smaller tactical units to take their place. The size of the new units ranged from 500 to 1,000. The number of ranks was reduced significantly from the 30 we found at Breitenfeld to ten or seven. Although the troops carried the same weapons, their firepower was increased by the shallower formations—which also reduced their vulnerability to artillery fire, another lesson from Breitenfeld. The troops were trained to fire salvos and the new formations increased maneuverability and simplified command and control.

Thanks to Swedish export of cannons which were sold on the Amsterdam arms market, the imperial army had acquired a substantial number of the regimental guns. It was a program favored by the Swedish government and industrial magnates much like the current situation in arms sales. These exports reached an annual level of 1,000 by 1657.

The cavalry regiments were grouped into squadrons of unequal size with new recruits usually making up the larger units while veterans were grouped in smaller ones. They were formed in five ranks, but this was still one or two ranks deeper than those of the Swedes.

BAMBERG

The Swedes attacked the city of Bamberg on 10 February 1632. While most sources acknowledge that the attack was ordered by Gustav Adolf, they differ as to the reason. Dupuy reports that it was an attack to punish the bishop of Bamberg for breaking his pledge of neutrality. Wilson on the other hand notes that Field Marshal Horn broke the truce with Bavaria by attacking Bamberg.[4] Although the city had been abandoned by Catholic League forces, the citizens mounted a short but determined defense until they ran out of ammunition. The Swedes were unsuccessful in their attempts to take the two nearby fortified towns of Kronach and Forshheim.

Tilly, who was still in his winter camp at Nördlingen at the time of Horn's attack on Bamberg, could not ignore the event. He quickly called in outlying garrisons and headed north with a mixed force of Bavarian militia and imperial forces, 22,000 total. The Swedes were surprised by his appearance at Bamberg in the evening of the last day of February.

Only two Swedish regiments were at Bamberg when Tilly's army appeared. The rest of Horn's 12,000 troops were raw recruits from Bohemia. The Bavarian militia quickly dispersed the cavalry outposts southeast of the city. The fleeing cavalry caused a panic among the raw recruits in the incomplete entrenchments in the suburbs on the east side of Regnitz River. The imperial troops quickly broke in and the defenders were overwhelmed. However, a fierce fight developed at a bridge leading to the main part of the town. The bridge changed hands several times as Horn committed his two Swedish regiments. The fighting continued well into the night when the Swedish rearguard, covering the extraction of the rest of the army, withdrew. Field Marshal Horn lost about a third of his army, mainly raw recruits who deserted. After the battle he withdrew to Schweinfurt.

While his disposition of forces begged for such a setback, Gustav Adolf was annoyed by the reverse at Bamberg. He had been involved in negotiations with Württemberg for an alliance. The shaky state of the Swedish alliance system is demonstrated by the fact that Württemberg hesitated to sign the alliance based on Horn's defeat at Bamberg. Gustav Adolf had to act quickly to sustain the Swedish string of successes, and he decided to strike at southern Bavaria. He moved from Mainz on 2 March by way of Swabia to link up with Horn, ordering General Banér and Duke William of Weimar to join him. This brought the Bavarian invasion army to 45,000 men.

The Swedes passed through Nuremberg and arrived at Donauwörth on 26 March. Though the town was taken quickly in a surprise assault, the victory was stained by the massacre of surrendering enemy soldiers and Protestant citizens who had come to welcome the conquerors.[5] After leaving garrisons in Bamberg and at Donauwörth, Gustav Adolf had 37,000 men and 72 pieces of artillery for the invasion of Bavaria.

Tilly had meanwhile left Schweinfurt and Würtzburg on the Main River and also moved south, hanging on the Swedes' flank at a respectful distance. He arrived at Ingolstadt further east on the Danube at the same time as Gustav reached Donauwörth. Tilly withdrew behind the Danube to await developments.

THE RETURN OF WALLENSTEIN

Emperor Ferdinand found himself in a desperate situation after Breitenfeld as there appeared to be no end to the advances of the Swedes. The Emperor found it necessary to endure the humiliation involved in asking Wallenstein to raise a second army.

Since his dismissal, Wallenstein had lived in Prague in regal splendor. He was the ruler of Friedland, a duchy consisting of lands given to him for past services. Montross writes that Wallenstein was *perhaps the first man in Europe to grasp the idea of the modern totalitarian state, organized for war.*[6] He put the entire population of his duchy to work making preparations for war, including making weapons, storing large quantities of food, and building roads. Within the short span of two years Wallenstein had accumulated military supplies sufficient to make a kingdom proud to own.

At the time of the Emperor's plea in December 1631 Wallenstein was reportedly considering offering his services to the Swedes.[7] He had been very offended by his unceremonious dismissal in 1630, and was prepared to exact

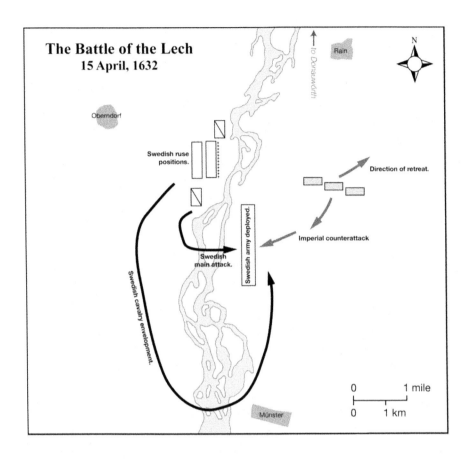

The Battle of the Lech
15 April, 1632

a high price for taking over the war effort. He turned down the initial pro-
posal, but accepted the renewed pleas in late December 1631.

The actual terms of Wallenstein's agreement with the Emperor are not
known since the documents have never been found. However, from subsequent happenings we can discern its broad outlines. He was apparently given
absolute control of the army but also much more. For example, he was given
full civil authority within operational areas, the right to impose punishment
as he deemed necessary, and the authority to engage in negotiations and
conclude treaties. For his service he was promised compensation in the form
of Bohemian and Brandenburg lands with the title of elector. Liddell Hart
describes Wallenstein's terms *so humiliating as no subject before or since has dared
to ask of his sovereign.*[8]

However, it did not take the energetic Wallenstein long to raise an army.

Former veterans, drawn by the allure of the name of the famous leader, flocked to his colors, as did a large number of mercenaries. By April 1632 he had a splendidly equipped army, drawing from his own stores, numbering between 40,000 and 65,000.[9]

THE BATTLE OF THE LECH

Gustav Adolf was aware that Wallenstein was back in charge of the imperial forces. By opting to continue his invasion of Bavaria he undoubtedly had three primary goals in mind. First, he wanted to bring Maximilian to terms or battle, thereby knocking Bavaria out of the war. Secondly, he may have decided to use the indirect approach to bring Wallenstein south and away from Saxony. He was hoping that both the Emperor and the Bavarian Elector would bring pressure on Wallenstein to come to the aid of Bavaria. Thirdly, Gustav Adolf hoped to gain large contributions and a great amount of supplies from this, up to now, virgin territory.

We are entering a period where the two greatest military leaders of the seventeenth century were pitted against each other. Each tried the indirect approach to bring on a battle under favorable conditions. Wallenstein, referred to by Liddell Hart as *the first grand strategist,* was more successful in using that approach than Gustav Adolf.[10]

While there were a number of bridges spanning the Danube, most were heavily guarded by Bavarian troops. Gustav Adolf decided to invade directly across the river at Donauwörth as this was the quickest route to Munich, the Bavarian capital. This would require that he make a second crossing over the Lech River which, coming south out of the Bavarian mountains and forming the border between Swabia and Bavaria, joined the Danube between Ingolstadt and Donauwörth, but closer to the latter. He could have crossed where he did and headed south to Augsburg along the western bank of the Lech, but that city was held by 5,000 Bavarians while other troops secured the crossing at Rain where the Lech joined the Danube.

Field Marshals Tilly and Aldringen made the same calculations as Gustav Adolf and arrived at the same conclusion: that the Swedes would avoid both Augsburg and Rain. Consequently, they entrenched their 21,000 men and 20 guns on the western bank of the Lech between Rain and Augsburg.

The Bavarian side of the Lech consisted of half-submerged woods and marshes, behind which the imperials were stationed. The Lech in this area divided into a series of fast moving parallel streams, varying in width from 60 to 100 meters. Heavy rains and melting snow had increased both the speed of flow and depth of the river. Crossing the Lech would be difficult even if the crossing was not contested, but with 21,000 imperial troops entrenched on the other side it became an enormous undertaking.

Gustav Adolf selected a crossing site about five kilometers south of Rain where the Lech split into two channels with a sizable island in the middle. The channel between the Swedes and the island was fordable, but the channel to the western bank from the island was deep. The Swedish commanders considered Tilly's position unassailable, but after a personal reconnaissance, Gustav decided to make a crossing of the Lech.

Gustav drew up his army in battle formation near the Lech directly opposite the imperial entrenchments. This deployment was on open ground very visible to the enemy. Then, under cover of an artillery bombardment, the Swedes began constructing a bridge. Most of the 72 guns were with the main Swedish army. This ruse worked. Meanwhile, other Swedes moved into the woods opposite the island and bridged the channel. Infantry troops and the rest of the artillery—18 guns—were deployed on the island the next morning to cover the next step in the operation.

Covered by the musketeers on the island and by a smoke screen created by *burning wet straw and gunpowder, 334 Finns, motivated by five months extra pay, rowed across to the Bavarian bank.*[11] This force was commanded by Colonel Wrangel. While the Finns occupied a tight perimeter on the Bavarian side of the river, pre-fabricated sections of bridging were pulled across the channel and secured. This allowed the rest of the Swedish army to cross, covered by fire from artillery hidden in the woods on the western side of the island. The crossing on 15 April had been discovered but the Finns held the perimeter until they were joined by the rest of the army. Gustav Adolf personally led two brigades of infantry across the river.

As soon as Tilly learned about the crossing, he sent troops to that site and a vicious battle developed south of his camp. In another brilliant tactical maneuver, Gustav had sent a force of 2,000 elite Swedish cavalry to ford the Lech about two kilometers south of the crossing site, near the village of Münster. This force surprised Tilly's troops and struck a decisive blow to the imperial left flank at the exact moment when the battle reached its climax around 1600 hours.

Field Marshal Johan von Aldringen was temporarily blinded by a head wound but survived. Field Marshal Tilly, on the other hand, was mortally wounded by a cannonball that shattered his right thigh. He was carried off the battlefield and Dupuy reports that Gustav Adolf sent his surgeon to attend to his opponent, but the wound was fatal and he died two weeks later.[12] The command of the imperial forces fell to Maximilian, the Bavarian elector.

The battle was for all practical purposes decided by evening after the surprise attack on the imperial left flank by the Swedish cavalry which had already driven the Bavarian cavalry from the field. Assailed from two directions, the imperial troops began to give way. They may have withdrawn temporarily to their camp, but made a quick retreat after darkness leaving their baggage and guns.

Wilson makes no mention of a Swedish pursuit, but both Liddell Hart and Dupuy deplore the fact that the Swedes failed to launch one. Montross, however, writes that the Swedes conducted a relentless pursuit but were unable to overtake and destroy the enemy due to a strong storm which left the roads blocked by fallen trees.[13]

Liddell Hart considers the crossing of the Lech a model operation, perhaps Gustav Adolf's tactical masterpiece.[14] It afterward became a model at military academies for forcing a river crossing in the face of a strong enemy in prepared positions behind it.

The losses in the battle are difficult to pin down. It appears that the Swedes sustained about 2,000 casualties and the imperial forces 3,000 to 4,000.

The Bavarian elector withdrew unmolested to Ingolstadt. A retreat in this direction left the door to southern Bavaria wide open for the Swedes. However, Gustav's failure to prevent Maximilian from getting away after the battle caused the Swedes serious problems later.

The defeat at Lech so demoralized the Bavarian garrison in Augsburg that they accepted the honors of war and marched out of the city ten days later. The Swedes' conquering advance had brought them from the shores of the Baltic to the foothills of the Alps. At the same time as the Swedes overran Bavaria, John George, the elector of Saxony, who had started an advance to Vienna through Bohemia, entered Prague without firing a shot. The lucky star had never shone brighter on the Protestant cause, but dark clouds were gathering.

MANEUVERING IN BAVARIA

Tilly's death only added to the many difficulties facing Emperor Ferdinand. His war treasury was practically empty and there were few prospects for a steady stream of income. He had no allies save Elector Maximilian, and the emperor did not trust his steadfastness in fighting for the Hapsburg Empire. Ferdinand's appeal to the Pope for monetary assistance was flatly turned down on the grounds that Pope Urban VIII had concluded that Ferdinand was waging a political, not a religious war. Spain and Poland could not help because they had exhausted their resources in other wars.[15]

After the Battle of the Lech, Gustav Adolf marched south about 20 miles to Augsburg, entering that city on 20 April. After paying a very large contribution, the city authorities took an oath of loyalty to the Swedish king. He did not continue the southward track to Munich, as was reasonable to expect, but turned back north toward Ingolstadt. That city was the strongest fortress in Bavaria and the place where the Bavarian elector had sought refuge after his defeat at the Lech. Ingolstadt is located on the north bank of the Danube. A stone bridge connected it to the south bank where there was a fortified bridgehead. It remains unclear why Gustav Adolf wasted almost two weeks after the Battle of Lech by going to Augsburg instead of immediately following Maximilian and his defeated army.

The Swedes tried to take the southern bridgehead on the Danube by storm on 29 April but were repulsed. Gustav thereupon camped his army around the fortifications. On 30 April, while on a reconnaissance, Gustav's horse was killed by a cannonball. Bruised but otherwise unhurt, Gustav promptly mounted another horse and continued the reconnaissance for a river crossing site. Soon thereafter, the Margrave of Baden-Durlach, riding beside the Swedish king, had his head severed by another cannonball.[16]

After sending an unsuccessful appeal to Wallenstein for assistance, Maximilian, leaving a strong garrison behind, departed Ingolstadt for Regensburg on 2 May. The Swedes made another assault on the southern bridgehead on 3 May and this time they were successful. They immediately crossed the river and invested the city.

Despite Maximilian's appeal for help, Wallenstein decided to turn his attention to the Saxons, the weak link in the Swedish alliance system. His plan was to eject them from Prague and Bohemia and then to move against Saxony proper. He ordered Maximilian to join him with his army rather than him joining the elector. This left Bavaria virtually defenseless—or so it seemed. In an excellent use of the indirect approach, Wallenstein had calculated that Gustav would be forced to quit Bavaria and come to the aid of the Saxon elector, John George.[17]

Gustav Adolf was fully aware of what was happening in Bohemia and Saxony, and knew that Wallenstein was moving against Prague and possibly the Saxon army in Bohemia. He also suspected that Wallenstein was hoping that Gustav Adolf would move north to assist his ally in order not to be trapped in southern Germany, isolated from his bases along the Baltic. This was a possibility that had haunted Gustav since he landed. However, Gustav hoped to bring Wallenstein to a showdown without abandoning his hard-won gains in Bavaria. He hoped that by moving deep into the heart of the Empire, Wallenstein and Maximilian would be forced to fight him by concentrating all their troops in southern Germany.

Having reached this conclusion, Gustav Adolf lifted the siege of Ingolstadt on 4 May and marched on Munich. The Swedes lost as many troops in their futile attempt to take Ingolstadt as they had in the Battle of the Lech. Field Marshal Horn was assigned the mission to eliminate any remnants of Tilly's army still in the area and to seize Landshut and other towns in Bavaria, north of Munich.

The Bavarian capital surrendered to the Swedes without resistance after the citizens were promised that their lives and property would be spared. The city did have to pay an immense contribution of 250,000 thalers, however, and large stores of war materials were seized.[18] Gustav stayed in Munich ten days. In what appears to have been a public relations move, the Swedish king attended a Catholic mass, a gesture that convinced no one of his tolerance.[19]

While the Swedes had little difficulty with the Bavarian towns, the deeply religious inhabitants remained hostile to the invaders and the peasants began a guerrilla war. This uprising, which soon spread into Swabia, was primarily a reaction to the plundering activities of the invaders.[20]

Cardinal Richelieu was forced to watch helplessly as the Swedes conquered Bavaria, his secret ally. The French could not risk a war with the all-conquering Swedes, and they also knew that Maximilian had brought the problems on himself.[21]

Gustav Adolf began having problems with indiscipline and criminal behavior among his German mercenaries during the campaign in Bavaria.

This was serious since these mercenaries accounted for more than 60 percent of his army. Gustav addressed his army as follows: *Had I known that you were a people so wanting in natural affections for your own country, I would never have saddled my horse for your sakes, much less imperil the life and my crown and my brave Swedes and Finns.*[22]

The same week that Gustav occupied Munich, Wallenstein was on the move. He was carrying out his plan to strike at the Swedes indirectly by attacking their ally, Saxony. He assembled his army at Znaim, on the road between Prague and Vienna, and marched the 240 kilometers to Prague. That city was held by a Saxon garrison but they offered little resistance and Wallenstein marched in on 25 May, leaving the Saxons to retreat. The retreat did not stop until they had left virtually all of Bohemia. Wallenstein moved to the Bohemian-Saxon boundary and halted. He now used the powers granted him by Emperor Ferdinand to offer the Saxon elector a separate peace on very favorable terms.[23]

Gustav Adolf had closely followed Wallenstein's activities and had correctly concluded that he was trying to convince Elector John George to break his alliance with Sweden. Gustav was aware that Field Marshal von Arnim, the elector's adviser, had conducted secret negotiations with Wallenstein. Gustav Adolf also concluded that the danger to Saxony and his line of communications had become acute and that he needed to act. His intelligence reports indicated that Wallenstein and Maximilian intended to join forces at Eger near western Bohemia.

Leaving garrisons in Munich and other Bavarian towns, Gustav Adolf marched north, reaching Donauwörth on 12 June. The earlier intelligence that Wallenstein and Maximilian were planning to join forces at Eger was confirmed when it was learned that Maximilian and his army had departed Regensburg and were heading to Eger via Amberg. This caused Gustav to change his plan. The danger to Saxony was no longer acute. Gustav decided to march rapidly to Weiden, between Eger and Amberg, hoping to inflict a decisive defeat on Maximilian before he could affect a junction with Wallenstein.

The Swedes were operating deep in enemy territory, and the population kept Wallenstein and Maximilian informed about the route and speed of the Swedish army. Based on this intelligence Wallenstein decided to change the junction point and have Maximilian speed up his march. While Maximilian managed to evade the Swedes, Wallenstein marched westward and the two armies joined at Schwabach near Nuremberg on 11 July.

It was noted earlier in this chapter that the dispersal of Swedish forces was a weakness in their dispositions. The forces under the command of the Swedish king had reached 150,000 by early 1632, but because they were so widely dispersed, he had a very small striking force at his disposal. He now found himself at the head of a force of 10,000 infantry and 8,000 cavalry and that force was obviously too small to move against the combined forces of Wallenstein and Maximilian, now numbering some 60,000 troops. His widely dispersed forces would not be able to join him for a week or more.

Gustav had hoped to confront each of his opponents separately. Against their combined armies he could not hope to prevail and was forced to take up a defensive posture near Nuremberg. The location selected was probably not the best from a military point of view, as he should have selected a place nearer to his other major force concentrations. He was not willing, however, to abandon the loyal and prominent Protestant city of Nuremberg on both political and moral grounds. Also, he was not willing to give up his hold on Bavaria since its psychological impact could lead to the loss of other allies, especially Württemberg and Swabia.

Having selected the concentration point, the Swedes set about fortifying their camp while Gustav Adolf sent out messages for Oxenstierna and generals commanding sizable forces to join him.

BLOCKADE OF NUREMBERG

The Swedes constructed a fortified camp around Nuremberg large enough to contain the army and its expected reinforcements. Over 6,000 peasants were used to dig a moat 12 feet wide and 8 feet deep around the camp. Redoubts were built at critical points using 300 cannon from the city's arsenal. The walled inner city of Nuremberg became the citadel of the defensive position. The cavalry was left outside the camp to keep communications open and to assist reinforcements on their way.

Wallenstein was meanwhile approaching Nuremberg but it seems not in a hurry, feeling that he had Gustav Adolf cornered. The Swedish cavalry was assembled near Fürth and they harassed the approaching imperial army in several hit and run engagements on the broad plains around Nuremberg.

Some writers claim that Wallenstein immediately decided to isolate and

Gustav II Adolf
(1594–1632), whose
tactical and strategic
skill as well as personal
bravery propelled
Sweden to great
power status on
the Continent.

Axel Oxenstierna
(1583–1654), the
Lord High Chancellor
of Sweden, whose
diplomatic skills
helped to cement
Sweden's status
during the Thirty
Years War and
beyond.

Field Marshal Johan Tzerclaes Tilly (1559–1632), perhaps the Holy Roman Empire's greatest general, was nevertheless defeated badly by Gustav Adolf at Breitenfeld.

Field Marshal Albrecht von Wallenstein (1583– 1634), commanded the Empire's army at Lützen, where the Swedes won the battle but lost Gustav II Adolf.

"Gustave Adolphe at Breitenfeld." The Battle of Breitenfeld in 1631 is considered Sweden's greatest victory during the Thirty Years War.

The Battle of Lützen. Gustav Adolf was killed while leading a cavalry charge and in the smoke and fog of battle became separated from his men.

Karl XII (1682–1718), also known as Charles XII. Like Gustav Adolf he assumed the Swedish throne as a teenager, and like his predecessor proved to be a military genius while brave to a fault on the battlefield.

The Battle of Narva, 1700, in which an impetuous
Swedish charge crushed a larger Russian army.

Karl XII crossing the Düna in 1701 during the Great Northern War.

Karl XII's greatest
opponent was
Russia's Peter
the Great (1672–
1725), who
finally defeated
the Swedish
army at Poltava
in 1704.

Bringing home the body of King Karl XII of Sweden.

starve the Swedes into submission.[24] This is generally true except he made one unsuccessful and costly attack on the western portions of the Swedish entrenchments shortly after his arrival. Thereafter, he constructed a fortified camp on the left bank of the Rednitz River around the old castle of Alte Veste, which was perched on the top of a hill rising 250 feet above the river and about six kilometers from the Swedes. Into this camp he crowded the nearly 60,000 men under his command.[25]

It was an elaborate camp based on the description provided by Colonel Monro. He and Wilson report that Wallenstein's camp was 16 kilometers in circumference, that 13,000 trees and 21,000 modern truckloads of earth were used in its construction. Some of the felled trees were used to form obstacles similar to modern barbed wire. The trees were placed on top of the abatements and trimmed in such manner that the sharpened ends of the branches pointed towards the enemy.[26]

Wallenstein knew that time was on his side since he commanded the Swedes' lines of communication. He decided to starve his enemy into submission. His forces controlled the roads from Nuremberg to virtually all points of the compass. Most importantly, Wallenstein's capture of Lichtenau isolated Gustav Adolf from important parts of his base areas. Swedish foraging operations became very difficult and there were many sharp cavalry engagements. Wallenstein's light Croat cavalry under General Hector Isolani (1586–1640), which devastated the surrounding landscape, was more suited for this type of warfare than the slower Swedish cavalry. Wallenstein also had the advantage of being supplied from nearby Bohemia and from Austria. It appeared that the Swedes were trapped.

To further complicate the food shortage, the Swedes had to feed not only their own 18,000 troops but also the citizens of Nuremberg. That city's population of 40,000 had swollen dramatically by over 100,000 refugees from the surrounding areas.

However, Wallenstein's strategy of starving the Swedes soon began to backfire with an unusually hot August. In his description of conditions in the imperial camp, Wilson writes that *the concentration of 55,000 troops and around 50,000 camp followers produced at least four tons of human excrement daily, in addition to the waste from the 45,000 cavalry and baggage horses. The camp was swarming with rats and flies, spreading disease.*[27]

Aggressive Swedish activities made things worse for Wallenstein. Colonel

Dubatel led a Swedish cavalry raid on Freystadt, 40 kilometers south of Nuremberg on 30 July, where a very large imperial supply base was located. The Swedes destroyed 1,000 wagonloads of supplies and fodder for the cavalry. They also took along several hundred wagons of supplies back to their base. The imperial cavalry took up the chase but Gustav Adolf took 2,000 of his cavalry and completely defeated the pursuers. Wallenstein's brother-in-law, Colonel Sparre, was captured in this engagement.[28]

Swedish reinforcements were also beginning to arrive. These reinforcements staged at Würzburg before proceeding to Nuremberg. Oxenstierna, with 7,000 troops, arrived there on 23 July, and other Swedish forces from the Weser, Rhine, and Elbe regions joined Oxenstierna in the weeks that followed. Oxenstierna brought these forces—28,000 strong with 3,000 supply wagons—to the fortified town of Bruck on 13 August. In Bruck they were joined by Gustav Adolf and his cavalry, and brought safely to the Nuremberg encampment. Wallenstein made no attempt to interfere with the Swedish relief efforts. By the middle of August his army was no longer fully operational because of disease and the effects of starvation. Wallenstein had become the victim of his own strategy as his strength decreased to about 45,000 men.

The reinforcements brought Swedish strength to 28,000 infantry, 17,000 cavalry, and an artillery force composed of 175 field guns—for a total of about 50,000—the largest army Gustav Adolf had commanded. It also meant that there were about 30,000 more mouths to feed as well an increased requirements for the cavalry. The effects of the imperial blockade were beginning to take their toll both among Gustav Adolf's troops and the civilians crowded into Nuremberg. Gustav decided to attack the imperial positions in what Liddell Hart describes as an act of desperation.[29]

BATTLE OF STEINAU

Before going on to describe the happenings around Nuremberg we should look at events taking place in Bohemia since they impacted both imperial and Swedish operations and are, for the most part, not covered in the accounts of this period. These operations also give an insight into the tensions that prevailed within the Swedish alliance system.

John George tried to improve his bargaining position by sending Field Marshal Arnim to invade Silesia. Arnim was given an army of 22,000 men for the task. These included 12,000 Saxons, 3,000 Brandenburgers, and 7,000

Swedes. The Swedish troops were commanded by General Jacob Duwall from Scotland where his name had been MacDougall. He was an aggressive daredevil who had been in Swedish service since 1607 and had raised two German regiments which formed part of the corps he brought into Silesia. Duwall's primary mission was apparently to ensure that von Arnim remained loyal to Sweden.[30]

Imperial forces were rushed into Silesia from Bohemia to reinforce the troops under the elderly Field Marshal Baltasar von Marradas (1560–1638). Marradas concentrated 20,000 troops at the Oder crossing at Steinau, between Glogau and Breslau. These troops were entrenched southeast of Steinau. Cavalry was posted west of town to observe the logical avenue of approach.

Von Arnim's advance guard under Duwall arrived at noon on 29 August, and without hesitation he attacked the Silesian cavalry and drove it back into their camp. Duwall's younger brother led 1,000 Swedish and Brandenburg infantry as they stormed the Steinau suburbs. The imperial forces set the town on fire and practically destroyed it. Duwall wanted to continue the attack but was overruled by von Arnim.

The allies marched south to Diebau where they built a bridge across the Oder. Marradas attacked Diebau on 4 September but was repulsed and withdrew leaving a small detachment at the Steinau Bridge to delay any pursuit. The allied losses in this campaign were minor while the imperial forces lost 6,000 men, mostly prisoners and deserters.

Von Arnim continued his drive and captured both Breslau and Schwidnitz, driving the imperial forces into the mountains. Arnim had conquered Silesia against greater odds than those facing Frederick the Great in his renowned invasion of the same area in 1740.[31]

In an effort to punish the Saxons for the Silesian invasion, Wallenstein sent Field Marshal Heinrich von Holk (1599–1633) with 10,000 men from Forchheim into southwest Saxony. Holk began to systematically plunder and devastate the region. Elector John George clamored for Swedish assistance and this increased the pressure on Gustav Adolf to break away from Nuremberg.

BATTLE FOR ALTE VESTE

A combination of disease and the detachment of Field Marshal Holk had left Wallenstein with a force of 31,000 infantry and 12,000 cavalry. In view of the fact that the Swedes had to seize a strongly fortified position, the odds were decidedly in favor of the imperials. After reviewing the situation, the Swedish king decided that the only feasible way to attack the fortified camp was from the north, a sector held by troops under Johan von Aldringen (1588–1634). This sector also presented the steepest approach to Alte Veste. The compensating factor was that securing this objective would allow Swedish artillery to dominate the battlefield.

To reach the northern slopes the Swedes decided to cross the Rednitz below the imperial camp. Fürth, held by imperial forces, was taken by the Swedes in a surprise night attack on the first of September. After crossing the river the Swedes took positions in a forested area close to the northern imperial lines.

Gustav Adolf and Wilhelm of Weimar were to lead the main infantry assault against Burgstall Hill while his dismounted cavalry under Bernhard of Weimar would work against the weaker defenses to his right. The attack had to be made without close artillery support as it had proved impossible to bring artillery into position in the rugged terrain. However, the Swedes had planned to pin down Wallenstein's forces with artillery fire from the opposite side of the river.

The initial assault began at 1000 hours on 3 September. The Swedes made every effort to bring up a few regimental guns. Wallenstein directed strong reinforcements to the threatened sector. The long-range Swedish artillery fire failed to silence the imperial guns and these raked the attacking Swedes with fire from nearly 100 tubes, adding to the damage caused by lines of musketeers. There was a drizzle that made the slopes exceedingly slippery for the Swedes.

Losses were heavy and many senior officers on both sides fell, showing the bitterness of the fighting and the fact that they were leading from the front. General Torstensson, leading one of the attacking columns, was captured. Duke Bernhard's horse was shot and the king had a narrow escape. General Banér was so severely wounded that he was out of action for the rest of the year.

During the next ten hours the Swedes, Finns, and Scots made two more attempts to capture Burgstall Hill but each time they were driven back with heavy losses by imperial counterattacks. The drizzle had turned to heavy rain late in the afternoon making footing on the steep slopes virtually impossible.

Gustav Adolf called a halt to the fighting and ordered his troops to stay in their positions.

The Swedes made one more attempt in the morning but were driven back in a counterattack by fresh imperial troops. Seeing his exhausted men driven back again, the Swedish king called a halt to the operation. He withdrew to Fürth. By most estimates the Swedes suffered 4,000 dead and wounded at Alte Veste while the imperial losses were less than half that number.

SWEDISH AND IMPERIAL WITHDRAWALS
For two weeks more the starving armies remained face to face, but stayed within their camps. There were virtually no military activities except for those of the burial parties which continued, as they had all summer, to dispose of scores of corpses every day.

Starvation was getting worse in both armies. Gustav Adolf realized that this prolonged contest of wills was getting him nowhere and decided to withdraw to the Main. A force of 4,400 infantry and 300 cavalry under General Dodo Knyphausen (1583–1636) was left in Nuremberg. The Swedish army marched out of their encampment on 18 September after having endured the blockade for 10 weeks. Gustav Adolf offered Wallenstein one last formal challenge to battle, but it was not accepted.[32]

Casualties and demoralization had taken their toll on the Swedish forces during their prolonged stay in the Nuremberg area. A total of 11,000 mercenaries deserted, and altogether over 29,000 people died in the Swedish camp. So many horses had died that only 4,000 of the Swedish cavalry had mounts by the time they withdrew. Total imperial casualties are not known but they were probably comparable to those of the Swedes, since when they left the Nuremberg area the imperial army had shrunk in size from its original 65,000 to 24,000.[33]

In European eyes, the Swedish king had received his first setback. Gustav himself must have recognized that it had been a mistake to remain in the Nuremberg area and that making the futile assault on Alte Veste had been a debacle. While Wallenstein is alleged to have remarked that *the King has blunted his horns,*[34] he would soon discover that they were not as blunted as he thought. The Swedish army stopped for a week in Windsheim. After deciding that Wallenstein was no longer a threat, Gustav Adolf marched towards Swabia, intending to spend the winter there.

Wallenstein abandoned and burned his camp on 21 September. He had so few horses remaining that 1,000 wagons of supplies were left behind in the inferno. He also abandoned all his sick and wounded and some of these perished when the camp was burned. Wallenstein marched north past Nuremberg to Forchheim, laying the countryside waste as he proceeded. The garrison of Nuremberg attacked the imperial rear guard and inflicted a large number of casualties, but this event was ignored by Wallenstein who continued into the rich farming area near Bamberg.

The Swedish king appeared a bit unsure about his next move. Part of that was due to his ignorance of his opponent's plans. He had received information about a peasant revolt about to break out in Austria and he toyed with the idea of marching south to be in a position to take advantage of internal unrest in the Empire. As before, he may have hoped that by threatening Bavaria and the approach to Austria, Wallenstein would be drawn away from Saxony and the Swedish communications with the Baltic. However, as Liddell Hart observes, Wallenstein was much better placed in this game of maneuvering against each other's rear since his base was Bohemia and he could operate on interior lines.[35]

Wallenstein and Maximilian had departed company in October, although first they had agreed to a trade of forces. Maximilian agreed to place Pappenheim under Wallenstein's command in return for Field Marshal Aldringen and fourteen imperial regiments.

RENEWED THREAT TO SAXONY

Wallenstein had left Field Marshals Holk and Matthias Gallas (1584–1647) in northwestern Bohemia and southern Saxony to ruthlessly devastate the Saxon possessions. In late October the Swedish king learned that Wallenstein was also moving into Saxony to join his other forces. It became obvious to Gustav Adolf that Wallenstein was still doggedly pursuing his aim of knocking Saxony out of the Swedish alliance. Liddell Hart, full of admiration for Wallenstein's keeping his eyes on Sweden's Achilles' heel, recognizes that both commanders were jockeying for advantage through maneuvering, and in so doing were violating the concept of seeking out the main forces of the enemy for a decisive blow.

Gustav Adolf immediately decided against any southern adventures in favor of moving back north to provide security for his Saxon ally. He left

Duke Bernhard with 8,000 men in Schweinfurt to protect Franconia and General Patrick Ruthven with 10,000 on the Danube and Lech to keep an eye on Maximilian and the remnants of his army. Field Marshal Horn had meanwhile captured Coblenz and Strasbourg and driven the Spanish and Lorraine troops out of Germany.

Holk captured Leipzig on October 31 while Wallenstein's cavalry raided the nearby territory and occupied several towns. Wallenstein was joined by Pappenheim on 6 November. This brought the size of the imperial forces in the vicinity of Leipzig to around 30,000.[36]

Gustav Adolf hurried north at an amazing speed. His army covered about 400 kilometers in 17 days at the cost of 4,000 horses.[37] On the way he sent orders for all detached commanders to join him. On the road to Erfurt the Swedes almost collided with Maximilian, who was heading in the opposite direction; the two armies were only 25 kilometers apart, but unaware of the fact. The main Saxon army was still with Arnim in Silesia. John George had only 4,000 men, plus 2,000 Lüneburgers and they had retreated into Torgau.

The Swedes reached Erfurt on 2 November with 20,000 veteran troops. Here they were given several days to rest. Again, we see another example of failing to quickly concentrate a strong striking force, since 20,000 troops represented only a small percentage of the troops available to Gustav Adolf.

Wallenstein was reportedly amazed at the speed with which the Swedes had moved from Bavaria to Erfurt. He is alleged to have exclaimed, *The Swedes came as if they had flown.*[38]

WALLENSTEIN'S LOST OPPORTUNITIES
The Swedish king continued his move toward Leipzig on 6 November 1632. He sent a message to Elector John George urging him to proceed to the Saale River with all his available forces. He sent a strong detachment ahead to seize the Saale defile at Kösen. Gustav Adolf crossed the Saale River at Altenburg and continued on to Naumburg, which he captured on 10 November. He paused here, about 100 kilometers from Leipzig, to concentrate his forces and await reinforcements. He began building an entrenched camp just north of the city as was his normal practice.

Meantime the weather had turned cold. Wallenstein, aware of Swedish activities at Naumburg, believed that they indicated that Gustav Adolf was preparing to go into winter quarters.

Wallenstein was at Eilenburg, about 16 kilometers northeast of Leipzig, when he learned that the Swedes had left Erfurth and were heading for Naumburg. He immediately sent troops to seize the defiles at Saale to block the Swedish advance, and at the same time he moved his army to Weissenfels, about 15 kilometers east of Naumberg.

When he arrived at Weissenfels, Wallenstein discovered that the Swedes had beat him to the Saale defines and had already taken Naumburg. He was surprised at the swiftness of the Swedish movements, and assembled his war council to consider what should be done. Based on the fact that the Swedes were entrenching their camp and waiting for reinforcements, there was unanimous agreement that the enemy did not plan to offer battle and would spend the winter in his camp. Wallenstein agreed with his council and on 14 November he started withdrawing his army north to Merseburg to go into winter quarters. He sent Pappenheim ahead to capture and hold Halle.[39]

Wallenstein has been criticized for his actions in November 1632. He was strategically located between three enemy forces and had numerical superiority over each of them—the Swedes at Naumburg, the Saxons at Torgau, and a Protestant force thought to be advancing from Brunswick-Lüneburg. The Lüneburg force had actually reached the far side of the Elbe near the Saxons at Torgau. Being centrally located he could have swiftly struck at each and thus at least prevent them from concentrating.

The second criticism is aimed at the fact that he decided to go into winter quarters and scatter his force in the presence of a strong enemy. The scattering of his forces with the Swedes in his proximity is impossible to defend despite Delbruck's best efforts.[40]

Wallenstein sent General Hatzfeld with 2,500 troops to watch Torgau. This force was too small to prevent the Saxons and Lüneburgers from moving west to join Gustav Adolf, and too large for just an observation and early warning force. Wallenstein also sent troops out to look for and gather food. Finally, he gave in to Pappenheim's wishes to return to Westphalia where the Swedes were picking off his garrisons, one at a time. Some historians have excused Wallenstein because he was suffering from gout and lacked the energy to argue with his restless subordinate.[41] He allowed Pappenheim to leave with a rather large force estimated at 5,800 to 8,000 troops. He did make arrangements for Field Marshal Gallas and his troops to replace those Pappenheim had taken away. However, Gallas was located in the south along the

Bohemian border and it would take some time before he could be expected.

All these missteps indicate that Wallenstein and his generals had seriously misjudged Gustav Adolf's intentions. The Swedish king had been eager the whole year to bring the elusive Wallenstein to battle, and that desire had increased since his repulse at Alte Veste, which he believed had tarnished his military reputation. He also wanted once and for all to remove the imperial threat against Saxony.

When Gustav Adolf learned that Wallenstein had withdrawn toward Merseburg, he abandoned his own camp and followed. Then, on 14 November, he received the news that Pappenheim had departed. He decided the time had come to strike, although outnumbered, and hastened his pursuit. Liddell Hart observes that *this instant seizure of the chance afforded by the enemy's dispersion is an admirable example of decisiveness and energy in fulfilling the principle of concentration du fort au faible.*[42]

Wallenstein learned about noon on 15 November that the Swedes were moving against him in force. He knew there was no way to avoid battle. The main force of his army was located at Lützen and it was there that Wallenstein decided to make his stand. He sent General Rodolfo Colloredo (1585–1657) with a detachment of 500 dragoons and Croats to delay the Swedes, and sent couriers after Pappenheim ordering him to return as quickly as possible.

Colloredo and his men blocked the Swedes at the marshy Rippach stream east of Weissenfels. They were able to hold up the Swedish advance for four hours on 15 September before being chased away. This four-hour delay had momentous consequences for the battle that followed. Gustav Adolf decided that the delay had made it too late for a battle on that day, and camped for the night. If the Swedes had been able to attack on the 15th, Pappenheim would have had no part in the battle and the imperial troops would not have had the additional time to prepare their positions. Under those circumstances a Swedish decisive victory was almost assured.

The land around Lützen is generally flat. In the seventeenth century there was an elevated road from Leipzig to Weissenfels that ran through the village of Lützen. There were deep ditches on both sides of this road.

ORDER OF BATTLE

Wallenstein deployed his army such that it has often been commented on by writers searching for his reasoning. Even Liddell Hart was puzzled by the unusual positioning. Wallenstein drew up his army parallel with the Leipzig road, facing southeast, rather than across it. In this way his right flank was exposed to the expected direction of the Swedish approach. However, he had anchored his right flank on the village of Lützen, straddling the road to Leipzig and consisting of 300 homes and an old walled castle. Wallenstein ordered this village burned before the battle began. The ground to the right of the imperial flank and Lützen consisted of marshy meadows through which ran the Mühlgraben stream, making a flanking movement by the Swedes virtually impossible.[43] The ditches were ready-made trenches and he lined these with musketeers. The imperial left flank was supposed to be anchored on Flossgraben stream. By the middle of the afternoon on September 15, the imperial troops had occupied their positions.

Earlier accounts (and some newer ones) have the imperial army organized into large "Spanish squares" as at Breitenfeld in 1631. This is not correct. As mentioned earlier in this chapter those formations were quickly being replaced as a result of Breitenfeld. Wallenstein had already made the transition to the linear formation, although he had not gone as far as the Swedes. He had reduced the 30 deep formations at Breitenfeld to 10 ranks for the infantry. He had also obtained light artillery and begun to mix musketeers with the cavalry.[44]

While the Germans had begun to close the tactical and technological gap, the Swedes continued their qualitative superiority. They had light muskets, and their formations were shallower. Finally, they enjoyed the advantage that the core of their army were Swedes and Finns, and even the disciplined mercenaries in the force enjoyed a distinct advantage every veteran army has over one that had just been formed.

The imperial infantry deployed in the center in two lines—10 deep—parallel to the Leipzig-Weissenfels road with 420 musketeers stationed in the ditches in front of them. Wallenstein placed the majority of his artillery on Windmill Hill, just to the north of Lützen, and also posted 400 musketeers at that location to cover the artillery and the town. About half the cavalry was behind the right flank while the rest was behind the infantry or on the right. The rest of the artillery was placed in front of the left flank.

There is much controversy as to the number of artillery pieces the imperials had but it was probably around 60 pieces when the lighter guns are included. Wallenstein did not have enough troops to cover the gap between his left flank and Flossgraben creek. This was the point where he expected the Swedes to try outflanking him. He ordered General Isolani to screen the open flank with his Croat cavalry, but there were not enough of them. Therefore, Wallenstein massed the baggage and camp followers behind the left flank to hold up sheets to represent flags for creating the impression of powerful forces in the rear. They were to carry out this activity until the arrival of Pappenheim, expected during the night.

Wallenstein took personal command of the center. Some sources recount that he had to be carried around the battlefield on a litter. There is no doubt that he suffered from gout but he was mounted on his horse and energetically directing his men. The left wing was commanded jointly by Field Marshal Holk and General Ottavio Piccolomini (1599–1656) who was promoted to Field Marshal in 1634. The right wing was commanded by General Colloredo.

There are some obvious reasons why Wallenstein drew up in what appeared to be an unusual position. First, the causeways served as ready-made positions and presented a serious obstacle to an attacker. Second, it allowed him to have a very secure right flank, anchored as it was on a village and impassable marshland. Third, the positioning would allow him to retreat to northwest Germany instead of Bohemia, which is what his strategic boldness dictated. The weakness in his position was his left flank where he should have been strongest because it was not anchored on any natural obstacles. This weakness was noted immediately by the Swedish king, who hoped that he would be able to turn this flank and drive the imperial forces away from a retreat to Leipzig. Imperial armies had customarily retreated to their left leaving that wing to cover their retreat. If the Swedes could turn the imperial left flank, they would have to withdraw in such a manner that they could be forced to winter in Saxony, a hostile region. Wallenstein accepted this risk with his eyes wide open but counted on Pappenheim's early return to rectify the weakness on his left.

As Wallenstein had expected, the Swedish army made an oblique turn to the right and Gustav Adolf formed his army very much as he had at Breitenfeld—infantry in two lines six deep and the cavalry on the wings. Before deploying, he received John George's refusal to join him with reinforcements from Torgau.[45] This news did not alter Gustav Adolf's plans, and he remained confident despite the absence of some of his best commanders—Horn, Banér,

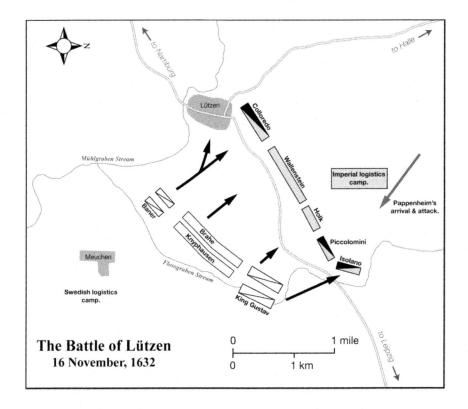

The Battle of Lützen
16 November, 1632

Torstensson, and Tott. These were either recovering from wounds or off on other assignments.

The Swedish left wing was commanded by Bernhard of Weimar. His cavalry consisted of about 3,000, primarily German mercenaries. The center was under the command of General Nils Brahe, who personally commanded the more experienced first line. It was his task to contain the imperial center while the king turned their left flank.[46] The second line was commanded by General Knyphausen. Each line consisted of four infantry regiments. Gustav Adolf personally commanded the right wing, consisting primarily of Swedish and Finnish cavalry. The army reserve, consisting of six squadrons of cavalry, was behind the center and commanded by Colonel Johan von Öhm. The heavier artillery—26 guns—was located in front of the center. Some 40 light infantry guns were with their respective units. The baggage train was located at the village of Meuchen, behind the Flossgraben and the left center of the Swedish formation.

There is considerable disagreement in the sources as to the strength of each army, even to which side had numerical superiority. The Swedes had a slight superiority until Pappenheim's cavalry, and especially his infantry, showed up. After that, the imperial forces had a slight superiority. The Swedes probably had about 13,000 infantry and slightly less than 7,000 cavalry at the start of the battle. The size of the imperial force is variously reported as 16,000 to 20,000 strong until the return of Pappenheim's forces.

The Swedish army spent the night of 15–16 November in battle order with the troops sleeping on the ground. The camp fires of both armies were clearly visible to each other, particularly in the glare of the fires consuming Lützen. As at Breitenfeld, the Swedish king spent the night with some of his principal commanders.

THE FOG OF LÜTZEN

The Swedish drummers roused the soldiers well before daylight. After the customary prayers and songs, the units were in their battle positions. The king galloped up and down the line. The wound he had received at Dirschau in 1627 was still painful and he wore only a sword-proof elk hide under his coat.[47]

A major battle has seldom been fought in visibility as low as that which prevailed on 16 November 1632. A heavy mist and dense fog shrouded the battlefield in the morning and periodically throughout the day. In the morning it was exacerbated by smoke from the smoldering village and later by the smoke from thousands of discharged weapons.

King Gustav Adolf had hoped to begin the battle at dawn but was forced to wait for improved visibility. It was important for the Swedes to attack early as they knew that reinforcements were on their way for Wallenstein. Conversely, the delay benefited the imperial forces because every second's delay brought Pappenheim closer. They also knew the Swedes could not expect any timely help from the forces at Torgau based on reports from their screening force.

The fog and mist finally began to lift shortly after 1000 hours and the two armies were barely able to see each other. Gustav Adolf immediately signaled his artillery to open fire and the imperial guns replied. After the artillery duel had lasted for about one hour, Gustav Adolf raised his sword and led his Swedish and Finnish cavalry forward. They quickly scattered the Croat cavalry screen.

Next in Gustav's path were the imperial musketeers in the ditches on both sides of the causeway. After some sharp fighting the musketeers were driven out of their positions. The Swedish cavalry wave now pounced on the imperial left wing and after some fierce fighting Field Marshal Hock's men were forced back. The shattering of the Croat cavalry screen had meanwhile led the "decoy" army consisting of conscripts, peddlers, and women to stream from the field. Wallenstein switched cavalry from his right flank to the left to stop the Swedish avalanche.

The Swedish attack on the imperial right wing was also the signal for the center and left wing to advance. The imperial musketeers were driven from the causeway and the Swedes moved on to capture the artillery in front of the imperial center. The Swedish attack was initially successful all along the front, but the visibility was again limited to a short distance as the fog settled in and mixed with the smoke produced by the combatants.

The success did not last long. First, Duke Bernhard had a tough going against the imperial right. Second, the Swedish center, which overlapped the imperial center, began an envelopment. This move by the right flank of the Swedish center opened a gap to the right of center, into which part of the imperial cavalry struck. The regiments on the Swedish right were now squeezed between the attacking cavalry and the imperial infantry. Despite desperate resistance they were pushed back across the causeways, which were quickly re-occupied by imperial musketeers. The captured imperial guns were lost in the process.

DEATH OF GUSTAV ADOLF

The battlefield was again shrouded in a thick fog. This heavy mist kept the smoke from the smoldering village and the discharge of the guns close to the ground, making for near zero visibility in some of the low-laying areas. This was the time when Gustav Adolf, who was still driving back the imperial left, received word that his center was in trouble. He sent orders for the second line to advance, and allegedly pulled one of his cavalry regiments out of the line and personally headed for the center. What followed is shrouded in as much literary fog as the natural fog on the battlefield.

One account has the king being wounded earlier during the battle by a musket ball that broke his arm—before 1030—but this is probably confused with the several wounds he received at the end.[48] Another account claims that the king was hit by a musket ball and lost control of his horse, which galloped into the enemy formations where he was killed.[49] Other explanations of what happened give as a reason that the king and his immediate escorts were riding faster horses and became separated from the regiment.[50] This is when the small group encountered a detachment of imperial cavalry and Gustav was hit and wounded by their pistol fire. He was either mortally wounded or killed instantaneously—we just don't know. He did tumble from his horse. Other accounts have him receiving several wounds before he died. We are left with several accounts of the king's end that attempt to accurately reconstruct events, but they are, for the most part, guesswork.

The simplest and most logical explanation is that the king and his party became lost in the heavy fog or that they did not realize how far back the Swedish center had been driven and therefore rode between the lines rather than behind the Swedish line. Duke Franz Albrecht of Lauenburg accompanied the king as a volunteer, and the Swedes never forgave the duke for abandoning the king's body, which was subsequently repeatedly stabbed and stripped by looters.[51] Liddell Hart's comment is correct in his observation: *The pitcher had been carried once too often to the well.*[52]

Gustav Adolf's horse without a rider and covered with blood galloped back to the Swedish lines. This is how the troops learned that their monarch was dead, despite assurances by Brahe and Knypenhausen that he was only wounded. They soon learned the truth but rather than becoming despondent, they became enraged.

The center commanders sent a message to Bernhard of Weimar that the king was dead and that he should assume command of the army. Knypnhausen advised retreat, but Bernhard decided to make another assault. The Swedish left wing was now placed under the command of General Brahe.

This was also the time—around 1400 hours—that Pappenheim arrived with 2,300 cavalry after riding hard for 35 kilometers through the night. He rode right into the victorious Swedish right. The confused sight that greeted him must have been dismaying. The imperial left was in full retreat and the baggage train was fleeing. The Swedish center was again ready to advance in a second attempt to dislodge the imperial center. Wilhelm of Weimar's bodyguard had fled and this panicked the Swedish baggage train, which also fled. Several imperial units had broken and both armies were losing cohesion. The battle had degenerated into isolated actions. Pappenheim became involved in a wild mêlée with the Swedish cavalry. He was mortally wounded early in the engagement and died while being evacuated to Leipzig. His cavalry, leaderless, fell back in confusion.

SWEDISH VICTORY

The Swedish command was reorganized after the king's death. Brahe took over the left wing, Knypenhausen assumed command of the center, and Bernhard took command of the Swedish right wing. One of the most difficult things in the midst of a battle is to assume a new command, and it speaks volumes about the professionalism of the Swedish officers that they were able to do so successfully.

The left wing under Brahe finally captured what was left of the village of Lützen, including the imperial artillery. Knypenhausen's center was engaged in a desperate struggle for the causeway. Despite severe losses, the cavalry on the Swedish right reorganized and pushed beyond the causeway.

Duke Bernhard ordered a general advance against the imperial troops. The Swedes, now aware of their king's death, were infuriated according to almost all accounts. The Swedish center swept forward and cleared the causeway after the second line of infantry moved forward to join the remnants of the first line. The advance in the center was assisted by the vigorous actions of the Swedish cavalry against the imperial left wing.

However, the battle was not over. As a complete victory appeared within grasp, General Piccolomini, who had managed to rally some of the imperial cavalry, launched a counterattack that completely stopped the advance of the Swedish right. However, it had taken seven charges by the cavalry to do so. Bernhard knew he had to regain the momentum, otherwise the Swedish center, advancing toward the imperial center, would be attacked in the flank. He led his cavalry forward again and slowly drove the imperial cavalry back. General Piccolomini, wounded four times, kept the withdrawal from becoming a rout. The Swedish cavalry pushed their opponents back past their abandoned baggage trains. These were set ablaze by the Swedes and wagonloads of ammunition *erupted in earth-shuddering blasts*.[53]

This took place at about the same time as the lead units of Pappenheim's infantry arrived on the scene, and although they were fed into the maelstrom, there was not much these 2,000 troops could do after their exhausting march. The imperial center was bracing for the onslaught of Swedes infuriated at the death of their king, and resolved not to lose the battle for which he had died. This was also the time that the ammunition wagons behind the imperial right began to explode. Rumors spread among the imperial infantry that the Swedes were attacking their rear and they began to fall back. Their heavy artillery was abandoned. However, the Swedes did not stop at the artillery position but continued their forward sweep. The imperial line began to disintegrate and the withdrawal soon became a flight.

One source[54] has the Swedes being pushed back to the causeways yet another time, but I believe this is because he does not have Pappenheim's cavalry arriving until around 1500 hours when they had arrived at least one hour earlier. I have found no convincing evidence that Wallenstein ordered another general assault after his center had been driven back and lost cohesion, which, according to most sources took place around 1700 hours.

Wallenstein, who was appalled at the heavy losses, including many senior officers, had in fact decided to withdraw as his army was hopelessly scattered. He abandoned his artillery and 1,160 wounded.[55]

While virtually all sources conclude that Lützen was a great Swedish victory, there is at least one dissenter, Peter Wilson. He makes the highly questionable claim that *Wallenstein showed far superior generalship, whereas Gustavus relied on an unimaginative frontal assault with superior numbers.*[56] Except for Wallenstein's successful use of the indirect approach to bring Gustav Adolf away from Bavaria and the selection of a battle position, most military historians agree that when it came to the battle itself, it was Wallenstein who made the most grievous errors.[57] It was Wallenstein who scattered his army while the enemy was in his immediate vicinity, a serious mistake and misjudgment of Swedish intentions. Geoffrey Parker calls this the most serious mistake of Wallenstein's career.[58]

Wilson also neglects the topographical layout of the battlefield. The Swedes could not envelop the imperial right because of the marshy ground in that area. They aimed instead for the imperial weakness, the left flank, and this is where the most important events took place. General Brahe's mission was to contain the imperial center, but as the battle progressed, heavy fighting developed in the center during the frantic mêlée that followed the death of the Swedish king and the return of Pappenheim. The eagerness of Gustav Adolf to fight in the miserable visibility is understandable. He expected both Pappenheim and Callas to show up and that would leave him with a distinct numerical inferiority. The old rule that it takes three attackers to one defender to successfully attack an enemy in defensive positions should not be forgotten.

Delbruck writes that Lützen was governed more definitely by luck than other battles. He concludes:

> Of course, Gustavus Adolphus had intended to attack the imperial forces at the very break of day. If that had been done, he would have been sure of a brilliant victory. But the fog delayed the Swedish attack, and during this time not only did the imperial forces strengthen their position by hard digging, but reinforcements were approaching . . . and the arrival of Pappenheim's infantry, which would have given Wallenstein numerical superiority, were late on their march from Halle . . .[59]

Most sources place the imperial losses as high as 12,000 while Swedish losses are generally listed as 6,000 to 10,000. Some of the companies on the imperial side were *reduced to two or three survivors,* and the failure of the Swedes to pursue was primarily because *several of their brigades had lost five-sixth of their strength.*[60]

The real tragedy for the Swedes—and for Protestant Germany—was the death of Gustav Adolf. The Swedes went on to fight in Germany for another sixteen years, but the leadership of the Protestant cause was soon assumed by the French. Wallenstein, nerves broken by his defeat, did not survive long, as Emperor Ferdinand had him assassinated in 1634.

NOTES

1. See Dupuy, *Gustavus Adolphus*, p. 116 and Montross, *op. cit.*, p. 280.
2. Wilson, *The Thirty Years War*, p. 495.
3. *Ibid*, pp. 493–494.
4. Depuy, *Gustav Adolphus*, p. 116 and Wilson, *The Thirty Years War*, p. 497.
5. See Monro, *Expedition*, p. 244.
6. Montross, *op. cit.*, pp. 280–281.
7. Dupuy, *Gustavus Adolphus*, p. 121.
8. Liddell Hart, *Great Captains*, p. 141.
9. B. H. Liddell Hart, *Strategy*, (New York: Praeger Publishers, 1972), p. 83 and Dupuy, *Gustavus Adolphus*, p. 121, report the size as 40,000 while Wilson, *The Thirty Years War*,

p. 501, places the number at 65,000. I don't know which is correct but it should be noted that Wilson's book was published decades after the other two.

10. Liddell Hart, *Great Captains*, p. 190.
11. Wilson, *The Thirty Years War*, pp. 498–500.
12. Dupuy, *Gustavus Adolphus*, p. 121.
13. Montross, *op. cit.*, p. 281.
14. Liddell Hart, *Great Captains*, p. 140.
15. Dupuy, *Gustavus Adolphus*, p. 121.
16. *Ibid*, p. 123.
17. Liddell Hart, *Strategy*, pp. 83–84.
18. Dupuy, *Gustavus Adolphus*, p. 124.
19. Wilson, *The Thirty Years War*, p. 500.
20. Monro, *Expedition*, p. 254–6.
21. Parker, *Europe in Crisis*, p. 164.
22. As quoted by Montross, *op. cit.*, p. 281.
23. Liddell Hart, *Great Captains*, p. 141.
24. See ibid, p. 146 and Wilson, *The Thirty Years War*, p. 501.
25. Dupuy, *Gustavus Adolphus*, p. 129.
26. Monro, *Expedition*, p. 278 and *Wilson, The Thirty Years War*, pp. 501 and 504.
27. Wilson, *The Thirty Years War*, p. 502.
28. Dupuy, *Gustavus Adolphus*, p. 130.
29. Liddell Hart, *Great Captains*, p. 143.
30. Wilson, *The Thirty Years War*, p. 502.
31. *Ibid,* p. 504.
32. Liddell Hart, *Great Captains*, p. 143.
33. Dupuy, *Gustavus Adolphus*, p. 135.
34. Liddell Hart, *Great Captains*, p. 192.
35. *Ibid*, p. 144.
36. Dupuy, *Gustavus Adolphus*, p. 137
37. Wilson, *The Thirty Years War*, p. 507.
38. Montross, *op. cit.*, p. 283.
39. Dupuy, *Gustav Adolphus*, p. 138.
40. Delbruck, *op. cit.*, volume 4, p. 209.
41. Wilson, *The Thirty Years War*, p. 507.
42. Liddell Hart, *Great Captains*, p. 145.
43. Delbruck, *op. cit.*, volume 4, pp. 207–208.
44. *Ibid*, p. 208 basing his information in Karl Deuticke, *Die Schlacht bei Lützen*, Giessen dissertation, 1917, p. 67.
45. Wilson, *The Thirty Years War*, p. 508.
46. R. Matthew Di Palma, "Battle of Lützen: Victory and Death for Gustavus Adolphus" in *Military History*, October 1988, p. 50.
47. Dupuy, *Gustavus Adolphus*, p. 142.

48. Di Palma, *op. cit.*, p. 51.

49. Gary Dean Peterson, *Warrior Kings of Sweden: The Rise of an Empire in the Sixteenth and Seventeenth Centuries* (Jefferson, North Carolina: McFarland & Company, Inc., 2007), Kindle edition, loc. 4043.

50. Dupuy, *Gustavus Adolphus*, p. 146.

51. Wilson, *The Thirty Years War*, p. 510.

52. Liddell Hart, *Great Captains*, p. 148.

53. Di Palma, *op. cit.*, p. 52.

54. *Ibid*, p. 53.

55. Wilson, *The Thirty Years War*, p. 510.

56. *Loc. cit.*

57. See for example, Fuller, *op. cit.*, volume II, p. 71; Liddell Hart, *Great Captains*, p. 149; and Delbruck, *op. cit.,* volume 4, p.209.

58. Parker, *The Thirty Years War,* p. 116.

59. Delbruck, *op. cit.*, volume 4, p. 209.

60. Montross, *op. cit.*, p. 284.

6
Swedish Military
Operations in Germany
from 1632 to 1648

*Retreat and defeat upset the financial
equation. Peace destroyed it.*

MICHAEL ROBERTS

The next two chapters provide the link between Sweden's rise to military preeminence and the beginning of its decline. This chapter focuses on Swedish campaigning in Germany from the death of Gustav Adolf in 1632 to the Treaties of Westphalia in 1648. Many important events happened in Germany and northern Europe in the 65-year period covered by these next two chapters, but because of limitations on the length of this book, military events can be covered only in a summary way. The focus is on Swedish military actions and brief descriptions of some of the campaigns and battles. French entry into the war and their campaigns will be covered only as they impacted Swedish activities. Therefore, there are a number of campaigns and battles that are not covered. However, the footnotes will assist readers to find sources that cover this period in greater detail.

THE SWEDISH GOVERNMENT

Gustav Adolf left only one heir, a daughter named Kristina who was six years old. However, there were no provisions in the constitution for a government without a monarch. The problem was solved by the creation of a regency of ten councilors until Kristina became of age in 1644. The Riksdag ratified the arrangements in early 1633 and the constitutional reforms drafted by Oxenstierna in 1634. Oxenstierna was confirmed as high chancellor and legate in Germany in January 1633 and he enjoyed extensive powers. He acted mostly on his own initiative since correspondence with Stockholm often took more than a month.

Relations between the young Kristina and Oxenstierna were good until after she became queen in 1644 at the age of 18. She is accused by some for having contributed heavily to the ruin of the Swedish economy. Her actions in inviting nobles from Germany, England, Scotland, and France to settle in Sweden and become members of the Swedish nobility added more than 300 families to the list of Swedish nobles. This resulted in more than half of the land being in the hands of nobility with no taxes being paid by the owners while there was a dire need to pay for military operations that the country had undertaken.[1]

MILITARY COMMAND

One item obviously had to be attended to immediately: the question of who should command the field forces in Germany. These forces were still engaged in hostilities and it was important to ensure proper loyalty and national control of what had become the most powerful army in Europe.[2] It was important to keep tight reins on the generals in order to keep them from becoming too autonomous and self-aggrandizing, as was the case with Wallenstein.[3]

Oxenstierna's preference for supreme commander was his son-in-law, Field Marshal Gustav Horn, who was also a councilor of state. However, Horn was a cautious commander, lacking the forceful character necessary to secure the unquestioned obedience of other capable field commanders, both Swedish and German.

Johan Banér, promoted to field marshal in 1634, was another logical choice for supreme commander, but he had not yet proven his ability as an independent leader and did not become a viable candidate until after Horn was captured in 1634. General Lennart Torstensson was another possibility but he had been captured at Alte Veste and imprisoned under deplorable conditions which led to medical issues. He was not back in service until 1635.

Even had one of the above been chosen, there was no assurance that he would have been accepted by the German allies. Wilhelm of Weimar was formally next in line since he had served as Gustav Adolf's deputy, but after Alte Veste he left the army, citing ill health.

Wilhelm's younger brother, Bernhard, became a problem for Oxenstierna. At least one German nineteenth century historian has presented him as the natural alternative to the other candidates.[4] He had great courage and his men showed him great loyalty. However, as revealed at Nördlingen, he lacked resoluteness; he was a person capable of making bold decisions but equally quick to change his mind.

After Lützen—a battle he was not reticent about claiming as his victory— he not only demanded the supreme command of all Protestant forces, but he wanted to be rewarded with his own principality in Germany since he was the youngest of several siblings and therefore could not expect receiving one through inheritance.[5]

Oxenstierna was fully aware of Bernhard's ambitions. However, he saw domestic complications in placing Swedish troops under German command. Promising the kind of rewards Bernhard demanded would also complicate his relations with other German leaders and make a strategy of extracting Sweden from the war more difficult. John George of Saxony was negotiating behind the scenes for acceptable terms for Protestant principalities to return to Emperor Ferdinand's fold. Wallenstein, still around, recommended peace, but Ferdinand was not ready to accept. With Gustav Adolf out of the way, Denmark now involved herself, and offered to mediate an end to the war, for a price of course—Bremen, Verden, and some other places occupied by Swedish troops. The emperor finally agreed to some of the Protestant demands, and Denmark's acquisition of Bremen and Verden.

It became necessary for Oxenstierna to take quick action before things led to the disintegration of the ever-shaky Protestant alliance. While some of the German states were inclined to end the war, France, Sweden, and Spain were not ready for its end. France was afraid of losing its foothold on the middle Rhine. Sweden wanted some form of compensation for all its efforts, and in accordance with the guidelines given by Gustav Adolf, that compensation was to be Pomerania. This was not likely without further successful war, as both Saxony and Brandenburg were expected to raise strong objections. Spain wanted to reassert is influence in northwest Germany and use it as a base against the Netherlands.

THE LEAGUE OF HEILBRONN
Oxenstierna continued Gustav Adolf's policy of trying to retain Swedish

dominance in a Protestant alliance. He was in fact on his way to Frankfurt on Main to attend a conference on the new alliance when he received word of the king's death. The conference was postponed until the following year.

The Saxon elector John George refused to attend the meeting. He insisted on a general agreement with Emperor Ferdinand. Most of the other Protestant princes opted to join the new confederation under Swedish leadership. The confederation became known as the League of Heilbronn. The members agreed to make regular contributions to maintain a force of 78,000 troops, but what they could pay was only 2.5 million thalers a year out of the estimated cost of 9.8 million.

French subsidies for Sweden had slowed in 1632 and came to an end in 1633 as France first wanted to see how things turned out politically in Germany. Richelieu was in fact considering dropping support for Sweden in favor of Saxony, a more pliant surrogate.[6] When the conference at Heilbronn appeared a Swedish success, France renewed the Treaty of Bärwalde, securing subsidies for Sweden for the time being. However, Richelieu continued to be irritated by Sweden's independent attitude and monetary support from France was on shaky ground.

Oxenstierna avoided making a decision on a supreme allied commander, other than to reject Bernhard of Weimar's suggestion that he assume that mantle. For the 1633 campaign, Oxenstierna appointed no overall commander, but he himself prepared the strategic plan in three widely separated areas. Bernhard, with most of the Swedish army and those of the allies, would operate in southern Germany (Swabia and Franconia) and move down the Danube. Field Marshal Horn, joining Bernhard from Alsace, was actually sent for the purpose of keeping an eye on the duke. A second army commanded by German and Bohemian exiles, was sent to assist Saxony and Brandenburg, and obviously to keep those states from defecting. Command in Silesia was entrusted to the elderly General Heinrich Matthias Thurn (1568–1640), but the actual commander was General Duwall. The real purpose was to insure that the Oder was protected in case of a Saxon defection. Duke George of Lüneburg and Landgrave Wilhelm had separate commands in Saxony and Westphalia. The best Swedish troops were sent to protect Mecklenburg, Pomerania, Bremen, Verden, and Mainz.[7]

The 1633 campaign was very indecisive and marred by a mutiny. Bernhard's and Horn's forces joined at Augsburg on 9 April, giving their combined forces 42,700 men and a two-to-one superiority over the enemy. However, the troops had not been paid in full since 1631. Breakdown of discipline in Bernhard's army was evident during his march through Franconia—particularly in a four-day sack of Landsberg where 300 of the surrendered garrison were put to the sword and over 150 civilians, including children, were killed.

The mutiny broke out on 30 April as the troops demanded 3 million thalers in arrears. To meet the soldiers' demands Oxenstierna felt it necessary to sell off conquered territories, a complete reversal of the policies of Gustav Adolf. Whole areas and bishoprics were given to leading commanders to keep or as places that could be "plundered" to compensate for owed pay.

Oxenstierna also capitulated to some of Duke Bernhard's demands by transferring to him Bamberg and Würzburg as hereditary possessions and giving him the title of duke of Franconia. Bernhard was to pay 600,000 thalers spread over four years, in addition to the normal contributions of those places based on their membership in the League of Heilbronn. Horn had opposed giving in to the mutineers and this widened the gulf between him and Bernhard. The problem of finding a durable solution to financing plagued the Swedes till the end of the war.

Wallenstein was still the nominal supreme commander of the imperial forces. His negotiations with Saxony and Sweden finally brought his downfall and death, although the particulars will no doubt remain shrouded in mystery.[8] It appears that Ferdinand put out an order to arrest the supreme commander and bring him to Vienna, dead or alive. When Wallenstein learned that he was about to be arrested, he tried to escape to nearby Protestant forces. Some of his own officers are alleged to have murdered him on 25 February 1634. Emperor Ferdinand quickly named his son Ferdinand III (1608–1657) as the new supreme commander.

FIRST BATTLE OF NÖRDLINGEN

The campaigning in 1634 appeared to be another year of indecisive results except for the first Battle of Nördlingen on 6 September. In fact, the battle was so one-sided that it appeared, like Breitenfeld, to be a turning point in the war.

The imperial troops under the command of Archduke Ferdinand (son of the emperor) and the military leadership of Field Marshal Gallas were besieging Nördlingen. The town was in desperate straits and Bernhard decided to march to its relief. The imperial forces alongside a contingent of Spaniards are variously estimated at 30,000–40,000.[9] The strength of the forces under Bernhard and Horn was roughly 25,000.

There was disagreement between Bernhard and Horn. Horn wanted to delay and wait for reinforcements of 6,000 men that were supposed to arrive within a week. However, Bernhard did not think Nördlingen would be able to hold out that long as they had fired flares indicating their situation was desperate. He was probably right. Bernhard's major mistake, however, was in delaying moving to Nördlingen by useless maneuvering which allowed the Spaniards time to join the besiegers.

Delbruck correctly notes that a decision to attack the besieging forces was never taken.[10] Horn had only agreed to press the besieging army in order to lessen the pressure on the garrison. The allied camp was at Bopfingen, less than 10 kilometers west of Nördlingen. The idea that was agreed to seems to have been to cut the imperial supply route from Donauwörth. This would at the same time simplify the Swedish supply route from Ulm and Württemberg.

The arch-like approach march from Bopfingen was another mistake. The circuitous route almost doubled the direct distance. It led directly west from Nördlingen to a ridge southwest of that town, called Arnsberg. Bernhard, who led the march with his units, appeared to have moved closer to the town than he and Horn had agreed. The route selected led through a difficult defile in a wooded area and the imperial troops became aware of the Swedish approach. They quickly sent strong forces to occupy the ridge southwest of the town, a total of over 8,000 troops.[11]

While Bernhard and his troops were able to partially occupy their positions, Horn, who was behind and supposed to form the right flank of the Swedish army, found that the ridge was already in enemy hands. Darkness fell during the initial struggle for this height, called Allbuch. The next morning Horn launched all his forces at the enemy holding the ridge. The Swedes made fifteen uphill assaults but were unable to dislodge the enemy. While this struggle was going on, Bernhard was conducting a holding action in his area. The fact that Bernhard and Horn had not brought all available forces to Nördlingen was another serious mistake.

Field Marshal Horn finally realized that he could not accomplish his task and that he would be forced to withdraw during daylight rather than wait for nightfall. He began his withdrawal covered by a cavalry screen. The imperial forces now launched their attacks and Bernhard's troops were also forced to withdraw. As a result, one of the worst possible situations in battle took place when the two units—Bernhard's and Horn's—became intermingled as Bernhard's retreating troops crossed through Horn's retreating troops who had fought with their backs to the Ulm road. If the battle had developed as the allied leaders had planned the two units would have been in roughly parallel lines—but they ended up at right angles since the enemy had occupied Horn's objective in force when they were alerted to the Swedish approach. Total confusion ensued as commanders lost control of their units. A total collapse followed and the allied infantry was practically wiped out. Horn was captured while Bernhard managed to escape.

Delbruck writes that he suspects Bernhard had moved so close to Nördlingen so that the battle that Field Marshal Horn was eager to avoid would be forced upon him.[12] If this is true it was a breach of the pre-battle understanding between the two commanders—that they would only threaten the enemy in order to ease the pressure on the besieged city. Bernhard was aware that the enemy was superior in numbers but he may not have known how great the discrepancy actually was. If a direct, rather than a circuitous approach had been taken by the allies, it is at least possible they would have been able to occupy the planned positions and it would have been the imperial and Spanish forces that would have had to attack uphill to try dislodging them. Since we don't know how and when the approach was discovered this is only speculation.

The losses were immense, and for the Swedes estimates range from 8,000 to 21,000, or more than half the forces engaged.[13] The lower number is probably closer to the truth since Duke Bernhard still had 14,000 troops at his disposal when he reached Heilbronn a few days later. The imperial and Spanish forces lost between 1,200 and 2,000 men.

Whatever the actual numbers, it was the worst defeat suffered by the Swedes in Germany. Most of the remaining disciplined national army that had been brought from Sweden perished. Although, the Swedish forces in Germany had always included a large number of mercenaries with a Swedish nucleus, from now on it was primarily Swedish in name only as the number of mercenaries—German, Scottish, English, Irish, French, and Polish—increased in relation to the Swedes. The troops fought increasingly for a particular general rather than for a cause or a nation.[14]

Some writers consider that the first battle of Nördlingen ended the Swedish period and ushered in the French period of the Thirty Years War. This is an artificial distinction and it can be persuasively argued that the period of full French partnership with Sweden did not take place until 1635 or even after the Battle of Rocroi in 1643, where a French army of 23,000 under the leadership of the twenty-two-year old Duke Henri of Enghien (1621–1686), later known as Prince of Condé, using the reformed army that Richelieu had created on the Swedish model, soundly defeated the Spanish army of 27,000 under General Francisco de Melo (1597–1651).

This Spanish defeat, coming close to the sinking of a Spanish fleet of 77 ships by Admiral Maarten Tromp (1598–1653), represented a monumental change in the political landscape of Europe. It confirmed the inferiority of the Spanish military system and signaled the fact that the long period of Spanish greatness was drawing to an end. It also ushered in a nearly unbroken period of French military superiority which lasted for the next two hundred years.

Some view the Battle of Nördlingen as important as Breitenfeld. However, Breitenfeld ushered in a new era in military tactics and weaponry while Nördlingen was merely a severe defeat due to mistakes and bad decisions by the Swedish commanders. Delbruck writes that there is nothing of tactical value to be gleaned from Nördlingen, only that neither side really wanted a general engagement.[15] Furthermore, the clash was not decisive. In some of the hardest fought battles after Nördlingen, the Swedes racked up impressive victories and we will take a look at some of them.

Cardinal Richelieu brought France into the Thirty Years War on the side of the Protestants in 1635. His objective was simply to prevent the Hapsburgs from regaining complete control of Germany. From this time on France was the senior partner with Sweden, as the war dragged on.

BATTLE OF WITTSTOCK

The next battle of consequence for our purpose was the Battle of Wittstock, fought on 4 October 1636. It came at a time when the Swedish army in Germany was down to 45,000 men, primarily located in Pomerania and Mecklenburg. It had been a cold winter and the Baltic had frozen, preventing both reinforcements and supply shipments from Sweden. The field force was down to 12,000 men under Field Marshal Johan Banér in Werben, and 6,000 men under Field Marshal Walter Leslie (1606–1667) in Westphalia.

After a long siege, a combined imperial army and Saxon (having switched sides in 1635) troops under the command of Field Marshal Melchior Hatzfeldt (1593–1658) captured Magdeburg on 13 July 1636. Banér left Werben on 12 August and moved west to join Leslie who was withdrawing through Lower Saxony. Hatzfeldt sent General Hans Kaspar von Klitzing (1594–1644) with 4,000 men to protect Brandenburg, which was on the verge of declaring war on the Swedes. Hatzfeldt also summoned General Rudolfo Marazzino (1585–1646) from the Oder to join the main imperial army assembled at Tangermünde for an invasion of western Pomerania and Mecklenburg.[16] The Swedish base area was in grave danger.

Field Marshal Banér ventured everything in a battle to save the base area. He marched northeast over the Elbe where he linked up with 3,800 troops detached from the Pomeranian garrisons. This increased his army to about 17,000 men. Banér now marched eastward cutting Hatzfeldt's communications, which forced him to recall General Klitzing, ordering him to join the main army at Wittstock, south of the Pomeranian lakes.

Banér marched his troops around the enemy and launched his attack from the southwest, after crossing the Dosse River. Banér's army numbered 16,000 to 17,000. His enemies were reported to have had 22,000 to 23,000 men, but more recent research appear to indicate that they may have had as few as 18,000, only a slight numerical advantage over the Swedes.[17] The discrepancy in imperial numbers is probably due to the fact that General Klitzing had not yet reached Wittstock and that was the primary reason why Banér was in a hurry to launch his attack.

The imperial forces occupied a strong position that had been field fortified. Instead of going against strength Banér decided to divide his army and carry out a simultaneous double envelopment of the enemy flanks. Whether intended or not, the operation turned into a staggered double envelopment and the Swedes ended up fighting with a reversed front during part of the battle.

Banér sent Generals James King (1589–1652) and Torsten Stalhansk (1594–1644) with 3,100 cavalry to turn the imperial right flank. General Leslie with 5,800 men was ordered to pin down the imperial center. Banér with the rest of the army fell on the imperial left.

If the reports of battle are true, Delbruck calls it *one of the most astonishing battles in world history. . . . and it would have to be placed even above Cannae with respect to the boldness of the plan and the greatness of the triumph.*[18] The general rule for double envelopments is that the weaker side should not attempt it unless its commander has absolute superiority in cavalry. It was therefore difficult to see how Banér thought he could bring on a victory in a decisive battle in this manner since he commanded the weaker side and had no superiority in cavalry.

The one advantage that Banér had was that the enemy flanks did not rest on natural obstacles and could thus be enveloped without large detours. Also, the enemy had taken up position facing a woods which shielded Swedish movements from view. The Swedish approach was not discovered until around 1430 hours. Banér was therefore able to launch a surprise attack with his right flank against the left flank of the enemy. The imperial troops held their ground against the Swedes and formed a new front to cope with the envelopment. Hatzfeldt sent aid from his right flank and center.

The Swedish envelopment of the enemy's right flank was not yet underway which, if intentional, makes this battle even more remarkable since that means the envelopments were staggered. Provided the relative numbers are correct, Banér's troops on the imperial left should now have been seriously outnumbered. Nevertheless, they withstood the enemy counterattacks for three hours with little loss of ground.

It was 1830 hours before General King fired a signal gun signifying that he was in position and launching his attack against the imperial right flank and rear. The surprised imperial right was driven back, losing its artillery, but darkness was setting in. The Swedish right flank had been able to hold its own and draw most of the enemy army against them.

Delbruck gives some reasons that are not so obvious for the imperial defeat. Banér had realized that the artificial frontal obstacles designed to protect the enemy also prevented him from counterattacking, particularly in the center, and this led Banér to risk dividing his army. This disposition negated the ability of the imperial commander to counter the envelopments at an appropriate time in a counterattack by the center. The imperial army also suffered the disadvantage of a divided command—shared by the Saxon elector John George and Hatzfeldt.[19]

Opinions differ as to the severity of the imperial defeat. There was undoubtedly considerable confusion because of the multidirectional attacks and the onset of darkness. However, that this was one of the most consequential battles of the war and that it was a Swedish victory cannot be disputed. An army does not abandon its artillery and supply trains unless it is in serious trouble. Before the battle the Swedes were on the ropes. By looking at what happened after the battle, we can get some idea of the severity of the imperial defeat. Their army broke up with the Saxons returning home and the imperial troops under Hatzfeldt having *lost cohesion, plundering their way westwards to the Lower Rhine*.[20] Panic broke out in Berlin and the court fled to Küstrin. Banér drove through Thuringia, relieved Erfurth, reopened communications with the Hessians, and continued into Saxony where he captured Torgau in February 1637.

LENNART TORSTENSSON AS SUPREME COMMANDER

The brief review of Swedish operations in the Thirty Years War after the death of Gustav Adolf would be incomplete without some mention of the lightning operations carried out by Field Marshal Lennart Torstensson (1603–1651). He took over operations in Germany after the death of Johan Banér on 10 May 1641, and his campaigns resulted in what might be called a period of Swedish revival based on mobility and iron discipline.

Torstensson was one of the last survivors of Gustav Adolf's great lieutenants. Due largely to his year of imprisonment after being captured at Alte Veste, he had become a sickly, dissolute, and prematurely old man. He was so racked by gout that he could barely walk and sign his name. He had been in Sweden and left that war-weary and financially strapped country with 7,000 raw recruits. Upon arrival he was confronted with another mutiny among the mercenaries, which, despite his ailments, he managed to put down.

After a period of reorganization, in 1642 he began his fast-moving campaigns that are second only to Gustav Adolf's in military achievement. The campaigns brought him to Saxony, Bohemia, Denmark, and Moravia. He won four notable victories that brought him to the very gates of Vienna. His fame as a successful military commander was marred, however, by destructiveness and brutality. He made no attempt to pay the troops, which comprised an open invitation for them to to plunder and which brought the worst thugs into his service. His method of enforcing discipline was little short of spreading terror as he routinely relied on the lash, the rack, and the gallows. He showed equal lack of pity for prisoners and noncombatants. In Saxony he left a trail of burning villages as he moved through the territory in 1642.[21]

What characterized Torstensson's military campaigns was relentless and rapid movement, and unpredictable maneuvers which left both friends and foes confused. The Saxon army was soundly defeated at Schweidnitz by a few speedy maneuvers followed by blows which staggered the opponents and put them to flight, minus their artillery. Having disposed of the Saxons, Torstensson moved into Moravia and laid the countryside waste. Olmütz was captured and the Swedish army advanced to within twenty-five miles of Vienna before falling back into Saxony when faced by a much stronger army under Archduke Leopold (1614–1662).

SECOND BATTLE OF BREITENFELD

The Swedes had already begun a siege of Leipzig when the archduke caught up with them. This time Torstensson did not withdraw but faced his pursuers in what is known as the Second Battle of Breitenfeld, on 2 November 1642. The imperial forces were commanded by Archduke Leopold and Field Marshal Ottavio Piccolomini (1599–1656). The imperial army is said to have numbered 26,000 men when the Saxon contingent of about 1,700 is counted. The Swedish army was inferior in numbers, having about 19,000 men.

The two armies camped for the night, with the imperial forces on the east side of Seehausen facing west. Torstensson was at Breitenfeld. Both armies advanced on the morning of 2 November with Torstensson drawing up in battle order in front of the village of Linkwald. Piccolomini recommended to Leopold that sixteen cavalry regiments be sent north around the woods to turn the Swedish left flank. This was done.

Torstensson shifted his army to confront the attack against his left, and the action was underway by 1000 hours. While the imperial attack was hampered because of an extension of the woods that split their advance, they made some progress against the Swedish center. However, the decisive action was taking place on the Swedish right where Generals Avid Wittenberg (1606–1657) and Torsten Stalhansk (1594–1644) led a devastating cavalry attack against the imperial right under General Hans Puchheim (1605–1657). The Swedish advance was so rapid that Puchheim did not have time to properly deploy his troops.

Several regiments of the imperial first line broke and fled even before contact was made, and this led the Saxons in the second line to also flee. Stalhansk led the pursuit of the fleeing imperial cavalry and Saxons while Wittenberg led the rest of the Swedish cavalry back behind the Swedish battle-line to assist the Swedish left under Colonel Erik Slang (1600–1642). That wing, which had advanced in a more deliberate manner, was under heavy pressure after Slang was killed as Croat cavalry were in the process of turning the flank. General Johan Königsmarck (1600–1653), commanding the cavalry in the second line, was able to hold the flank long enough for Wittenberg to arrive around noon. The Swedes swept around the enemy flank and drove it back on the center.

Archduke Leopold and Piccolomini led their bodyguards in an unsuccessful and desperate counterattack to try to restore the situation. The archduke almost lost his life. The infantry south of the woods was trapped and surrendered after a short resistance.

The Swedes had won the battle through smashing cavalry charges. Leopold escaped, but only after losing half his army in killed or prisoners, who immediately took service with the victor. One source reports that Torstensson himself—virtually bound to his horse and reins—led the charge against the imperial left wing, separating it from the infantry.[22]

The Swedish losses were 4,000 killed or wounded while the imperial losses were 8-10,000 dead and captured. They also lost all their artillery—46 guns—their field treasury, and supply train. Leipzig fell to the Swedes on 7 December 1642, and this time it remained in their hands until 1650. News of the defeat struck fear in Catholic Germany.[23] However, like so many other battles, it did not lead to decisive strategic results.

Torstensson returned to Moravia but was then ordered against Denmark, which had begun to side with the Empire during the last years of the war. The reason for the Swedish surprise attack on Denmark and Norway was to punish Denmark for joining with the emperor and to insure that their attempts to mediate an end to the war ceased.

The emperor had sent an army north to help his new ally. Leaving a force to hold Denmark, Torstensson turned back south, eluding the imperial forces and spreading devastation through Hapsburg holdings in the north. The imperial forces finally caught up with Torstensson, but suffered a major defeat at the Battle of Juterborg.

Despite now enjoying naval superiority, the war did not initially go well for the Swedes in the Scandinavian Peninsula. Field Marshal Horn was recalled from retirement to lead an army of 10,600 men against Skåne, the Danish held part of southern Sweden. Horn captured Helsingborg and blockaded Malmö while another army occupied the Norwegian province of Jämtland. The local Skåne militia stopped Horn's advance and began raiding Swedish territory. The Norwegian army blockaded Gothenburg from land while a Danish fleet was stationed outside the harbor.

The first Danish-Swedish naval engagement ended in a Danish victory over a Dutch mercenary fleet in Swedish service. A 41-ship Swedish fleet was trapped in Kiel Bay when it withdrew after a long-range bombardment by the Danish fleet. The Danes landed guns and bombarded the Swedish ships from the shore. The Swedish ships were now under command of General Karl Gustav Wrangel (field marshal from 1646) and he managed to slip out of the trap with lights extinguished. The emperor had meanwhile sent an army under Field Marshal Gallas to assist the Danes, although there was no formal alliance.

King Kristian IV prepared to ferry an army to Sweden to relieve Malmö and drive Horn out of the province. A Norwegian counterattack had already driven the Swedes out of Jämtland.

Meantime the Swedish fleet had been repaired and had linked up with the remnants of the Dutch mercenary fleet. With a combined force of 37 ships the Swedes found the Danish fleet under Admiral Mundt at Fehmarn Island on 23 October 1644. Half the Danish fleet had already been laid up for the winter, leaving them with only 17 undermanned ships. The surprise attack succeeded completely and only three of the Danish ships escaped, Admiral Mundt was killed.

The Swedish attack on Denmark did not make their French ally happy. They had reached agreement with the Dutch Republic in January 1644 to limit Swedish gains since they did not want Sweden in complete control of the entrance to the Baltic. Peace talks opened at the border town of Brömsebro in southern Sweden in February 1645 and the treaty was signed in August. Sweden gained virtually all her demands, despite not having had any spectacular results in the land war. She was awarded the Baltic islands of Ösel and Gotland, and Denmark had to relinquish the province of Halland on the western Swedish coast for 30 years as an assurance that the peace would be kept. The Norwegians lost the provinces of Jämtland and Härjedalen.

BATTLE OF JANKAU

After Juterborg, Torstensson invaded Bohemia where he met another army of imperial and Bavarian troops at Jankau, on 6 March 1645. The imperial and Bavarian troops that Torstensson faced at Jankau were of higher quality than any he had yet encountered. The two armies were evenly matched in number at 16,000 each, with Field Marshal Hatzfeldt holding a slight advantage in cavalry while Torstensson had a similar advantage in infantry. However, the Swedes had a substantial superiority in artillery—60 to 26 tubes.[24]

The Swedes won the battle through superior and steadfast leadership at the same time as the other side made several errors and failed to coordinate actions. Torstensson's maneuvers, shielded by woods, confused the imperial commander, allowing the Swedes to eliminate enemy detachments one by one. Torstensson reported that he lost only 600 men. The imperial troops lost half their army, including 4,000 prisoners. Field Marshal Johan Götz was killed along with five senior officers—two colonels and three lieutenant colonels. The imperial commander, Field Marshal Hatzfeldt, was captured along with five generals, eight colonels and fourteen lieutenant colonels.[25] Nearly all of the veteran Bavarian cavalry perished.

The ransoming of captured senior officers had become commonplace at this stage of the Thirty Years War. The warring parties saw no advantage in keeping these prisoners, and their exchange had become a source of revenue. Field Marshal Torstensson allowed the whole imperial general staff captured at Jankau their freedom in return for 120,000 riks-dollars.[26]

Transylvania entered into an alliance with Sweden in 1643, and agreed to invade Hungary and Silesia. The Swedish purpose in encouraging this was to divert the emperor's attention while Torstensson dealt with Denmark. While Transylvania's entry into the war caused considerable alarm, the Hungarian incursion ran into more resistance than had been expected. The Transylvanians were not ready to do anything further until they had active support from Sweden. In the meantime they accepted Ferdinand's offer for negotiations.

Transylvania became more active in the wake of Jankau and the receipt of French subsidies. News of the imperial debacle Jankau caused considerable alarm in Vienna. Most forces were withdrawn behind the Danube, and the militia, consisting of 5,500 citizens and students, was called up to reinforce the 1,500 man garrison.[27]

Torstensson encountered problems when he reached the Danube. His Finnish engineers were accustomed to securing boats to build bridges, but all the local boats had been moved to the southern bank of the river. The 14,200 Transylvanian troops which had joined him were proving unreliable, and he was worried about the link to his base. It was decided to capture Brün while he waited for reinforcements. An outbreak of plague resulted in the loss of 8,000 Swedes and Transylvanians during the siege.

Negotiations between the Empire and Transylvania had meanwhile resumed, and the Emperor's offer for peace was accepted in August 1645. This forced the Swedes to lift the siege of Brün but, encouraged by the peace treaty between Sweden and Denmark, Torstensson decided to try once more to take Vienna. The imperial forces south of the Danube had now grown to over 20,000 while Torstensson, now seriously ill, had about 10,000. He cancelled his attempt and moved his forces north through Saxony and into Thuringia. Here he turned over command of the Swedish army in Germany to Field Marshal Karl Gustav Wrangel (1613–1676).

The Thirty Years War was beginning to wind down. The cautious French Marshal Turenne combined with Field Marshal Wrangel to devastate Bavaria, forcing the 73-year-old Maximilian to sue for a truce. Fearing that such a truce would lead to a French withdrawal from the war, Wrangel opposed granting a truce but finally relented. The Truce of Ulm was agreed to on 14 March 1647.

Brandenburg and Saxony had already been forced to conclude truces with the Swedes—Brandenburg, now under Elector Friedrich Wilhelm, in 1641 and Saxony in 1645 after its isolation following the Battle of Jankau. The terms were rather lenient. Sweden accepted Saxon neutrality in return for a payment of 11,000 thalers a month for the Swedish garrison in Leipzig and freedom of movement through Saxony. In return Sweden agreed to lift their siege of the Saxon garrison of Magdeburg.[28]

Field Marshal Wrangel's doubts about the wisdom of the Ulm Truce proved to be correct, since the French stood to benefit most from it. Swedish-French relations were also soured by the defection of six French cavalry regiments during a "lack-of-pay mutiny." These regiments took service with the

Swedes! The Emperor was able to bribe Maximilian to break the Ulm Truce on 7 September 1647.

Maximilian's breach of the truce had the effect of improving Swedish-French relations to the point where Marshal Turenne and Field Marshal Wrangel united to invade Bavaria. The imperial troops were under the command of Field Marshal Peter Melander (1589–1648), a very capable officer. He was now commanding the last Hapsburg army left in Germany, a force of less than 16,000 with only enough horses for about one third of his cavalry. The allies, who had a clear superiority with 22,000 troops, caught up with the imperial army in heavily wooded terrain near the village of Zusmarshausen. General Raimond Montecuccoli (1609–1680) commanded the rear guard of the withdrawing imperial army and carried out his task in a spirited manner. Pursued by six Swedish and three French cavalry regiments, he was finally outflanked. Melander turned around with part of his force to extricate his rear guard, but was mortally wounded in the chest. The action of the rear guard had bought the time needed to get the demoralized remnants of the imperial army behind prepared entrenchments, from which they continued their withdrawal after darkness, abandoning their guns and trains.

Although the allies had failed to destroy the imperial forces at Zusmarshausen, the end was inevitable. The imperial remnants repelled several allied attempts to cross the Lech River until Field Marshal Wrangel, in an attempt to repeat Gustav Adolf's success, had his cavalry swim the river. Luck was on his side as the imperial outposts reported that the allies were across the Lech in force. General Jobst Gronsfeld (1598–1662), now in command of the imperial forces, withdrew to Ingolstadt, abandoning southern Bavaria to the allies. The imperial army dissolved during the retreat, dropping to 5,000 effectives.

In a sure sign of an empire in trouble, Gronsfeld was fired and he was followed by a number of successors until Field Marshal Piccolomini was settled on. Meanwhile the allies devastated Bavaria, sparing only Munich, in order to force Maximilian to terms. He and his court had already fled to Salzburg.

The imperials and Bavarians were eventually able to recover somewhat to a combined strength of 24,000. Turenne and Wrangel retired slowly to avoid a possible reverse that would complicate peace negotiations. The Swedes were still besieging Prague.

PEACE OF WESTPHALIA

The emperor finally agreed to sign what became known as the Treaties of Westphalia, documents that had been negotiated over several years. There were actually two treaties, with the empire settling with Sweden in the Peace of Osnabrück and with France in the Peace of Münster. The treaties were formally sworn and signed on 24 October 1648.

However, almost six years passed before the last foreign garrison left, since the countryside now swarmed with unemployed and lawless mercenaries. And despite the end of the Thirty Years War, peace did not return to Europe. England and Scotland were in the middle of a rebellion, and France became embroiled in the civil war of the Fronde. In addition, waves of Swedes, Russians, and Cossacks invaded Poland and Lithuania between 1648 and 1656. As much as one third of the population was left dead in their wake. Poles remember the period as *the Deluge* and consider it the worst catastrophe in their tragic history of calamities.[29]

Sweden received several important territories in north Germany by the Treaties of Westphalia, primarily in Pomerania. The acquisition of Bremen gave Sweden a base on the North Sea. The treaties also assured that the Baltic had become a Swedish lake, at least temporarily, as hoped for by Gustav Adolf. The Swedish forces in Germany numbered about 70,000 in 1648. Almost half were scattered in 127 garrisons or strongpoints, strategically located.[30] The localities where the troops were located were required to pay maintenance fees as long as the troops were present. Germany and the Empire had to pay huge sums for their withdrawal or disbandment—15 million thalers from the Empire and 5 million more from the local German communities. Accelerated withdrawals called for additional payments.[31]

The only power to totally reject the Peace of Westphalia, not surprisingly, was the Papacy. Pope Innocent X denounced it as *null, void, invalid, iniquitous, unjust, damnable, reprobate, insane and empty of and effect for all time*.[32] He was politely ignored by the Catholic powers.

Pagden writes that it was defeat on the battlefield that forced the Christian churches in Europe to relinquish their hold over individual judgment.[33] It can be argued that we have now, in the 21st century, returned to a period where organized religion is very active in influencing the political leanings of individual believers, with the rise of Islam being a case in point.

THE HUMAN COST

That the Thirty Years War was a very destructive affair is not in doubt. The degree of destruction and number of dead is a hotly debated subject.[34] Some of the earlier stories of mass atrocities, pestilence, and mind-boggling loss of life may well have been exaggerated for various reasons, but the recent tendency to gloss over contemporary accounts can be equally damaging to historical accuracy. The "it wasn't that bad after all" school is based on mostly ignoring contemporary accounts and using questionable statistics about assumed populations before and after the war.

What is often forgotten is that even the percentages batted around by some recent researchers would still be the equivalent of 18,000,000 deaths in Germany alone based on current populations. That is more loss of life than Germany experienced in the two world wars. It is also more than the fatalities experienced during the Black Death where urban data suggests a mortality figure of 25% to 30%, with less in many rural areas.[35]

Montross, writing in the 1950s, paints an appalling picture of conditions in Germany at the end of the Thirty Years War:[36]

> *Plague and famine carried off thousands of victims every month, in addition to those maimed and butchered by a wanton soldiery. Cannibalism grew so rife that bodies were torn from the gallows by hunger-maddened folk, and throughout the Rhineland the very graveyards were guarded because of the traffic in human flesh.*

Some of what Montross writes about cannibalism is undoubtedly based on unreliable sources. However, his conclusion that *it is certain that no other European people of modern centuries have ever had such a concentrated experience of war's brutality* is undoubtedly on the mark.[37] He goes on to mention that Bohemia claimed the loss of 75 percent of its people, Nassau of 80 percent, Württemberg 83 percent, Bavaria estimated that 80,000 families were wiped out, and only 20 percent of population of the worst devastated regions of the Palatinate survived. He agrees that these figures were undoubtedly somewhat exaggerated.

C.V. Wedgwood rejects claims that the population of the German Empire dropped from 16 to 4 million, pointing out that in 1618 the population was around 21 million and probably less than 13.5 million in 1648, leaving a net loss of 7.5 million—or over 33 percent. He admits that figures are difficult to establish with any certainty because of faulty statistics and temporary emigration.[38] It should also be remembered that some areas—particularly the large towns in northern Germany—were spared from the worst ravages of war, while areas like the Palatinate and Bohemia were heavily devastated.

S.H. Steinberg, one of the most ardent revisionists, concludes his short book on the following note:

> *In short, cannibalism has to be struck from our history books, as have the colossal losses of population, the complete economic ruin, the collapse of civilization and all other myths of the 'Thirty Years War'.*[39]

QUEEN KRISTINA

Axel Oxenstierna, as Chancellor and guardian for the under-age Kristina, had in fact, if not in name, been the ruler of Sweden for the eight years following the death of Gustav Adolf. At first, his relationship with Kristina was good, but this changed as she grew up. Disputes with the crown princess eventually led to a decline in his power.

Kristina turned eighteen in 1644 and was then old enough to become queen. From all accounts, she was not a person of the people. She is accused of ruining Sweden's economy by increasing the nobility and making the new nobles exempt from taxes for the state-owned lands they were given. The resources of the government came mainly from the vast crown lands, and Kristina's distribution of these lands to her favorites led to a permanent annual loss of income to the state of not less than 200,000 pounds.[40] The condition of the farmers was deplorable, and a failed harvest in 1649 due to the cold weather that prevailed for most of the seventeenth century worsened the situation. The farmers demanded that the nobility return all lands they had acquired from the state, and they were joined by the lower nobility and the clergy. The higher nobility, on the other hand, requested protection from the farmers' demand for reduction in their holdings. Both sides appealed to the queen. She was caught in the middle of a political struggle.

Kristina had no children and no plans to marry. In the early 1650s she arranged that her cousin Karl Gustav[41] succeed her, and the Swedish nobility agreed. Then, in 1654, Kristina abruptly abdicated and converted to Catholicism! After leaving the country in the hands of Karl X Gustav, she moved to Rome and died in 1689.

WAR FINANCING

A large and powerful military establishment and its consequent wars cost money—a lot of money. Gustav Adolf's basic principle on how to pay for his conquests is mentioned in Chapter 3—war should pay for itself. That idea succeeded beyond the wildest imagination and goes a long way to explain how a small and poor country could finance major wars and maintain a strong military establishment. The principle boiled down to others paying the costs of Sweden's wars—enemies, friends, and even neutrals.

The main source of financing was Germany. Huge amounts were extorted in the form of money and supplies from both occupied enemy and allied territories. Cities purchased their protection and safety with money. Allies or friends—such as France and the Dutch—contributed to the conflict which they themselves wished to avoid. While these subsidies were a minor factor in the overall financing of the war, they were extremely helpful at critical points. Neutrals were also indirect contributors. They had to pay large duties in Baltic ports that were taken over by the Swedes during the war or in the earlier Polish campaigns.

Sven Lundkvist has estimated that in the period after the Battle of Breitenfeld, Germany contributed annually as much as ten to twelve times the regular Swedish budget.[42] The astonishing impact of this method of financing war is perhaps best illustrated by the fact that whereas in 1630 the Swedish government had to pay out 2.8 million riks-dollars from taxpayer sources for the German war, by 1633 that amount had dropped to 128,000.[43]

As long as the Heilbronn League played a role, Chancellor Oxenstierna was very successful in transferring Swedish expenses to the league members. Vast donations of conquered territories were also used, traded, or sold in return for large payments to the Swedish treasury.[44] The Swedes still had to find money from its own resources for defense of the homeland and the Baltic provinces, for the navy, and for domestically produced armaments. In the closing years of the war in Germany, these expenditures did not exceed 35 percent of the state budget, and only 4 percent of that budget went to the support of operations in Germany.[45]

Enormous amounts of confiscated or pillaged booty also flowed back to

Sweden. The amount sent north from Prague in 1648 is reported by Robert Frost. The long list of figurines, valuable clocks, jewelry, mathematical instruments, and paintings by the masters are accompanied by 12 barrels of gold coins and 2.5 tons of silver.[46]

The "contribution" system may have worked well in the early period of the war, but not in the post-Gustav Adolf period when very extreme measures were used by his followers. Also, repeated campaigns in the same rich territories were beginning to lessen opportunities for advantageous looting.

The "contribution" system only operated satisfactorily as long as Swedish arms produced victories. At the low ebb of the war that we saw after the Battle of Nördlingen and up to the Battle of Wittstock, "contributions' dried up and it was only through French subsidies that Sweden was able to turn that situation around. As Roberts observes: *As long as Sweden continued to win victories she could count on winning them at little cost to herself. Retreat and defeat upset the financial equation. Peace destroyed it.*[47]

NOTES

1. Sprague, *op. cit.*, pp. 128–129.
2. Wilson, *The Thirty Years War*, p. 513.
3. J. V. Polisensky, *The Thirty Years War*, Translated from the Czech by Robert Evans. (Berkeley: University of California Press, 1971), p. 198.
4. Wilson, *The Thirty Years War*, p. 514, referring primarily to G. Droysen's two volume work titled *Bernhard von Weimar*, published in 1885.
5. Montross, *op. cit.*, p. 285.
6. Wilson, *The Thirty Years War*, p. 516, referencing J. Öhman, *Der Kampf um den Frieden. Schweden und der Kaiser im Dreissigjährigen Krieg* (Vienna, 2005), pp. 51–54.
7. Wilson, *The Thirty Years War*, p. 515 and Dupuy, *Gustavus Adolphus*, p. 150.
8. See Golo Mann, *Wallenstein: Sein Leben erzählt* (Frankfurt am Main: S. Fisher Verlag, 1971), pp. 1087–1127 and Liddell Hart, *Great Captains*, pp. 196–203.
9. Delbruck, *op. cit.*, volume 4, p. 211 puts the strength of the imperial and Spanish troops at 40,000; Wilson, *The Thirty Years War*, p. 545 gives the combined strength at 35,500; Montross, *op. cit.*, p. 285 reports that the strength was 30,000.
10. Delbruck, *op. cit.*, volume 4, p. 210.
11. Wilson, *The Thirty Years War*, p. 547.
12. Delbruck, *op. cit.*, volume 4, p. 211.
13. *Loc. cit.* gives the Swedish losses between 10,000 and 12,000; Dupuy and Dupuy, *op.*

cit., p. 540. place the number of dead, wounded and captured at 21,000; Wilson, *The Thirty Years War*, p. 549 writes that only around 8,000 were killed.

14. Montross, *op. cit.*, p. 285.
15. Delbruck, *op. cit.*, volume 4, p. 211.
16. Wilson, *The Thirty Years War*, p. 581.
17. *Loc. cit.*
18. Delbruck, op. cit., volume 4, pp. 212–213.
19. *Ibid*, p. 214.
20. Wilson, *The Thirty Years War*, p. 583.
21. Montross, *op. cit.*, p. 289.
22. *Ibid*, p. 290.
23. Wilson, *The Thirty Years War*, pp. 636–638.
24. Delbruck, *op. cit.*, volume 4, p. 215.
25. *Loc. cit.*
26. Parker, *Thirty Years War*, p. 203. The going rate for ransoming an enemy general was approximately 25,000 riks-dollars.
27. Wilson, *The Thirty Years War*, p. 696.
28. *Ibid*, p. 705.
29. Pagden, *op. cit.*, p. 306.
30. Parker, *The Military Revolution*, p. 168.
31. Wilson, *The Thirty Years War*, pp. 770–773.
32. Theodore K. Rabb, *The Struggle for Stability in Early Modern Europe*, (New York: Oxford University Press, 1975), p. 81.
33. Pagden, *op. cit.*, p. 308.
34. Stephen J. Lee, *The Thirty Years War*. Lancaster Pamphlets (New York: Routledge, 2001), pp. 53–58.
35. Robert S. Gottfried, *The Black Death: Natural and Human Disaster in Medieval Europe* (New York: The Free Press, 1983), pp. 68–69.
36. Montross, *op. cit.*, p. 285.
37. *Ibid,* p. 286.
38. Wedgwood, *op. cit.*, p. 496.
39. S. H. Steinberg, *The Thirty Years War and the Conflict for European Hegemony 1600–1660* (New York: W. W. Norton & Company, Inc., 1966), p. 122.
40. R. Nisbet Bain, *Charles XII and the Collapse of the Swedish Empire, 1682–1719* (Nabu Public Domain Reprints, 2010), p. 7.
41. Karl Gustav's parents were Johan Kasimir of Zweibrücken and Katharina, Gustav Adolf's sister.
42. Sven Lundkvist, "Svensk krigsfinasiering 1630–1635", in 1966 *Historisk Tidsskrift*, p. 410 as quoted in Roberts, *The Swedish Imperial Experience*, p. 52.
43. *Ibid*, p. 385.
44. Roland Nordlund, *Krig genom ombud. De svanska krigsfinaserna och Heilbronnförbundet 1633* (Uppsala, 1974), as quoted by Roberts, *The Swedish Imperial Experience*, p. 53.

45. Roberts, *The Swedish Imperial Experience*, p. 53.
46. Frost, *op. cit.*, p. 134.
47. *Ibid,* p. 54.

7
Defending an Empire—
The Reigns of Karl X
and Karl XI

The exalted position achieved by 1648 had
been maintained in difficult circumstances
against a coalition of the greatest powers
in central and eastern Europe.

ROBERT I. FROST

This chapter is the second of two covering the period from the rise of Sweden as a pre-eminent military power to the start of a rapid decline during the Great Northern War at the beginning of the reign of Karl XII in 1697. The previous chapter covered the Thirty Years War after the death of Gustav Adolf in 1632. This chapter covers the period from the ascension of Karl X in 1654 to the ascension of Karl XII in 1697. Many important events for the future history of Europe took place during these 49 years, but, like the previous chapter, they have to be condensed because of space restrictions.

The end of the Thirty Years War did not bring an end to European conflicts. For Sweden, the end of that war inaugurated a period covering two generations devoted to defending its hard-fought gains as predators—former foes and friends alike—tried to separate Sweden from those gains. The 70 years of virtually incessant war that came to a close with the Peace of Westphalia saw the beginning of another 70-year period of almost constant warfare.

BEGINNINGS OF SWEDISH DOMESTIC REFORMS

Karl X Gustav found the realm not very far removed from bankruptcy when he began his reign in 1654, a reign that ended only six years later with his death in 1660. Mismanagement at home under Queen Kristina had led to a reduction in the tax base and the squandering of enormous sums of money. The expanded magnate class, both military and non-military, had grown enormously rich as a result of the war. Palatial residences had sprung up throughout the country, particularly in and around Stockholm. The distribution of crown land led to a reduction of the tax base and the shortfall was, as always, shifted to the middle and lower classes which had less political power. In 1655, the magnate class controlled 72 percent of Sweden's farmland and this was all exempt from taxation.[1] The lower nobility was also alienated because this class found advancement almost impossible as the higher nobility maintained a virtual monopoly on higher offices.[2]

Karl X Gustav took unanticipated action, against the advice of his council, to deal with the financial problems of the state. He reversed a trend, begun under Gustav Adolf and greatly accelerated under the reign of his daughter, by forcing the magnate class to agree to a partial reduction in their land holdings. This action made him exceedingly popular with the lower classes and the lesser nobility but not so much among the magnate class. The end result of this reform, continued by his successor, was rather spectacular. By the end of the century, the non-taxable lands in the hands of the upper aristocracy had fallen to 33 percent while the number of tax-paying workers and farmers who owned their own land had doubled.[3]

The lands that were returned to crown control became the basis for a reorganization of the recruiting system—*indelningsverket* or the system of apportionment. A new governmental department was created to carry out the reforms. Downing's explanation of this system is short and concise:[4]

> *Each soldier and officer was granted either a tract of land* [from those taken back by the crown] *or a percentage of the revenue from one. What emerged was a network of yeoman militias that could field almost a hundred thousand troops, integrated into a meticulous national mobilization plan, and able to acquit itself well on the field of battle with only a small amount of centralized organization.*

The weakness of this organization, which persisted in a modified form until compulsory military service was introduced in 1901, was the lack of an efficient supply service. The supply magazines were few, and quickly emptied in an emergency. There was no central logistic command structure, domestic resource extraction system, or provisions for foreign resource mobilization which had worked so well for Gustav Adolf. Wars during the reign of Karl X were primarily financed on credit.[5]

A centralized standing national army, as Prussia and France had opted for, would have been preferable from the standpoint of military efficiency. A centralized system was a great advantage for those countries where farmers were not free-holders; the relation between lord and peasant was a repressed one. It was much simpler and more secure for Prussia, France, and Austria to opt for standing armies whose loyalty to the crown was much stronger than to rely on militias with questionable and shifting loyalties. It also allowed for forced extraction of taxes, a centralized logistic system, and the full and systematic exploitation of national resources. Domestic resource mobilization was not a system that Sweden was ready to accept—it would have undermined freedoms and the constitutional legitimacy on which the monarchy rested. In Prussia and France, the system they adopted led to military-bureaucratic absolutism with its well-known consequences in the eighteenth and nineteenth centuries.[6]

Sweden's government and constitution survived virtually intact through the Thirty Years War. While having brushes with monarchical absolutism during the reigns of Karl XI and Karl XII, the essential components of the constitutional system remained intact.

Whatever absolutism existed was based on populism and exercised through functional local governments and the Riksdag. There were no social upheavals as we find in those countries where military-bureaucratic absolutism existed. When Swedish farmers and workers were dissatisfied they had a political route for venting their frustrations that avoided social disorder. In short, Sweden entered the eighteenth century with its constitutional liberties intact.

KARL X'S BALTIC CAMPAIGNS

The Baltic Campaigns of both Karl X and his son Karl XI are exceedingly difficult to deal with for a military writer. Western military historians only began to show an interest in east Europe after the rise of Russia and Prussia, since those events had a direct impact on happenings in western Europe. Western (Anglo) military historians do not cover eastern Europe, and the popular military histories—even the multi-volume work by Hans Del-bruck—make virtually no reference to the east before Poltava. This is a seri-ous oversight since it was the long and bloody struggles in the Baltic, Poland, and Russia, eventually ending in Swedish defeat, which served as a necessary precursor to the rise of both Russia and Prussia. While I have used a variety of Swedish, Norwegian, and German sources I have relied heavily on the writings of Robert I. Frost. I have only footnoted when I felt it was necessary to do so.

After celebrating his marriage with Princess Hedwig Eleonora of Hol-stein, Karl X embarked for the continent to begin a war that he was never to finish. He had set his mind on completing Gustav Adolf's policy of making the Baltic Sea a Swedish lake. Toward this goal he desired to create a land-bridge between Livonia and Pomerania, and this required the addition of all intervening Polish territory.

Poland had tried to take advantage of Sweden's involvement in the Thirty Years War. King Wladyhslaw (Sigismund III's son) had assembled an army of 24,000 and threatened war, while at the same time negotiating. To avoid war, Sweden agreed to the Treaty of Sztumsdorff in 1653 which provided for a 26-year truce and the restoration to Poland of all East Prussia as well as Livonia south of the Dvina River. These lands, and more, were what King Karl X wanted to restore to Swedish control.

The Swedish king felt the time was opportune as Poland was dealing with a Cossack revolt and involved in war with Russia. The situation appeared to promise an easy triumph. It had to be quick, however, because Sweden could not afford to rely on an expensive mercenary force for long. Karl X opted for a multi-prong attack, thus avoiding a risky landing on the Prussian coast. Gen-eral Magnus de la Gardie would invade Poland from Livonia with a force of 7,200 troops. Field Marshal Arvid Wittenberg meantime marched east across Brandenburg with a force of almost 14,000 men and crossed the Polish fron-tier on 21 July. By the time Karl X left Pomerania for Poland at the end of July with an additional 12,700 men, Wittenberg had won his first victories.

The Poles were in a hopeless situation, beset by enemies in the east, south, and now from the west. The Russians were pressing their advance in Lithuania, driving back the hopelessly outnumbered Lithuanian forces under Field Marshal Janusz Radziwill. The Lithuanians withdrew to their capital of Vilna which fell on 8 August. Tsar Alexis Michailovitsch made a triumphant entry the following day.[7] Any attempt by the Swedes to reach an understanding with King John Casimir, the grandson of Sigismund III, so as to make a joint effort against the Russians continued to founder on rival dynastic claims as they had earlier.

The Poles had virtually nothing with which to counter the three-pronged Swedish invasion. Most of the Polish regular army of slightly more than 9,000 men was still in the Ukraine trying to deal with the Cossacks and Russians. Wittenberg's advance was virtually uncontested, and the Polish levies surrendered at Ujscie on 25 July, followed by the cities of Poznan and Lalisz. These towns had Swedish garrisons by the time Karl X joined Wittenberg on 24 August. The whole of Poland lay open before the Swedish king.

At the same time, Radziwill carried out a plan that had been brewing for some time. He considered the Polish surrender at Ujscie the ultimate betrayal of Lithuania by Poland and he entered into the Treaty of Kiejdany on 17 August, accepting Swedish protection. On 20 October Radziwill signed a second treaty recognizing Karl X as Duke of Lithuania and proclaiming a union with Sweden. Karl was undoubtedly aware that his actions with respect to Lithuania would bring him into conflict with Russia, but it appears he willingly accepted this possibility.

The surrender of Radziwill was important only in appearances. Most of the Lithuanians did not agree with Radziwill's actions and soon become involved in conflict with the invaders. Much of the Lithuanian army rallied behind Hetman Pawel Jan Sapieha and, reinforced by peasant militia, carried out successful hit-and-run campaigns against the small and vulnerable Swedish garrisons.

The Polish government was in total disarray and at the point of collapse. The council of state even offered the crown to the Hapsburgs in the hope of receiving support from the Empire. With Russian and Cossack forces approaching Lwow, King Casimir abandoned Warsaw and moved to confront the Swedes. After a few skirmishes with the Swedish advance guard, the Poles withdrew toward Cracow. King Karl entered Warsaw on 8 September but left almost immediately to pursue the Polish king.

John Casimir made a stand at Zarnow on 16 September. The Swedes repulsed one Polish cavalry charge before heavy rain interrupted the action. Generals Lanckoronski and Koniecpolski made a vigorous effort to come to the relief of Cracow but were defeated by the Swedes on 3 October, as John Casimir fled to exile in Silesia. The ancient Polish capital surrendered on 19 October and the regular Polish army gave up the struggle. Koniecpolski surrendered near Cracow with 5,385 men on 24 October and this was followed two days later by the surrender of Lanckoronski with 10,000 men.[8] Nearly all of Poland proper was now in Swedish hands.

In Berlin, the Great Elector of Brandenburg, Frederick William, witnessed what appeared to be the total collapse of Poland and became worried about Royal Prussia which he held as a Polish fief. He had built up his army in Brandenburg to 14,000. In October 1655 he marched it from Brandenburg into Royal Prussia. In the Treaty of Rinsk of 12 November he concluded a defensive alliance with the Royal Prussian nobility. Karl X could not let stand this interference in his plan to secure the southern shore of the Baltic. He intended to turn Royal Prussia, too, into a Swedish province.

Karl X moved north from Cracow in October to bring Prussia under Swedish control. By December the Swedes had occupied all of Royal Prussia except for Danzig and Marienburg. Cities, such as Thorn and Elbing, which were not part of the alliance agreed to at Rinsk, surrendered to the Swedes in November 1655, and Marienburg fell in March 1656. Karl X launched a pursuit of Frederick William. The Brandenburg military commander, George Friedrich von Waldeck, urged the Great Elector to confront the Swedes in battle, but Frederick William decided instead to accept Swedish terms and signed the Treaty of Königsberg on 17 January 1656. This treaty restored Royal Prussia to its former status as a fief of Poland and made the Great Elector a vassal of Karl X as "the protector of Poland." This was all accomplished by January 1656 and, as a Swedish vassal state, Brandenburg now became a Swedish ally in the war.

Like so many before and after, King Karl X found it easier to beat the Poles in battle than to subjugate the nation. Problems arose as a result of the behavior of the troops under Karl's command, but his personal responsibility was almost as great. Although King Karl X's troops were supposedly well disciplined, it is reported that a large number of men were executed within one month, mostly for minor infractions.[9] The Poles were inflamed by Swedish atrocities, murder, desecration of churches and monasteries, and plunder of public and private property, including properties of the nobility which Sweden needed on its side. The nobility soon formed military detachments throughout the country and the partisans harassed the Swedes in guerrilla warfare.

The demand for exorbitant payments to pay his mercenaries added to the popular conflagration that was brewing. A payment of 240,000 zloties was demanded from Warsaw, a sum several times the annual tax revenues. From Cracow, 300,000 zloties were demanded. When Karl X was told that such a sum could not be raised, he ordered that churches be stripped of their valuables to meet his demands.[10]

In addition to having to pay their own mercenaries, Polish regular soldiers who had surrendered also demanded back-pay from when they were serving in the Polish army. The policy that war should pay for itself did not work in Poland as it had in Germany during the Thirty Years War. First, the behavior of the Swedes was less disciplined and, second, the "contributions" demanded were too large. They may have been suitable for the wealthy principalities and towns in Germany, but the Polish towns were not wealthy.

The behavior of the Swedes rekindled Polish resistance, and soon John Casimir returned from exile and the Polish troops who had taken service with the Swedes also departed. The new patriotic fervor reached a peak by April 1656. However, things did not look promising for the Poles. All major cities in the country, with few exceptions, were in enemy hands—either Russian or Swedish. One of the exceptions was Danzig, but its trading routes to the interior had been severed.

The news that John Casimir had returned caused Karl X to rush back to Poland from Prussia with an army of 10,000. After some minor successes, the Swedes were repulsed at the fortress of Zamosc and were then blocked by superior enemy forces near Sandomierz in the triangle formed by the San and Vistula rivers. With extraordinary skill, but with heavy loss, Karl X was able to break out of the trap before it closed and retreated to Prussia. He was harassed by Polish cavalry on the way and by partisan guerrilla activities. He reached Prussia with only 4,000 men. The rest of the Swedish troops were in garrisons spread throughout Poland.

John Casimir took Warsaw in June 1656, capturing the small Swedish garrison. Karl X, now reinforced to 18,000 troops by his new ally, Frederick

William of Brandenburg, launched another campaign to recapture Warsaw at the end of July 1656. Karl X and the Great Elector had signed an alliance at Marienburg on 25 June 1656. While Frederick William still remained Karl X's vassal, in Royal Prussia he received additional territories with full hereditary rights.

The Swedes had learned from their earlier wars in Poland and from their experience in The Thirty Years War. The forces the Swedes brought to Poland in 1655 were exceedingly cavalry heavy—over 40 percent of the Swedish army was cavalry and this ratio grew as new reinforcements arrived on the scene. Karl's infantry strength in the Battle of Warsaw was only 5,500. While this allowed for mobile warfare, rather than having a campaign plan Karl X appears most of the time to have reacted to what the enemy did rather than the other way around.

The size of the forces under John Casimir and Field Marshal Stefan Czarniecki at Warsaw is reported to have numbered 50,000.[11] Frost, relying on Polish sources, puts the number at about 40,000. Using either number, the Poles had a decisive superiority of more than two to one since the allied armies numbered only 18,000. The Poles were also very cavalry heavy, having only 4,500 infantry. Czarniecki had cautioned against an open battle in view of Swedish firepower, but was overruled by his king.[12]

The forces of Karl X and Frederick William were on the east side of the Vistula, about ten kilometers north of Warsaw on the opposite side of the river. John Casimir crossed the river in the vicinity of the capital with the intention of attacking the Swedish flank. Czarniecki, with 2,000 cavalry, was detached and sent up the west bank of the river as security against a Swedish attack from that direction.

Despite being heavily outnumbered, Karl X seized the initiative. He marched his army south along the east side of the Vistula in the morning of 28 July in a frontal attack against the Polish infantry which had dug in along an open area near the river. The frontal attack failed.

The next day, in a brilliant and risky maneuver which was only possible because of his highly mobile army, Karl X moved his whole force to the left through the Bialolecki forest which brought the Swedes down on the Polish right flank. When the Swedish movement was discovered the Poles launched a counterattack with their hussars. The attack was directed against the Swedish *Uppland* and *Småland* cavalry regiments. The Swedish cavalry was arranged in three lines, as it usually was during the Thirty Years War, and this gave them both depth and elasticity. The hussars, exposed to fire from the allied infantry, tore into the Swedish cavalry and penetrated the first line but became stuck and were repulsed when they tried to break through the second line.

John Casimir did not follow up the cavalry charge or give it any support from his reserves. He had apparently already concluded that the battle was lost and began to withdraw his army across the bridge spanning the Vistula, leaving a cavalry screen on the east bank to protect that operation.

On the third day of the battle, 30 July, the Swedes swept across the open plain on the east side of the Vistula, scattering the Polish and Lithuanian cavalry screen. These forces fled to the south and north along the river. John Casimir abandoned Warsaw for the second time in one year. No figures on casualties are available but they do not appear to have been significant.

While the three-day battle of Warsaw was a magnificent Swedish victory that set off alarm bells throughout Europe, it was not decisive and had little effect on the war. The allied pursuit captured Random on 10 August but Friederick William refused to advance deeper into the Polish interior. Since the Brandenburg forces made up about half of the allied army, Karl X was forced to give up his campaign. There were probably two reasons for the Great Elector's actions. First, it was risky to undertake operations into the Polish interior. Second, it was not in his long-term interest to see Sweden prevail.

Karl X decided to withdraw to Royal Prussia, taking some of the small isolated garrisons from the Sandomierz area with him while strengthening the garrison in Cracow. Danzig was still holding out and there was no hope of forcing that city to surrender as the Swedish naval blockade had been broken in late July with the arrival of thirty Dutch warships, joined by a smaller Danish fleet. The Dutch also brought in 1,300 troops to reinforce the Danzig garrison. All this was done to ensure free trade and without a declaration of war by either country.

John Casimir sent a cavalry force of 13,000, under Field Marshal Wincenty Gosiewski into Royal Prussia in August 1656 to punish Frederick William for his treachery in joining Sweden. He overran a smaller Swedish-Brandenburg force, causing about 5,000 casualties among the allies. He was in turn defeated by 9,000 Swedes at Philipowo on 22 October and withdrew to Lithuania.

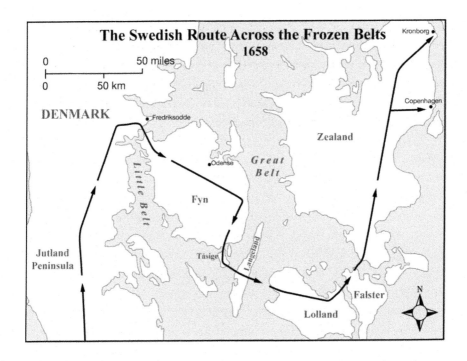

In February 1657, Transylvania, under Prince George Rakoczy, intervened on the side of Sweden. They crossed the Carpathian Mountains with 30,000 men; however, the intervention was a disaster. The Transylvanian invasion force was surrounded by Polish forces in July and forced to surrender. The remnant of the army was destroyed by Tartar cavalry as they withdrew back to Transylvania. Rakoczy escaped with only 400 horsemen.

Things were beginning to unravel for the Swedes. Their Baltic operations were seen as a threat to the fragile and delicate political settlement of the Peace of Westphalia. Old foes were also bent on revenge. Russia declared war on Sweden in May. One of the tsar's aims was to secure the Polish throne after the death of John Casimir. There were not enough Swedish troops in the north to cope with the large three-pronged Russian invasion. The main Russian army, 35,000 strong, captured Dünaburg in July and Kokenhausen the following month, before laying siege to Riga. They were unable to capture that strongly fortified city. A Russian army numbering 15,000 besieged Dorpat's small garrison and it surrendered in October after a valiant defense. Heavy raids were launched in Estonia, Ingria, and southern Finland.

The Empire also intervened in the spring of 1657 by sending 12,000 troops to aid the Poles in recapturing Cracow. Denmark declared war on Sweden on 1 June 1657 and launched simultaneous invasions of Bremen and southern Sweden. Denmark's attacks were soon followed by Elector Friederick William who deserted the Swedes. The Swedes withdrew from Poland in order to protect other areas around the Baltic.[13]

KARL X'S SCANDINAVIAN CAMPAIGNS

Rather than suing for peace, Karl X astonished Europe by attacking the archenemy—Denmark. In July 1657 he crossed the borders of Holstein and drove the Danes out of Bremen. The unexpected attack on Denmark from the south while most of the Danish troops had been moved into the Scandinavian Peninsula for their expected conquest of Sweden, taking advantage of the Swedish army being busy in the Baltic provinces, was nothing short of a strategic masterstroke. It could well have ended the coalition that had formed against Sweden except for the intervention of an outside power.

After securing Bremen, Karl next set his eyes on the Jutland Peninsula. Field Marshal Karl Gustav Wrangel's force of 4,000 men stormed the Fredriksodde fortress, across the strait from the island of Fyn, on 24 October 1657. Danish Field Marshal Bilde was killed in the battle and more than 3,000 of his men surrendered. Those were the last effective troops on the Danish mainland.

Jutland is separated from insular Denmark by two of the three straits connecting the North Sea to the Baltic Sea—the Little Belt (Lillebælt) runs between Jutland and the island of Fyn while the Great Belt (Storebælt) separates Fyn from the largest island—Zealand—where Copenhagen is located. The third strait is located between Sweden and Denmark and called Øresund in Danish. In English it is commonly referred to as the Sound.

Little Belt is about 800 meters wide and 75 meters deep in the vicinity of Fredriksodde. The Great Belt is about 16 kilometers wide at its narrowest point. Øresund and the eastern channel of the Great Belt were made international waterways by the 1857 Copenhagen Convention.

Karl X knew that he could only bring Denmark to its knees by attacking the insular part of the kingdom. He also knew that time was not on his side since the Danes were sure to bring troops from southern Sweden back to Zealand.

In a daring and masterful move without parallel in military history, Karl X decided—against the advice of his generals who did not think the ice had sufficient load-bearing capacity, as several soldiers had broken through it and drowned while on reconnaissance—to cross the frozen belts with his army. However, instead of taking the direct route, he chose one that involved some island-hopping. The Swedes moved first from Fyn to Langeland via Tåsige, then to Lolland and Falster before reaching Zealand.[14] Karl X knew that the ice would prevent the Danish-Norwegian fleet from contesting the crossing.

The crossing was successful and the few Danish detachments barring the way to Copenhagen were easily brushed aside. The terrified Danes agreed to the humiliating Peace of Roskilde (8 March 1658) dictated by Karl X. The terms of the treaty were exceedingly degrading and ruinous for both Denmark and Norway, and apparently were the first step in Karl X's pan-Scandinavian scheme:[15]

1. The immediate transfer of the Provinces of Skåne (Scania), Blekinge, Bornholm, and Halland to Sweden. Halland was already held by Sweden as a 30-year guarantee for the 1645 Treaty of Brömsebro.
2. The immediate transfer of the Norwegian Province of Båhuslen to Sweden. The provinces of Jämtland and Härjedalen had already been transferred to Sweden by the terms of the 1645 Treaty of Brömsebro.
3. The immediate transfer of the Norwegian Province of Trøndelag to Sweden. At that time Trøndelag encompassed what today amounts to four provinces—North Trøndelag, South Trøndelag with the nation's ancient capital of Trondheim, Møre, Romsdal, and much of Nordland. Norway was thus cut into two parts.
4. Danish withdrawal from all anti-Swedish alliances.
5. Danish prevention of any warships from nations hostile to Sweden from crossing through the straits into the Baltic.
6. A promise by Denmark to restore the estates taken from the Duke of Holstein-Gottorp.
7. Denmark to pay for the cost of Swedish occupation forces.
8. Denmark to provide military forces to serve in Sweden's wars outside Scandinavia. The 2,000 men that Denmark was required to provide deserted rather than serve for the Swedes.

The Swedish demands are probably one of the worst examples in history of political overreach following a military victory. Karl X should have known from past history that neither England nor Holland—the primary maritime powers—would allow Scandinavia to become one power with control of the entry to the Baltic.[16] They had previously intervened to prevent this, and England continued this policy of keeping Scandinavia divided in a balanced fashion until well into the Twentieth Century.

At the time of the Roskilde Treaty, a war between England and Holland had just concluded—the Second Anglo-Dutch War, 1665–1667. Denmark took no part in the war but had a defensive alliance with Holland dating back to 1649 which called for the two countries to assist each other with 4,000 troops in case of an attack.[17]

Queen Kristina of Sweden had entered into an alliance with England in 1654, the year she abdicated. The purpose was basically to offset the Danish alliance with Holland. To further complicate the mind-spinning diplomacy of this period of history, England, Sweden, and Holland signed The Triple Alliance on 13 January 1668. The purpose of this treaty was protection against French aspirations in the Spanish Netherlands, and it was apparently considered so urgent that it spurred the Dutch and English to quickly conclude their naval war. While it never came to armed conflict, the threat alone was enough to bring Louis XIV to negotiate and sign the Treaty of Aix-la-Chapelle with Spain.[18]

Although allied with Sweden in the Triple Alliance, the Dutch secretly urged the Danes not to ratify the Treaty of Roskilde.[19] This led to six months of procrastination, and Karl X, who had grown impatient, renewed the war. Karl was now determined to completely terminate the Danish monarchy. While the new conflict started out well, it did not go as well as the original one.

Karl X left Kiel with 10,000 men on 16 August and observers guessed that he was heading for Prussia to punish it for its treachery and to try to re-store a deteriorating situation in the Baltic Provinces. To everyone's surprise, he landed the next day on Zealand and was soon back at the walls of Copenhagen. The Swedish tried for a quick capture of the Danish capital but the attempt failed and they had to resort to a bloody siege. Swedish troops quickly captured the Kronborg fortress in September and the Swedish fleet was used to blockade the Danish capital from the sea. With the capture of Kronborg, the Swedes controlled both sides of the Sound.

The English were the first to intervene when a fleet of 35 warships under Admiral Ordam joined the Danish fleet on October 29, 1658 to temporarily lift the sea blockade of Copenhagen, but they did not stay long. In early November 1658 a Dutch fleet of 45 ships under Admiral Van Weisenaer forced its way through the Sound after a six-hour naval engagement. Having driven off the Swedish fleet, the Dutch landed supplies and reinforcements in Copenhagen.

Intervention by the maritime powers was decisive in frustrating Karl X in achieving his goals. The departure of the naval forces led the Swedish navy to resume its blockade of the Danish capital. This led to a Dutch intervention in February 1659. The combined Dutch and Danish fleets again drove the Swedish navy away. The Dutch stayed around throughout 1659.

General Philip von Sulzbach, with 6,000 Swedes, mounted a tenacious defense of the islands of Fyn and Langeland. However, intervention by the Dutch fleet under Admiral Michiel de Ruyter again proved decisive. His ships ferried 9,000 Danish troops from Jutland to the island of Fyn in early November 1659. The Swedes were forced to evacuate after the defeat of their cavalry in the Battle of Nyborg on 24 November 1659.

The Swedish forces sent against Norway also sustained several reverses. Swedish troops had advanced into Trøndelag and occupied that province. The Swedes tried to integrate the province, and initially the Norwegians did not resist since they were not all that happy under Danish rule. Trondheim, the ancient Norwegian capital, had played a secondary role to Bergen as the primary Norwegian port. They therefore saw a possible economic advantage in being under Swedish rule.

However, the Norwegian attitude changed when the Swedes began levying taxes and recruiting troops for other purposes than local defense. A total of 2,000 young Norwegians were drafted for service in Sweden's Baltic provinces. The Norwegian draftees were quickly shipped to the Baltic front. About 600 deserted en route and none of those who reached the front ever returned to Norway.[20] Higher taxes and the forced recruitment of boys as young as 15 led to unrest in Trøndelag.

With many of the regular Norwegian forces serving with the Danes, the forces in Norway were under the command of General Jørgen Bjelke. He planned to mount an immediate offensive against Trøndelag while maintaining a defensive posture in the southern part of the country. Ninety company-size units were mobilized.

With a force of 3,500 men, Bjelke invaded Trøndelag from three directions. The Swedish forces under General Stiernsköld numbered only 800, a sign of the manpower strain in Sweden with forces thinly spread all around the Baltic. Stiernsköld retired to Trondheim where he was besieged. A cavalry unit of 500 was sent from Sweden as reinforcement but it was intercepted by the Norwegians and driven back into Sweden. The Swedes now entered into negotiations and were afforded the honors of war. They withdrew from Trondheim to Sweden on 17 December 1658 and were escorted back across the old border by Norwegian troops.[21]

Karl X had decided that the town of Halden was the key to southern Norway. With its defenses eliminated the road would be open to advance on Kristiania (now Oslo). Colonel Tønne Huitfeld was the commander in Halden, under the overall direction of Bjelke. He had 2,000 Norwegian troops at his disposal. Between September 1658 and January 1660, these troops repelled three Swedish attempts to take the fortress and town.

The first attack was made in September 1658. It was poorly organized as no serious opposition was expected. The attack was repelled before it reached Halden. A Norwegian counterthrust into Båhuslen failed when General Stake launched the second Swedish attack in February 1659 with 4,000 troops. The Swedish attack failed. In the far north, Colonel Preben von Ahnen conducted a raid into Sweden in the Nasafjell area in 1659 and destroyed Swedish mining industries.

The most powerful Swedish attack against Halden was launched in January 1660 by General Kagg with 4,500 troops. The Norwegian defenders had also received reinforcements from the north after Trøndelag was recaptured. Several attempts to storm the Norwegian positions failed and the Swedes withdrew.[22]

The Swedish position in the Baltic was also deteriorating. The Poles captured Thorn in 1658 but the Swedes still held Marienburg and Elbing. In Pomerania, an Imperial (Austrian) army of 17,000 joined 13,000 Brandenburgers to besiege Stettin. The Swedes were in retreat on all fronts.

Karl X had finally decided that—beset by revengeful enemies on all fronts—the time had come to sue for peace. He summoned a Riksdag session in Gothenburg and it was agreed to seek international mediation to bring about a settlement with Denmark, Holland, and Poland in order to concentrate military efforts against Russia and Brandenburg. Karl X's unexpected death on 13 February 1660 deprived the country of his leadership in extricating itself from the precarious situation in which the country found itself.

THE REIGN OF KARL XI, 1660–1697

The regency appointed for Karl X's four-year-old son Karl was selected by the king before he died and he had every reason to believe that he left his infant son in good and strong hands. It consisted of the Queen Dowager and five senior members of the magnate class. However, Nisbet Bain writes that *this regency was the weakest and most mischievous Sweden ever had,* and calls the Chancellor, Magnus Gabriel de la Gardie, *always the evil genius of the regency.*[23] The chancellor had a background of brilliant service during three successive reigns, but had never displayed any particular ability to rule a nation with wisdom and steadfastness. He was immensely rich. There was a return to the extravagant wasteful spending and corruption of Queen Kristina's reign, with friends of the chancellor growing rich at public expense. The regency left the military reforms of Karl X in limbo.

When Karl X died the Swedish government immediately put out peace overtures. If the many enemies had known the sad state of Swedish affairs they would probably not have been as quick as they were in accepting these overtures. However, the dramatic victories achieved by Karl X had inspired Europe with a healthy fear of Swedish arms and were therefore instrumental in obtaining surprisingly good terms.

The first successful negotiations were those to settle Baltic issues with the Polish-Lithuanian Commonwealth, the Empire, and Brandenburg-Prussia. These negotiations, which had actually begun in the fall of 1659, resulted in the signing of the Treaty of Oliva in Royal Prussia on May 3, 1660. The negotiations were difficult, as was to be expected between these long-standing enemies, and were led by a French diplomat, de Lumbres. He had to use all his skills to keep the conference from collapsing due to attempts by the Danes, Dutch, the Empire, and Brandenburg to derail it. Sweden was fortunate to have its ally France involved. The recalcitrant countries wanted Sweden out of Germany while France needed Swedish military power to stay there. The Brandenburg and Austrian invasion of Swedish Pomerania, mentioned earlier, was labeled a breach of the Peace of Westphalia, and France used this to threaten to send an army of 30,000 to assist the Swedes to recover lost territories. The same threat was used against Poland when that country's demands were increased after the news of King Karl X's death reached the conference. The French stated pointedly that the threat of force would be carried out unless all parties came to agreement.[24]

Under the terms of the Treaty of Oliva, Swedish sovereignty over Livonia was confirmed. Brandenburg was confirmed as the sovereign in Royal Prussia. King John Casimir withdrew his dynastic claim to the Swedish throne, although he was allowed to retain the title of hereditary Swedish king for life. All occupied territories were restored to the rulers before the start of the Second Northern War (1655–1660) and special provisions were inserted to protect religious freedoms. The signatories were Emperor Leopold I, the Great Elector, and Chancellor De la Gardie.

The issues between Sweden and Denmark were settled by the Treaty of Copenhagen, signed on 3 June 1660. The negotiations had begun in earnest at the end of March, 1660. By that time Admiral Michiel de Ruyter and the Dutch fleet that had blockaded the Swedish navy had left for home. A Danish request for support to recover the province of Skåne was supported by Poland, Austria, and Brandenburg but not by Holland. Here, again, we see Holland's sensitivity to having one nation control both sides of the Sound.

The other sticking point in the negotiations was the future of Bornholm Island. Denmark demanded that it be returned but it was not until Denmark provided compensation in the form of several noble estates in Skåne. The owners would be compensated by the Danish government. Later, the negotiations threatened to derail because of intrigues by the representatives of the mediating countries. The issue was finally settled after Denmark and Sweden agreed to negotiate directly.

Sweden retained all territories seized from Denmark except for Bornholm and received exemption from the Sound dues. She gave up all claims to Norwegian territories except for retaining Båhuslen. The borders between the three Scandinavian countries have remained essentially unchanged since the Treaty of Copenhagen.

The last Treaty was that of Kardis, in Estonia. It was signed in July 1661 and ended the war between Sweden and Russia (1656–1658). All territories taken from Sweden were returned and in so doing it confirmed the earlier

Treaty of Stolbovo. Russia also agreed to destroy all vessels built in the Baltic.

It can be argued that the only real winners from these treaties were Sweden and Brandenburg. Brandenburg, which had not risked its army in any prolonged conflict, gained a duchy (Prussia) and would soon become a powerful, ambitious, and militaristic monarchy. It was the beginning of an army with a state instead of a state with an army.[25]

Sweden had all her losses returned, thanks to strong support from France. Frost writes that . . . *Sweden's military reputation had never been higher. The exalted position it had achieved by 1648 had been maintained in difficult circumstances, against a coalition of the greatest powers in central and eastern Europe.*[26] This statement is correct and many Swedish writers agree, but there were warning signs, fully recognized in retrospect, on the horizons.

First, the obvious one was the lack of an adequate population to support military operations. It was a fact that could not be altered. While the new territories expanded the recruiting base, the reliable nucleus continued to be Swedish and Finnish troops and they were spread exceedingly thin.

Second, war could no longer pay for itself. Mercenaries still made up the majority of Swedish forces abroad. These required payment in cash or kind. The system established by *indelingsverket*, payment in land or through the incomes from land, was not suitable for sustaining mercenary armies. A continuation of the "contribution" system was not appropriate in the poorer countries and only created animosities. Sweden had to rely increasingly on a credit system—both domestic and foreign. This worked well when Swedish arms were producing spectacular successes, but not as well when the country's long-term success was called into question. The fall of mineral prices in the second half of the seventeenth century, particularly copper, severely reduced incomes from the mining industries.

Third, most countries had caught up with Sweden in military technology and tactics so that her earlier edge was for all practical purposes lost. Other states which had opted for standing national armies were becoming better trained and disciplined.

Fourth, Swedish wars were for the most part aggressive, and few reliable friends or allies can be found under those conditions. This was as true then as it is now—nations have no permanent friends or enemies, only permanent interests. The unstated goal of the Vasa kings of a permanent Scandinavian union was ill served by continual nibbling away at Danish and Norwegian territories, acts that brought foreign intervention and attacks by foes on other Swedish holdings.

Fifth, the stumbling approach in the implementation of *indelingsverket* because of the influence of the magnate class was detrimental. While the system worked to protect constitutionalism, it had inherent flaws which were obvious in the late 1600s and early 1700s. No steps were taken to make it militarily functional—the major flaw being the lack of a functional logistic system and an overall logistic command. The lack of an overall logistic command was exacerbated by the lack of a rational system for extracting and mobilizing domestic resources.[27]

Sweden was able to remain basically on the sidelines during the major wars that took place in western Europe during the regency. These wars were mostly due to the ambitions of Louis XIV. Chancellor De la Gardie was an unabashed Francophile but his opponents in the Riksdag were in favor of neutrality and a policy that would draw the country nearer to England and Holland to counterbalance the designs of France. Both warring camps campaigned to win the support of the great northern power. However, Sweden's financial difficulties drove her foreign policy. In the words of Nisbet Bain, Sweden *now became what she had never been before, a mere mercenary of France.*[28] Sweden had to walk a fine line and that is why we find her simultaneously a member of the Triple Alliance, designed to arrest French ambitions, and a continued ally of France. While De la Gardie's opponents appear to have initially prevailed, it was Gardie's policies that won after the Triple Alliance had served its purposes, largely due to Swedish membership.

In the Treaty of Stockholm in April 1672 Sweden *virtually sold herself to Louis XIV* by agreeing to maintain an army of 16,000 troops in Germany for his use in return for large subsidies.[29] It was an initiative launched during the end of the regency government, so the blame should not be placed on France. This was actually the last major act of the regency since Karl XI had become the king in his own right on 18 December 1672. Sweden tried, in vain to mediate between the belligerents until Louis XIV grew impatient and demanded that Sweden invade Brandenburg in return for the generous financial assistance already provided.

Field Marshal Wrangel finally moved into Brandenburg in December 1674 and went into winter quarters. The Swedish force under Wrangel was ill-prepared for a fight. Instead of waiting for a Swedish attack, the Great

Elector surprised the Swedes near Fehrbellin on 28 June 1675.

Fehrbellin was nothing more than a large skirmish—total losses being only 600—and not a true test of Swedish and Prussian arms. But propaganda in central Europe heralded it as a major victory and the signal to again pounce on the Swedes.

The German allies of Sweden became hesitant and her traditional foes—the Empire, Holland, Brandenburg, and Denmark—immediately declared war. The Great Elector invaded Swedish Pomerania, capturing Stettin, Stralsund, and Greifswald between December 1676 and November 1677, while the Duchy of Bremen was seized by Denmark. By the end of 1676 Sweden had lost nearly all her possessions in Germany.

Kristian V of Denmark, although it had been announced in June 1675 that his sister was engaged to marry Karl XI, nevertheless declared war on his future brother-in-law three months later. Nothing happened in southern Sweden in 1675 because Denmark was waiting for the arrival of a Dutch fleet under Admiral Tromp. Holland was at this time involved in a war with France. The Danes had increased their fleet to 70 ships, mostly new or rebuilt, because of their experience in the 1650s when the Swedes blockaded Copenhagen.[30]

A large naval battle was fought on 1 June 1676 at Jamsund near Öland. The combined Dutch and Danish-Norwegian fleets, under the command of Danish Admiral Niels Juel, one of the most capable admirals in Danish history, defeated the Swedish navy. This victory gave the allies control of the sea and the Danish army could be transported to Sweden in safety.

The Danes landed in Skåne in 1676 with an army of about 15,000. The town of Helsingborg was captured on June 29. The Swedish forces of 5,000 were thinly spread throughout the province. The Danes had great success initially, forcing the Swedes to withdraw to Sweden proper. By August, only the town of Malmö in Skåne remained in Swedish hands.

Norwegian forces under Governor-General Ulrik Fredrik Gyldenløve had anticipated the war, and Norwegian forces numbering 12,000 were in position along the border. The general plan was to force the Swedes to fight a two-front war.

A Norwegian force of 4,000 under General Russenstein was concentrated at Fredrikshald with a dual mission—protect against a Swedish invasion of southern Norway while threatening to recapture their former province of

Båhuslen. They were opposed by the Swedish General Ascheberg with 2,000 men at Svarteborg. Operations in Norway in 1675 were primarily limited to skirmishes to test defenses and probe the strength of defenses in the mountain passes. The only exception was a seaborne coastal force sent south along Sweden's west coast to try cutting General Ascheberg's supply route. The Swedes learned about the plan and the operation failed.

In 1676 Gyldenløve took personal command of the field army. The Norwegians took and fortified the pass at Kvistrum. Then they moved south, capturing Uddevall against weak resistance and proceeded south to invest Gothenburg. However, after the defeat of a portion of the Danish army at Halmstad on 17 August 1676, Gyldenløve was forced to retreat northward.[31]

Kristian V traveled to Copenhagen to spend the winter, but Karl XI had different plans. He had increased his army to 16,000 and was preparing to invade Skåne. The population in Skåne was very pro-Danish and kept the Danes informed. For these actions they paid dearly. Few of those who actively supported the Danes and were unlucky enough to be captured survived, and after Sweden regained control of the province, a brutal integration program was carried out in 1679–1680.

The Danish army left its winter camp and was ready when the Swedes advanced into Skåne during the night of 23–24 October 1676. The two armies shadowed each other for over a month. The Swedish army was suffering from illness and hunger. Karl XI decided to venture all on one gamble. The Swedes attacked the Danish army just north of Lund. The day-long battle that followed was one of the bloodiest engagements of its time, not only in Nordic military history but also on a European scale. The sources differ not only as to the number of combatants but also on the number of casualties. The number of participants is given as 16,000 to 20,000. Most agree that 8–9,000 lay dead on the field as the battle ebbed out. The number of wounded is not known. The two armies were in no condition to continue the fight the next day, and it is considered a Swedish victory because the Danes were the first to withdraw.

In 1677 9,000 troops led by Karl XI routed 12,000 Danes in the Battle of Landskrona. This was the last pitched battle of the war. In September, Kristian V withdrew his army back to Zealand.

The war was not going so well against the Norwegians. Gyldenløve had 15,000 troops in Norway in addition to 2,000 garrison troops and those who manned the seaborne coastal fleet. The Norwegians opened fronts both in Båhuslen and in Jämtland. Gyldenløve moved against Marstrand and the Karlsten fortress supported by the coastal fleet. After a successful siege the Norwegians were able to capture both the city and the fortress. A Swedish force was also defeated north of Uddevalla. An army of 8,000 Norwegians tried to take Båhus fortress in 1678. It was the hardest siege that fortress had experienced, but the Norwegians failed to take it despite heavy destruction.

However, the war was being decided on other fronts. Sweden sustained two crushing naval defeats in 1677. One took place at Fehmaren as the Swedish fleet was returning to the Baltic from a blockade of Gothenburg when it encountered a larger Danish-Norwegian fleet under Admiral Juel. The result was another great Danish victory in a battle that lasted all night.

The second naval defeat was also administered by Admiral Juel at Køge Bay, near Copenhagen. The Swedes lost over 3,000 men while Danish losses were 375. Denmark now had complete control of the sea, and Sweden could not move troops between its homeland and Germany.

General peace negotiations to end the many interlinked wars had been going on since 1672, but took on a sense of urgency starting in 1676. The negotiations were again led by France. An uninterrupted series of victories had made Louis XIV the arbiter of Europe. With a victorious standing army of 100,000 battle-hardened veterans, Louis XIV could pretty well dictate terms to everyone, and this is what happened. The Treaties of Nijmegen were signed between August 1678 and December 1679, and served as a basis for settling various conflicts that had grown out of the conflict between France and Holland. In the Treaty of Saint-Germain-en-Laye in June 1679, France and Sweden made peace with Brandenburg. In the Treaty of Fontainebleau in August 1679, France dictated peace terms between Sweden and Denmark-Norway. These dictated terms were confirmed in the Peace of Lund at the end of September 1679 by Sweden and Denmark. The peace stipulated that all territory lost by Sweden should be returned. Denmark received minor war reparations and returned Swedish Rügen. The treaty with Brandenburg likewise demanded that all territories taken from Sweden be returned.

It was in French interests to have a strong ally in the north, and this was achieved by the generous terms Sweden received. The settlement with Brandenburg involved holding back a few slivers of prior Swedish territory without requesting Swedish agreement. Karl XI became furious and wrote a letter to Louis XIV in a dictatorial and contemptuous tone that produced a negative impression on the Grand Monarch that was difficult to forget. Karl XI, for his part, grew to dislike and distrust the French.[32] There was no display of gratitude to Louis XIV for having pulled his irons out of the fire.

BUREAUCRATIC REFORMS

Karl XI devoted most of his time after the conclusion of peace in 1679 to putting the Swedish state in order. He threw himself into this work with the same zeal he had displayed in war and it became an obsession of his that Sweden's greatness could only be restored and maintained through economic reforms.

Sweden had become a splintered society. The aristocratic class had taken on a growing dominance since the days of Gustav Adolf, and it had become increasingly a military-based class. This element of society was allocated the bulk of the state lands and in the process impoverished the state and the lower classes. Because the classes continuously bid for the king's support, both noble and non-noble, it had reached a point where the Riksdag was even willing to give the crown more than what was asked for. As a result of this situation, Karl XI found himself one of the most absolute rulers in Europe. In its eagerness to curry favor with the king, the Riksdag became nothing more than a mouthpiece for the crown, forgetting its constitutional function.

This voluntary surrender to the crown reached its climax in 1693 with the Riksdag issuing the Declaration of Sovereignty (Suveranetets-forklaring) which stated that the king was "an all-commanding sovereign responsible for his actions to none on earth and with powers to rule his realm as he saw best." It is not often in history that a duly selected/elected legislative body, representing all parts of society, voluntarily surrenders its constitutional prerogatives to the executive, but that is what happened. Usually, that type of change occurs only after a coup or a great amount of blood has flowed in the streets.

To his credit, King Karl XI—and for the good of Swedish democracy—used the powers handed to him on a silver platter wisely. Michael Roberts writes that most of *the abuses in the Swedish system were not corrected until the absolutism after 1680 placed the arch-bureaucrat Charles XI in effective control of the bureaucracy.*[33] Karl X, his father, had started the land recovery program and the military apportionment system, but they had taken on a state of dormancy during his own regency. Karl XI now set about carrying out these reforms

212 | A WARRIOR DYNASTY

and did so with firm resolve, day and night. At first the sweeping reforms had an unsettling economic effect but soon produced lasting benefits for the country. Common sense regulations were promulgated in the areas of finances, budgeting, trade, and agriculture. Some of these reforms, when applied in the Baltic territories, were not as welcomed or successful.

The apportionment system (*indelingsverket*) was modified, but the main flaws mentioned earlier in this chapter were not adequately addressed. Defenses were improved and strengthened to the point *that when Karl XI died in 1697, he left his son a well-armed and highly-trained army of 90,000*. The navy had been increased to 34 ships of the line and 11 frigates.[34] No Swedish king had left finer instruments of war for his son.

The military was intended for defense, and as such was more than adequate, but it proved inadequate for taking on most of Europe. As pointed out by Gustav Jonasson, *the military left to Karl XII were never intended to be led to Dresden, Kraków and Pultava,* and shortened the lifespan of Sweden as great power.[35]

Bain points out that the moral improvements in Sweden under Karl XI were even more astonishing than in the material aspects. Almost everyone came to recognize that the thrifty, hard-working, and common sense monarch was working for the good of the country as a whole, and his example had an infectious effect on the national character.[36]

The domestic stability also led to the renewed importance of the nation abroad. The king had a dislike for diplomacy—regarding it as little more than lying on a grand scale—and therefore left foreign affairs in the hands of the now-aging Chancellor, Bengt Oxenstierna. Since the chancellor shared the king's distrust of Louis XIV, relations with France soured. Sweden signed the Treaty of Hague with Holland in September 1681. Its aim was to serve as a brake on the ambitions of France and Spain, and the Empire joined in 1682.

Louis XIV took immediate action against his former ally by providing arms to Denmark and Brandenburg. A Franco-Danish fleet actually appeared in the Baltic, but Holland quickly reacted by demonstrating its willingness to assist her new ally. The Treaty of Regensburg addressed the growing unrest in Europe and restored tranquility for a few years.

A new coalition against France was formed in 1688, and this led to another European war. Both sides tried to draw Sweden in but the overtures were turned down. Instead, in a switch of its usual role, Sweden became the primary mediator that brought the war to an end during the reign of Karl XII.

NOTES

1. Ingvar Andersson, *A History of Sweden* (Stockholm: Natur och Kultur, 1962), p. 216.
2. Downing, *op. cit.*, p. 202.
3. Andersson, *op. cit.* p. 216.
4. Downing, *op. cit.*, p. 203.
5. Roberts, *The Swedish Imperial Experience*, pp. 46, 52–53.
6. For more information on the indelingsverket see Downing, *op. cit*, pp. 203–211; Roberts, *The Swedish Imperial Experience*, pp. 140–146; and Hatton, *op. cit.*, pp. 113–114.
7. Frost, *op. cit.*, p. 167.
8. *Ibid*, pp. 168–169.
9. Patrick Gordon, *Tagebuch des Generals Patrick Gordon wärend seiner Kriegsdienste under den Schweden un Polen* (Moscow, 1869), pp. 17–18 as quoted in Frost, *op. cit.*, pp. 169–170.
10. Frost, *op. cit.*, quoting Polish sources.
11. Dupuy & Dupuy, *op. cit.*, pp. 568–569.
12. Frost, *op. cit.*, p. 173.
13. Bain, *op. cit.*, p. 8.
14. Frost, *op. cit.*, p. 180.
15. Ersland, *op. cit.*, volume 1, pp. 205-213; Andrina Stiles, *op. cit.*; and Jill Lisk, *The Struggle for Supremacy in the Baltic, 1600-1725* (New York: Funk & Wagnalls, 1992).
16. It was not only an interest in free trade that was behind the policies of the maritime powers. They were also in great need of the enormous amounts of lumber that came primarily from Norway and Finland for building and maintaining their fleets.
17. Ersland, *op. cit.*, volume 1, p. 207.
18. For a more detailed discussion see John A. Lynn, *The French Wars 1667-1714* (London: Osprey Publishing, 2002) pp. 361-366.
19. Bain, *op. cit.*, p. 9.
20. Erslad and Holm, *op. cit.*, volume 1, p. 207 and note 66, p. 319.
21. *Ibid,* volume 1, p. 208.
22. *Ibid*, volume 1, p. 213.
23. Bain, *op. cit.*, pp. 10-11.
24. For further information see Frost, *op. cit.*, p. 183 and Lucien Bély (editor), *L'Europe des traits de Westphalie: esprit de la Diplomatie et diplomatie de l'esprit* (Presses universitaires de France, 2000), pp. 511f.
25. David Ogg, *Europe in the Seventeenth Century*. Eighth Edition (London: Adam & Charles Black, 1960), pp. 449 and 451. See also Walter Goerlitz, *History of the German General Staff 1657-1945*. Translated from the German by Brian Battershaw. (New York: Praeger, 1957), pp. 1-4 and Frost, *op. cit.*, pp.198-200.
26. Frost, *op. cit.*, pp. 200-201.
27. Downing, *op. cit.*, pp. 203 and 206-207.

28. Bain, *op. cit.*, p. 11.
29. *Ibid*, p. 12.
30. Ersland and Holm, *op. cit.*, volume 1, p. 225.
31. *Ibid*, volume 1, p. 226.
32. Bain, *op. cit.*, p. 14.
33. Roberts, *The Swedish Imperial Experience*. 1979 Edition, p. 59.
34. *Ibid*, p. 141, quoting Sven Årgren, *Karl XI:s indelingsverk för armén. Bidrag till dess historia åren 1679-1697* (Uppsala, 1922).
35. Roberts, *The Swedish Imperial Experience*. 1979 Edition, p. 146, quoting Gustav Jonasson's review of Cavallie's *Från fred till krig*, in *Historisk Tidsskrift*, 1975, p. 492.
36. Bain, *op. cit.*, p. 17.

8

Karl XII's Danish, Baltic, and German Campaigns

I have resolved never to begin an unjust war, but also never to end a just one without overcoming my enemy.

STATEMENT BY KARL XII

When Karl XI died in April 1697, the war clouds were already gathering for what seemed to be an endless series of wars. When he died he left a 15-year old son destined to be considered the greatest among the Vasa dynasty's long list of warrior kings.

Karl XII was the first-born son of Karl XI in his marriage to Ulrika Eleonora, the daughter of Fredrik III of Denmark and Sofie Amalie of Brunswig-Lüneburg. She was therefore the sister of King Kristian V. Their engagement was officially announced in mid-June 1675, three months before her brother declared war on Sweden.

There was heavy pressure on Ulrika to renounce her engagement, but she refused, considering herself as honor-bound. There was also opposition within Sweden to the proposed marriage, and one of the opponents was none other than Karl XI's mother, Hedwig Eleonora. Nevertheless, the marriage took place on 6 May 1680. The couple had seven children, the first child being a girl and the second being Karl XII, born on 17 June 1682.

Karl XII's mother died in 1693, when Karl was only eleven years old. His father appeared to have seriously grieved over the loss of his wife. On his deathbed in 1697 he confessed to his mother that he had not had one happy day since she died.[1] Her loss was also hard on the eleven-year-old son, and their mutual sorrow brought the two very close. After her death the actual tutor of the future king was Karl XI himself. Karl XII's strong-willed grandmother, Hedwig Eleonora of Holstein, was also influential in his upbringing after his mother died. He was happiest, however, when honing his military skills or while accompanying his father on hunting expeditions.

THE EUROPEAN SITUATION AT THE
END OF THE 17TH CENTURY

The treaties "dictated" by Louis XIV of France left many issues unresolved. A number of states were only waiting to settle scores. The relatively long period of tranquility for Sweden following the Peace of Lund was due to both internal and external forces. Karl XI's policy was to avoid involvement in warfare on the continent as long as Swedish interests were not threatened. For much of this period Poland-Lithuania and Russia were preoccupied in the south by wars against Turkey and the Tartars. In northern Europe severe problems were just below the surface.

The countries of Europe were increasingly concerned about what would happen when Spain's childless King Charles II went to his grave. Now that the Turkish wars were winding down, Emperor Leopold I was preparing to ensure that Louis XIV would not reap any harvest from Charles II's eventual passing.

Frost notes the passing of an age with the death of many of the leaders we encountered in previous chapters. Karl XI's death in 1697 was followed two years later by the death of Kristian V of Denmark, who was succeeded by his son Fredrik IV who ruled until 1730. Tsar Alexis had died in 1676, followed by two relatively short reigns by his sons Fedor II and Ivan V, who died in 1696. This brought Ivan's half brother Peter (1682–1725), to become known as Peter the Great, to power. The elector of Saxony, Frederick Augustus,[2] managed to get himself chosen King of Poland in 1697, and assumed the name Augustus II. Brandenburg went through more than a leadership change; its very status was transformed. Elector Frederick William died in 1688 and Frederick III became elector. He successfully petitioned the Emperor to change the status of the electorate to a kingdom. Thus, in 1701 he became Frederik I, King of Prussia.

Peter of Russia was at first eager to prosecute the war against the Ottoman Empire and to secure the shores of the Black and Caspian seas, but he was unwilling to fight the Turks alone. When Austria, Poland-Lithuania, and

Venice settled their war with Turkey in January 1699, Peter quickly opened negotiations and a 20-year truce was arranged in June 1700.[3]

Charles II of Spain died on 1 November 1700 and this led to war. In the same year Denmark, allied with Russia and Poland, began the Great Northern War. This war was somewhat different than the previous ones in which Sweden had taken the offensive. This time Sweden's enemies were the aggressors.[4] These two actions—the Great Northern War and the War of the Spanish Succession—marked the beginning of the great military conflagration that consumed the first two decades of the eighteenth century. Every nation in Europe resorted to arms, and the colonies in Asia, Africa, and the Americas were swept up in the conflagration. Montross notes that it was a world war in every respect, except that the armies were in the 100,000-man rather than the 1,000,000-man range. Nevertheless, the impact was proportional when one considers the much smaller population in the early eighteenth century.[5]

THE GREAT NORTHERN WAR—THE DANISH CAMPAIGN

If Denmark and its allies counted on Swedish weakness and the inexperience of her young ruler, they were sadly mistaken on both counts. Karl XI had left his son the finest military that nation had produced. It is true, as pointed out by Professors Gustav Jonasson and Robert Frost, that this military instrument was primarily for defense and not intended for an invasion deep into Russia.

However, it was intended to defend the Swedish Empire and here one encounters a military quandary. No nation can expect to win a war solely by defensive actions. After almost two centuries of wars had produced nothing but temporary pauses, I believe that it had become clear to the young king that a new approach was in order. The core issues that caused the wars had not been adequately addressed. We get a glimpse of Karl XII's view in his statement *I have resolved never to begin an unjust war, but also never to end a just one without overcoming my enemy.*[6]

If I am right about Karl's thinking, it goes a long way toward explaining his total proclivity for offense and his stubborn dismissal of peace offers from both Augustus II and Peter the Great. He knew, based on his reading of history, that these offers would only lead to temporary pauses.

Denmark and her allies discovered almost immediately that the moment they had chosen to strike was not as propitious as anticipated. The young king may have had war thrust on him by the treacherous attacks of his neighbors, but he had ripened with unusual rapidity, surprising his enemies. Karl XII did not wait to be attacked; he delivered the first blows. These blows began a series of campaigns that many writers have described as among the most brilliant in military annals.

Karl XII is not viewed by his critics as a great strategist or tactician, and he is not considered one of the great captains of history, probably because he lost his final campaign. He caught the world's attention and admiration by being a superb leader of soldiers, by his fabulous audacity, and by his perseverance. As will be obvious from these last two chapters, I place his strategic and tactical skills much higher than most other writers.

It was in Holstein-Gottorp where the fuse for the war was lit. The Holstein-Gottorp supporters in Sweden were powerful, led by Hedwig Eleonora, Karl XII's grandmother. She came from Holstein-Gottorp, being the daughter of Duke Fredrik III and therefore the sister of Duke Fredrik IV who was married to Hedwig Sofia, Karl XII's older sister. The dynastic bonds were therefore strong.

The bone of contention was whether the duchy's rights, confirmed in previous treaties since 1645, included the right to fortify its border. Denmark considered this a provocation since the duchy provided easy access to Denmark's southern frontier. Sweden had upset Holland and England by staying neutral in the Nine Years War (1688–1697).[7] The fact that Sweden was the principal mediator at Rijswijk only earned her the animosities of both sides, particularly the maritime powers. The Danes exploited the resentment against Sweden by the western powers by razing, within a month of Karl XI's death, the fortresses built by Holstein-Gottorp. This was a breach of the 1689 Altona agreement guaranteed by the maritime powers, but Denmark calculated that their current unhappiness with Sweden would lead them to ignore Denmark's action.[8]

To shore up their security the Danes entered into alliances—the first with Augustus II, who had his eyes on Livonia. A defensive alliance between Denmark and Saxony was signed in March 1698 and reconfirmed in 1700. Russia signed a defensive alliance with Denmark in April 1699, but this alliance would not come into force until Russia had made peace with Turkey, which happened in June 1700.

The Danes moved their army into Schleswig-Holstein at the end of 1699 but did not move into Holstein-Gottorp until their ally Augustus attacked Livonia. Augustus' attempt to seize Riga failed, but he did take Dünamunde, on the other side of the Dvina on 23 March. It was at this time that Fredrik IV moved into Holstein-Gottorp and laid siege to the town of Tønning. Having concluded peace with Turkey, Tsar Peter made his move against Sweden in late August.

None of the allies expected a long war, as the odds were immensely in their favor. The Swedes, facing a war on three fronts, seemed doomed to a quick defeat. They had not yet come to know Karl XII.

The young Swedish King singled out Denmark as the object of his first strike. In early January Sweden had made a diplomatic move that proved very beneficial and dashed Danish hopes that the maritime powers would not react to the breach of the Altona agreement. Sweden committed itself to support the maritime powers in upholding the Treaty of Rijswijk against Louis IV. Consequently, she was now able to call on them for help to uphold the Altona agreement.

Fredrik IV at first refused to believe that the maritime powers would intervene on the side of Sweden. It was not until diplomatic dispatches arrived confirming that an Anglo/Dutch fleet was on its way that his great miscalculation set in. His reaction was to try attacking the Swedish fleet before the allied squadron arrived. The Swedish fleet stayed in harbor, and the Danish attempt to take Gothenburg also failed.

The prospects for Denmark seemed to grow dimmer each time news arrived. Fredrik IV discovered that Dutch troops were on their way to join the Swedes in Germany. He also learned that Hanoverian troops had begun to cooperate with Field Marshal Nils Gyllenstierna, the Swedish commander in Germany. Fredrik IV decided to rush the siege of Tønning by storming the fortress. The assault launched on 22 May failed, and since the Swedes and Hanoverians had crossed the Elbe into Holstein, Fredrik terminated the siege and marched to meet the invaders who were commanded by the Elector of Hanover and numbered nearly 20,000.

When it appeared that the Elector of Brandenburg might also intervene on the side of Denmark, William III of England threatened to invade the Duchy of Cleves along the lower Rhine. Danish expectations of having to deal with Sweden alone had not come to fruition. There were no clashes between the Danes and Hanoverians, only much useless maneuvering.

Karl XII soon discovered that help from the maritime powers was both calculated and limited. No doubt, these powers were grateful for promised Swedish support against Louis XIV, and therefore did not want to see a weakening of Sweden by the alliance it was facing in case that support should be needed. However, as always, they did not want to upset the balance in the north. They made it known to Russia, the Empire, and Brandenburg that they were acting only as guarantors of Altona to restore the Duke of Holstein-Gottorp to the lands taken from him by Denmark, and not as allies of Sweden. Karl XII left it up to Duke Fredrick whether or not to accept the many offers of mediation that were flowing in, but he also realized that the actions of the maritime powers had upset his plans to quickly knock Denmark out of the war.

Karl XII learned just how limited the assistance of the maritime powers would be when their fleet—13 Dutch and 12 English warships—arrived off Gothenburg on 9 June 1700. They moved close to the northern entrance of the Sound by the middle of the month and waited for the Swedish fleet to join them. At the same time Karl XII approached the southern end of the eastern entrance to the Sound with 38 ships of the line, carrying 2,700 guns.[9]

The planned junction of the fleets proved difficult, and so did agreement on a single naval commander. The allies would not agree to a Swedish commander unless it was Karl XII himself. The very capable Danish Admiral Juel took up a position with the Danish-Norwegian fleet—40 ships of the line—between the Swedes and the maritime powers' squadron, keeping their fleets from joining. Whoever attacked him would be operating under adverse conditions.

Karl XII finally took a very risky action to break the stalemate. He ordered Admiral Hans Wachtmeister to take most of the fleet through the treacherous Flintrännan channel so as to slip by the Danish fleet on the night of 13–14 July and join the maritime powers squadrons on July 17. The passage succeeded and this forced Admiral Juel to withdraw to Copenhagen harbor.[10] The Swedes could not persuade the Dutch and English to join them in an attack on Juel's ships in the harbor.

Fredrik IV, hoping for the news of some spectacular successes by his Polish and Russian allies, procrastinated. His obstinate behavior led the Dutch and English admirals to go along with a Swedish plan that called for transporting a Swedish army of about 10,000 from Sweden to Zealand.

The preparations for the landing were made quickly but the transport was delayed by two days because of storms. A successful landing was made on 4 August against only light opposition. There were only 5,000 Danish troops on the whole island and just 800 at the landing site. The landing was a strategic surprise for the Danes, as they had expected that the Swedes would head for Holstein to join their allies. The combined fleets kept Admiral Juel bottled up in Copenhagen while the warships escorting the transports provided fire support for the landing. The bridgehead was quickly expanded by 12 August to make room for the 10,000 troops.

The Danish forces on Zealand withdrew to Copenhagen. It was decided not to storm the town but to keep it blockaded and under bombardment from both sea and land. It was also realized that the Danes would scuttle their fleet rather than let it fall into the hands of the Swedes if an assault were to be made. The city was not prepared for a blockade, and food was already in short supply after less than two weeks.

On 21 August a message arrived from the Hanoverian elector, George Ludwig, that King Fredrik IV was willing to make peace. Karl XII was requested to cease all hostilities and prepare for the evacuation of Zealand. The Danish king had agreed to all the demands of the guarantors. Danish promises led to the conference at Travendal, and by the time Karl XII received the message, peace had been signed on 18 August between King Fredrik IV and Fredrik IV, Duke of Holstein-Gottorp. The treaty, also signed by the Altona guarantors, provided for an indemnity of 260,000 riks-dollars and contained an important clause whereby the Danish king promised not take hostile actions against Sweden or help Sweden's enemies.

Karl XII was concerned that without the Danish-Norwegian fleet being destroyed, Denmark could opt to invade southern Sweden at the earliest opportunity. There was friction between civilian officials in Stockholm and Karl XII as to the stance they should take with respect to the Danish offer. Karl XII wanted to continue his advance on Copenhagen until he read a copy of the Travendal Treaty and was satisfied that Denmark had really withdrawn from the enemy coalition.

The civilian officials told him that with his brother-in-law having signed the treaty and being restored to his duchy,

Sweden ought to accept the treaty regardless of the exact wording of the document—otherwise there would be a falling-out with the maritime powers and, in the eyes of Europe, Sweden would appear to be the aggressor. They also reminded him that there were things to attend to on the other side of the Baltic where Augustus had made a direct attack on the Swedish empire.

Karl XII grudgingly accepted the arguments of the chancellery officials and some of his own military commanders, and the Danes were informed on 23 August that the Swedes would evacuate Zealand. Copies of the Travendal Treaty arrived the following day and the king was satisfied that it left no loop-hole for Denmark to continue its support of Augustus II.

The Treaty of Travendal was a serious setback for the anti-Swedish alliance. Denmark, a principal member, had been knocked out of the war before any meaningful gains had been made by Augustus, and before Peter's armies even reached the theater of operations.

THE BALTIC CAMPAIGNS

Karl XII spent much of September 1700 at his headquarters in Sweden con-ferring with his advisers and the high command about how to best deal with Augustus. Since the armistice between Russia and Turkey was now known, the tsar's intentions were not certain. Peter had actually issued a declaration of war on Sweden on 30 August but it did not become known in Sweden until much later.

It was obvious that additional Swedish troops had to be sent to the Baltic provinces. However, the most thorny question was how and where to strike back at Augustus. One option was to begin an offensive from Livonia. The second option was a direct attack on Augustus in Saxony.[11]

The second option was the soundest from a military standpoint and the one that Karl XII favored. Swedish forces would be going against a root of the current problem—Saxony. Forces could be augmented from those already in Germany—in Pomerania, Bremen, and Verden. The forces in Germany had gone through a strengthening program during the summer, and even if almost half were left in garrisons, over 10,000 could be provided for an in-vasion of Saxony. By further strengthening from the army used on Zealand, a force easily capable of dealing with the Saxons could be rapidly assembled. Furthermore, an offensive into Saxony would keep the Baltic provinces from becoming a battlefield. Livonia, for example, still had not recovered from the destructive effects of the great famine that had swept through the province in 1695–1696, leaving more than 50,000 dead.[12] The problem of crossing

Brandenburg territory was initially believed manageable since Brandenburg had allowed Saxon troops to cross its territory. An order was sent to Field Marshal Gyllenstierna in Germany to be prepared for the operation, either as a main attack or as a diversion in case the Livonian option was chosen.

The option to attack Saxony directly ran into a hornet's nest of foreign policy problems. The Dutch and English opposed it vigorously. They were primarily concerned about the effect of such an action in case the issue of the Spanish succession turned into war. King William III was primarily worried that he would lose his traditional recruiting ground for mercenaries. The Dutch were also providing quantities of supplies to Sweden for use in their war with Augustus. This welcomed help could be jeopardized by an invasion of Germany.

The Saxon invasion of Livonia was a breach of the 1660 Treaty of Oliva, for which France was a guarantor. Sweden suggested to Louis XIV that he might want to cooperate in the proposed invasion as guarantor to the treaty which had been broken. Help was not expected but Sweden wanted to know the French attitude on the issue. The French were not willing to go further than to offer their good offices for mediation. In view of the strong views of Holland and England, particularly William III, those powers were informed that Karl XII would attack Augustus through Livonia.[13]

The final nail in the coffin of the planned Saxon invasion was news from Ingria that a large Russian army was approaching its border with obvious intentions to invade. To regain Ingria was a primary Russian goal since its earlier loss had excluded them from access to the Baltic. The Russian declaration of war was received in late September. There was no way of countering a Russian invasion by going after Saxony. Winter was approaching and all available troops were quickly embarked to defend against the attacks by Augustus, now joined by Russia.

Swedish operations in Livonia had been too reactive and tame for Karl XII, despite the fact that Riga had held and General George Johan Maidel had inflicted a significant defeat on a part of Saxon army, forcing it to retire back behind the Dvina. The major worry was that the Livonian nobility was showing signs of unrest, and the Swedes did not fully trust their troops led by a Swedish officer, Count Otto Vellingsk.

Augustus made a second attempt in July to take Riga with an army of 17,000. A Swedish success was required to keep the loyalty of the Livonians.

The news that Denmark had been knocked out of the alliance caused Augustus to halt his operation against Riga. Augustus was the epitome of duplicity and double dealing among a number of like-minded rulers of that time. He sent an urgent message to Tsar Peter for help while at the same time appealing to Louis XIV to arrange an armistice with Karl XII. Simultaneously, he shrewdly reinforced garrisons that had to be held to keep a line of communication open to his Russian ally.

Karl XII did not know about the Saxon withdrawal from Riga until he reached Pernau, but he knew about a mediation offer from Louis XIV. This led to a debate about the king's methods concerning foreign policy by chancery officials both at his headquarters and in Stockholm. These complaints began at the time the king returned from Zealand, and centered on his openness and naiveté in dealing with foreign diplomats, and in not leaving adequate instructions and sufficient power for others to act in his place.[14]

There is probably truth to these complaints. We have seen in the previous chapter that Karl's father had a strong dislike for diplomacy, and this probably extended to his son. Karl was very direct and a person of few words. His advisers would present him various options; he thanked them and told them he would let them know his decision. This he did, but what apparently did not sit well with them is that he did not tell them why he had selected one option over another.[15]

The chancellery officials felt that he was too preoccupied by military matters at the expense of diplomacy, and that when he did venture into that field failed to follow the elaborate customs that had come to characterize that craft. But it also sounds a bit like sour grapes. Karl XII sought and listened to advice from both military and civilian leaders who had more experience, and in the case of both Denmark and Saxony he bowed to foreign policy necessities.

Gustaf Jonasson provides an example of the difficulties between the civilian chancellery officials and the king. Karl graciously accepted Louis XIV's offer to mediate between Augustus and himself. However, to the officials in the chancellery, who had to negotiate the offer, he insisted that Augustus had to evacuate Swedish Livonia before an armistice was signed. To the civilians this was the same as throwing down a gauntlet, showing that he did not want peace.[16]

Chancellery papers and correspondence with the king and among themselves have been used to paint a monarch who preferred the sword to the pen. Professor Hatton provides some very rational explanations for these difficulties. The first is that the king was young and inexperienced. She observes that the king was naturally more concerned with short-term objectives, and that this is the natural difference in attitude between a soldier and a diplomat. It is an early example of the difficulties in civil-military relations. She also notes that the officials who prepared letters and documents did so with an eye for the future. She writes: *In times of crisis, therefore, and in times of decision, officials tended to emphasize Charles XII's sole responsibility for the course adopted and to set down their objections and fears on paper as a form of insurance for the future.*[17]

Andrina Stiles, among others, considered Professor Hatton an apologist for Karl XII and his obstinacy. As an example Stiles quotes Hatton:[18]

> *If anyone could have saved Sweden's great power position he [Karl XII] would have been the man, with his gifts as a commander, with his capacity for inspiring loyalty in his maturity, and with his dedication to the task fate had allotted him.*

Karl assumed, probably correctly, that the reason for Augustus' peace feeler was to delay the departure of Swedish forces from Sweden until it was too late in the season. Karl felt he would be negotiating from a position of weakness until he had his army in Livonia. This is shown by the fact that after landing in Livonia he expressed himself ready to proceed with an armistice while Augustus still held three Livonian forts. He was also willing to conclude an armistice at this time for another important reason—it would leave him free to deal with the Russians. It was clear thinking and correct strategy.

Vellingk reported to Karl XII that Augustus had become alarmed when the Russians appeared to concentrate their effort in Ingria while ignoring his pleas for help. Augustus had put his army in winter quarters in Courland while he traveled to Warsaw. Karl XII and his military advisors decided that pursuing the Saxons in Courland was probably a waste of time in view of the Russian threat to Ingria. The Swedish king found the recommendation of the French emissary, Count Louis Guiscard-Magny, who arrived in mid-November, convincing. He agreed with Karl XII that Augustus should return the forts he had seized and pay restitution costs before ratification of any treaty.[19]

The decision had already been made to turn against the Russians with all forces that could be spared, since the threat from Augustus seemed rather remote. The Swedish forces—8,000 cavalry and 7,000 infantry—were to be marshaled at Wesenberg. Magazines to support a six-week campaign were established, including winter clothing. Colonel Henning Horn, the garrison commander at Narva, was told that help was on its way.[20] When Karl XII was asked where he intended to go into winter quarters, he answered simply that winter quarters would not be necessary since the army would be on the move.[21]

At this time a Russian army of about 40,000 had begun the bombardment of Narva. The Russian army was not a rabble as some writers would have us believe, but included seasoned veterans from the war with Turkey, and there were many highly qualified foreign advisers.[22] Among those was Field Marshal Charles Eugen de Croy, a former imperial general. The expectation was that Narva would fall to the Russians by the end of November. Tsar Peter sent General Boris Sheremetev (1652–1719), promoted to field marshal in 1701, with 5,000 men to destroy the Swedish supply depots at Wesenberg, but General Vellingk's Livonian troops stopped him before he reached the depots. However, he turned the territory between Wesenberg and Narva into a wasteland to delay the Swedish advance which had started on 13 November with less than 11,000 troops—despite arguments by some at headquarters that marching to the relief of Narva would risk a battle with the huge Russian army.

The march to Narva was grueling as troops waded, hungry and tired, through mud from autumn rains halfway up their legs. At night they slept in the open. King Karl XII demonstrated his supreme confidence in victory by ordering a regiment that had not reached Wesenberg by the designated departure date not to hurry after the army but instead take up position at Lake Peipus to prevent the beaten Russian army from bringing their artillery safely across the lake. Such optimism was infectious and caused rising morale among the troops.

The Swedes were encouraged by the news that about 400 Swedish cavalry commanded by the king had encountered Sherementev's force and put it to flight. The engagement is reported that way in a number of earlier books including books from the 1960s,[23] but the initial reports on which they relied were not accurate. General Sherementev had already received orders to withdraw from a pass where he was posted and not to engage the Swedish army.[24]

The force the king encountered was therefore only a rearguard. The Swedes did capture a number of guns and supplies. However, the word spread through the ranks of the Swedish army that the king had won a major victory, and this helped to further raise their morale.

The Swedish army was within two kilometers of Narva by 19 November and a series of shots were fired to let Colonel Horn know that the help he was waiting for had arrived. The Russians had been warned by General Sheremetev that the Swedes were approaching, but they were not expected to launch an immediate attack on an adversary outnumbering them almost four to one. Instead the Russians expected the Swedes to undertake the customary build-up of forces before a battle took place.

This lack of urgency may have been the reason for a historically controversial event. Tsar Peter left his army on the night of 17–18 November for Ingria, ostensibly to organize reinforcements and meet with Augustus. Not only did he depart on the eve of the battle, but he took the nominal army commander, Field Marshal Fedor Golovin, with him. Peter turned the command over to the very reluctant Eugen Croy. Some have described Tsar Peter's departure as an act of cowardice, but Massie takes exception to this charge.[25] However, it seems highly unusual for Peter and his principal deputy to choose the eve of battle to leave. Some accounts have—incorrectly—the tsar fleeing with his defeated army.[26]

The Russian army was positioned in a large fortified camp on the southern side of Narva. It is generally agreed that the Russian army numbered 40,000 and that the Swedes had 10,000.[27] Croy, when he saw how small the approaching Swedish army was, wanted to take a strong force and leave the fortified camp to meet them in open battle, but the reluctance of his Russian subordinates forced him to change his mind. The Russian army remained within their camp. It was protected by a wall nine feet high, and a ditch about six feet wide. The artillery numbered some 140 cannon. The weakness of their position, pointed out to the tsar by Croy, was that they were spread out for seven kilometers, leaving open the possibility that a concentrated enemy attack at one point could achieve local superiority before reinforcements could arrive on the scene.

Croy watched the Swedish approach with growing alarm. All had expected that the Swedes would start digging their own trenches and establish a camp, but instead he saw through his telescope that the Swedish soldiers were carrying equipment needed to cross obstacles. He was beginning to realize that the Swedes, contrary to all rules for an inferior force, were about to storm his position.

The Swedes had noticed the weakness of the Russian deployment and the king ordered General Karl Gustav Rehnskiöld to quickly prepare a plan of attack. It was decided that the infantry would launch the main attack against the center of the Russian camp in two groups. After breaking in, one group would turn north and one would turn south, rolling up the Russian line. The Swedish artillery, positioned on a slight rise, would support the attack. The cavalry was to remain outside the camp to deal with possible sorties or flight. Rehnskiöld would command the left wing of the Swedish army while Vellingk commanded the right. King Karl commanded a separate small force on the far left in the company of Colonel Magnus Stenbock (promoted to field marshal in 1713).

The Swedish attack began at 1400 hours in the middle of a snowstorm that was more of a problem for the defenders than the attackers as the wind blew the snow into the defenders' faces. The Swedish infantry halted thirty paces from the breastworks and fired a devastating volley that made the defenders *fall like grass*. Throwing bundles of twigs and brush into the ditch, the Swedes climbed over, scaled the breastwork, and killed everyone they found in what one Swedish officer described as *a terrible massacre*.[28] Within fifteen minutes the Swedes had broken into the center of the fortified camp and a furious battle ensued.

The first part of the Russian army to give way was their right wing. Many thousands fled toward the river, so many in fact that the bridge collapsed. The rest defended themselves within a wagon fort until darkness. The Russian left held out until dawn when it found itself completely surrounded and surrendered. There were so many prisoners captured that the Swedes found themselves unable to feed them. They were divided into groups. Those who had fought bravely were allowed to keep their arms while those who had not proven themselves worthy of that honor were disarmed. All soldiers were permitted to return home. From 0400 on the 21st until far into the next day a steady stream of Russians left and marched east. High-ranking officers were detained; the non-Russian officers were freed without ransom; the Russians were sent to Sweden in the hope that they could be used in a future prisoner swap.

The Swedish losses were 677 dead and 1,205 wounded.[29] Some of the Swedish casualties were incurred by friendly fire in the night battle.[30] The most reliable figure on Russian casualties is that between eight and ten thousand were killed.[31] The rest of the Russian army were wounded and/or captured. The wounded were freed along with the prisoners but it is doubtful that many reached their homeland. Field Marshal Croy and nine other generals were captured, along with ten colonels and thirty-three other senior officers.[32] The most important booty captured was the Russian artillery: 145 guns, 12 mortars, and 4 howitzers. Also captured were 10,000 cannonballs and 397 barrels of powder.[33] The captured standards were sent to Stockholm.

The young king acquitted himself well. He was one of the first over the entrenchment, lost his horse and sword in the ditch, mounted a new one provided by a cavalryman, and had three shots fired at him—one failed to penetrate his water-soaked uniform while the second bullet was found after the battle in his neckerchief. Word of his courage spread like wildfire among the troops.

The magazines of food in the Russian camp were welcomed additions to the meager Swedish supplies, and the Swedish soldiers moved into the abandoned Russian tents. Before long, this proved to have been a grave mistake because of disease (see below). The victory, particularly its magnitude, astonished Europe.

Many historians consider that Karl XII made a strategic mistake in not following up his victory at Narva despite the urgings of his advisers. They felt that the Russian realm was demoralized after Peter's already brutal reforms and that a Swedish invasion might have begun a revolt against the tsar.

Karl, in choosing to turn instead against Poland, made the right military decision based on what he knew at the time by going after what he considered his strongest opponent, Augustus. He had little respect for the Russian army after Narva, and could not have known that the feverish activities carried out by Peter the Great over seven years would result in a vastly improved and well-equipped army. Only in retrospect, and with the knowledge of what Peter was going to do, can it be remotely considered a strategic mistake. Even then, to leave the undefeated Polish-Lithuanian-Saxon armies on his flanks and rear would have been a perilous gamble.

The decision made by Karl XII is very much like that made after the Battle of Breitenfeld when Gustav Adolf opted not to risk a drive against Vienna with unreliable allies in his rear and a hostile Bavaria hugging his flank. Most historians, with the notable exception of General Fuller,[34] apparently fail to see the similarity in the strategic decision made by Karl XII. Finally, it should be noted that the forces available to Karl XII in 1700 were totally inadequate for an invasion of Russia.

Happenings at the other end of Europe created difficulty for Sweden's operations against Augustus. About the same time as the battle of Narva, Charles II of Spain died, thus triggering the struggle over his succession. The French changed their attitude to the war in the Baltic almost overnight. The French emissary Guiscard had worked hard to bring about an armistice between Augustus and Sweden. With a possible war looming on the horizon it was in French interests to see the war in the Baltic continue so as to keep either Sweden or Augustus from joining the maritime powers.

The splitting of the continent into pro-French and anti-French states served to complicate things for Sweden. Sweden found herself driven by the need for international loans—which came from the maritime powers—and by the need to have the Travendal Treaty upheld by them.

Sweden was obligated by the Travendal Treaty to help the maritime powers in case they were attacked. In February 1702 Karl XII promised both defensive and offensive help as soon as his own war was concluded. We now run into a situation where everyone saw their own problems clearly but not those of others. The maritime powers became annoyed when Karl XII did not end the war in the Baltic and join them.

Karl XII could not gain freedom of action lest he upset relations with the maritime powers, and that he could not do since their cooperation was what kept Denmark-Norway in place. He could not move against Augustus in Saxony for fear of upsetting England and the Dutch Republic. After the enemies of France gained substantial victories in 1706 they could no longer claim that Karl XII was spoiling their war by entering Germany. When this opportunity came Karl XII immediately invaded Saxony. The calculated risk worked and immediately knocked Augustus out of the war. If this could have taken place much earlier the many years of Swedish war in Poland could have been avoided and forces released for use against Russia in the 1702–1706 period.

Swedish campaign plans had to be changed considerably. An infectious disease had ravaged the Russian camp at Narva before the battle, and unfortunately it spread to the Swedish soldiers when they moved into the Russian tents. It spread like wildfire among the Swedes, causing untold deaths.[35] Karl XII determined to avoid enclosed camps from then on.

It proved impossible to bring reinforcements from Sweden until spring, and the same was true for equipment and money. As a result the Swedish army was forced to go into winter quarters in Livonia and Estonia.

There were no indications that the defeat at Narva would lead Peter to the negotiating table. He became thoroughly determined to rebuild his shattered army. Church bells were melted down to make cannons, taxes were increased, and training was intensified.

The tsar and Augustus concluded a treaty when they met at Birsen in February 1701. Augustus had been wooed by both France and the Empire, and he had entered into a secret understanding with Emperor Leopold in return for a guarantee of his position as king of Poland. He was therefore able to demand stiff conditions from Tsar Peter who had just sustained a major defeat at the hands of the Swedes. In the Treaty of Birsen the tsar agreed that Estonia and Livonia would pass to Augustus when Sweden's Baltic possessions were divided. The Russians also agreed to pay heavy subsidies and provide an auxiliary army of up to 20,000 troops to assist Augustus. Ingria was to go to the Russians.[36]

Augustus was now in a seemingly strong position. He had secured a very favorable treaty with Russia, and the Emperor had guaranteed his Polish crown, as had Prussia. Augustus also held up hopes that Denmark-Norway would re-enter the war provided Sweden suffered defeats in the Baltic.

Montross writes that Augustus, Karl XII's cousin, typified the worst German despotism of the age:[37]

> *Called Augustus the Strong because of his gross appetites, he left 354 illegitimate children as his chief claim to historical fame. The moral tone of the court at Dresden is suggested by the fact that one of his natural daughters became his mistress after marrying her half-brother.*

The strong position of the Saxons meant that for Karl XII, they had become the primary enemy. The Russians were kept in their place by their defeat and by Swedish garrisons spread along their borders. Augustus falsely professed his peaceful intent to the emperor and the maritime powers, but he had set his sight on delivering a serious defeat to the Swedes, and his troops raided southern Livonia from their base in Courland.

Reinforcements from Sweden in the spring brought the strength of their army to about 24,000. This was not enough to mount simultaneous attacks against Augustus and the tsar. It was important, however, to keep both enemies guessing as long as possible. In the end it was planned to make a crossing of the Dvina that would bring on a main battle with the Saxons. After the hoped for victory, the Swedes could then clear out Courland with part of their forces while the majority of the army took on the Russians in the dry weather of the late summer or after the roads had frozen in mid-winter. The rainy season had to be avoided. In this way the battlefields would be moved away from the provinces.

The Swedish crossing of the Dvina was well prepared. A pontoon bridge was constructed in Riga in the spring, strong enough to support cavalry. It would only be floated into position at the last moment. Diversionary plans were also made to confuse the Saxons and protect the operation. Furthermore, troops were stationed so as to protect Estonia and northern Livonia from invasion, while other forces were sent north to test Russian defenses in preparation for future operations.

There was a narrow window for beginning the operation. It could not start until the roads had dried out after the spring thaw but before the fall rains. It also could not begin until the grass was high enough for horses to eat and, most important perhaps, until more reinforcements from Sweden had arrived. Ten thousand soldiers landed in Reval in May, and the forces already in the Baltic provinces were ordered to leave their winter quarters. The army began its southward march from the Dorpat area on 17 June, which also happened to be Karl XII's nineteenth birthday. The army followed the road to Riga, but at Wenden it turned right towards Kokenhausen in an attempt to draw the Saxons away from the planned crossing site over the Dvina. When the army had reached a point about five kilometers from Kokenhausen on 3 July, it turned left and headed for Riga at maximum speed. Everything was ready at Riga.

Since Augustus was in Warsaw, General Adam Heinrich von Steinau commanded the Saxon forces. He had at his disposal 9,000 Saxons plus some Russian auxiliaries under General Repnin. He did not know where the Swedes would cross and had spread his troops thin to cover the likely crossings. This operation demonstrates the superiority of the offense against a defense when the main point of attack is unknown. He could only concentrate his forces once the enemy intention was known, and by then it could be too late. Steinau also fell for a Swedish feint against Kokenhausen by sending reinforcements to that fort. He was further misled by another Swedish feint towards Dünamunde the night before the crossing. The crossing began at dawn on 9 July.

The Swedes had achieved tactical surprise. The river was crossed using a dense smoke screen as Gustav Adolf had done at the Battle of the Lech in 1632. The boats made the crossing behind the smoke screen. In addition, there was a screen of small boats piled high with bales of hay to absorb musket and cannon fire. The troop transports were provided with large rectangular sheets of leather to absorb musket fire.

The Riga fort and armed merchant ships provided excellent covering fire by engaging enemy gun positions. The fire support was so effective that General Steinau gave them high praise for the Swedish success. An important part of the assault plan miscarried. The pre-constructed bridge, built in sections, to span the 2,000-foot-wide river could not be launched in a timely manner since a strong northwesterly wind prevented its deployment. The failure of the bridge prevented the use of most of the Swedish cavalry.

The crossing of the infantry and small units of cavalry was meantime a complete success. About 6,000 Swedes were eventually in the bridgehead. Karl XII went across in the first wave despite the protests of his aides and advisers. There was some hard fighting as the Saxons tried to drive the Swedes back. However, after a battle that lasted several hours the Saxons decided to withdraw. Due to the absence of most of their cavalry, however, the objective of forcing a decisive battle on the Saxons through pursuit could not be carried out. Although the Swedes improvised in getting their cavalry across after the bridge failure, it took such a long time that it was too late to launch a pursuit.

The Swedish infantry showed great discipline under heavy fire. They carried the fight to the enemy in such a determined manner that the experienced Saxon troops were astonished. This was particularly true at the beginning of the battle when the Swedes were heavily outnumbered as they tried to establish a beachhead.[38]

The Swedish victory in crossing the Dvina made an even greater impression in Europe than the victory at Narva because the Saxon army was viewed as more experienced and had a high reputation. The conduct of the Russian auxiliary troops was a disappointment for the Saxons. The four Russian regiments that General Steinau had placed in reserve panicked and fled before taking part in the battle.[39] The losses in the battle were relatively light. The Swedes lost 500 in dead and wounded; the Saxons lost 800 dead and wounded plus 700 captured.[40]

The failure to get the cavalry across the river in a timely manner robbed the Swedes of the decisive victory they had hoped for. Consequently, they were forced to change their campaign plan for the year.

The planned pursuit of Peter the Great was contingent upon first having knocked Augustus out of the war, and the failure to do so upset the plans. There was no way the Swedes could move against the Russians with a full strength Polish-Saxon army in their rear or flank. The Swedes spent the rest of the year securing Courland and Swedish Livonia. The Saxons abandoned the forts of Kokenhausen and Kobron without a fight, but they had to be forcibly ejected from Dünamunde. The main Swedish army took up positions in Courland from which they could foil any Saxon attempt to link up with the Russians, and which were also centrally located for the defense of the northern territories. It was also a good location for the receipt of reinforcements and supplies from Sweden.

Swedish relations with the maritime powers were soured by English, Dutch, and Prussian suspicions that Sweden's intent was to incorporate Courland into their empire, despite Swedish assurances to the contrary. In fact such a step was on the long-term Swedish calendar. The Swedes also launched an expedition against Archangel on the White Sea but it failed and the Swedes accused the Dutch of revealing their plans.

Naively, Karl XII was drawn into the complicated politics and internal squabbles in Poland. Up to now Karl XII had basically fought Augustus as the elector of Saxony, but now that he had withdrawn his army into Poland the Swedes were presented with a problem. Cardinal Michael Stephan Radiejowki, the Primate of Poland, wrote a letter to Karl XII at the request of Augustus, warning the king not to enter Poland. Letters were also received from Poles of the opposite opinion, primarily James Sobieski who lived in exile in Silesia after his unsuccessful attempt to gain the Polish crown in 1697.

The idea of Augustus' dethronement and his replacement by Sobieski originated at the Swedish Chancery. The chancellor had raised this with the king on several occasions.[41] Karl XII therefore proposed that the Poles be told that if they wanted to get rid of Augustus, Sweden would help. This went too far for the diplomats who wanted the Poles to sort out their own affairs. They urged caution in dealing with Polish groups.

For Karl XII's military campaign against both Augustus and Peter the Great, it was important to get this issue settled without waiting for the slow diplomatic route. He therefore answered the Polish Primate's letter by coming out in the open with his demand that the Poles dethrone Augustus, unwisely promising he would not enter Poland until an answer was received. The king did not realize—as he admitted—that Radiejowski would make the letter public in preparation for the Diet in December 1701.[42]

In the long run what Karl XII had done made little difference. His dilemma was that he could not undertake a campaign against Russia with an undefeated Augustus in his rear. Karl XII felt he had the blessings of the chancery, but admitted that he should not have put the dethronement demand on paper.

The answer to Karl XII's July letter to the Polish Primate did not arrive until the middle of October, and it turned down his suggestion and warned against any encroachment of Polish territory. The war against Saxony had now also become a war against Poland, because Augustus had sought sanctuary in that country and the Poles were not willing to expel him. Karl XII was furious but it was too late in the year to do anything about it and this was probably the reason for the three-month delay in the Polish answer.

Russian forces were also going into action against Swedish territory in the north, destroying Swedish hopes of keeping the war away from their provinces. Colonel (later General) Anton von Schlippenbach had been left to defend Livonia with 7,000 troops. Field Marshal Boris Sheremetev fought an indecisive battle with Schlippenbach near Dorpat. Each side suffered about 1,000 casualties but the Russians captured 350 Swedes that were sent to Moscow. This caused great joy in a city used to being constantly defeated by the Swedes.[43]

The Russians, under Sheremetev, administered a severe defeat to Schlippenbach at Hummelshof six months later (18 July 1702). The Swedes were virtually annihilated—2,500 casualties from a total force of 5,000. An additional 300 were captured while the Russian losses were placed at 800. The virtual destruction of Schlippenbach's army left Livonia wide open to the

Russians except for a few garrisons in the main cities. Sheremetev's army had free reign in the Swedish province. The savage Kalmuk and Cossack cavalry moved at will through Livonia laying the countryside waste, burning villages, and taking thousands of civilian prisoners.

Among the captives was a 17-year old peasant girl named Martha Shavronska who was not sent to work on the Azov fortifications as the others. Instead she begun an amazing "career" as a concubine, first to Sheremetev, then to Menshikov, and finally to Peter the Great himself who married her in 1707 and crowned her Empress Catherine I of Russia.[44]

The Russians also took control of Lake Ladoga and Lake Peipus south of Narva. Finally, they captured the Swedish fort of Nöteborg at the southern end of Lake Ladoga where it connects with the Neva River. The fort controlled the trade from the Baltic to the Russian interior via a network of rivers. Nöteborg, with a small garrison of only 450, was captured after a 10-day siege on 22 October 1702, and renamed Schlüsselburg. The whole length of the Neva River to the Gulf of Finland was occupied, and Peter founded a city at the mouth of that river named St. Petersburg.

Despite holding the military advantage for the next five years and winning every engagement, Karl XII was unable to achieve final victory. He became mired in the same wars and political maneuvering as his predecessors. When his campaigns are reduced to lines on a map, it looks like a spider's web of maneuvering. The Swedes being mired down in Poland and Lithuania was like a gift on a silver platter for the Russians. It gave Peter the Great seven precious years between the defeat at Narva and the Swedish invasion to rebuild and strengthen his army. He also did his best to keep the Swedes mired down by generous subsidies to factions opposed to Karl XII, even entering into an alliance with Lithuania in 1702.

Karl XII marched on Warsaw in 1702 and occupied it on 14 May with no opposition. Then he marched westward seeking out Augustus, who had finally reappeared to defend his crown. The armies met in the battle of Klissow. The Swedes were outnumbered almost two to one, with their army consisting of 8,000 infantry and 4,000 cavalry. Opposing them in strong positions difficult to assault were 7,500 Saxon infantry, 9,000 Saxon cavalry, and 6,000 Polish cavalry. Almost all the Swedish artillery was behind struggling through the mud to keep up with the army. There were only four guns available at the start of the battle. The Saxons had 46 guns.[45]

After viewing the Saxon positions, Karl XII changed his battle deployment by thinning out his center and right to mount a risky envelopment of the Saxon right. The weakened Swedish center and right were barely able to repulse heavy assaults while the envelopment was in progress. Eventually, the Swedes fell on the Saxon right flank as the center and right moved forward to pin down the troops to their front. The Saxons were hopelessly caught in a pincer and forced back on the marshland in their rear. When it was all over the Swedes entered the enemy camp. They had lost 300 killed and about 500 wounded. The Saxons had about 2,000 killed and 1,000 captured. One of those killed on the Swedish side was Karl's brother-in-law, Fredrik IV, the Duke of Holstein-Gottorp. Augustus escaped by fleeing through the swampy marshland.

The next substantial engagement with the Saxon army came about a year later, in June 1703, at Pultusk. After a rapid forced march the Swedes pounced on the surprised Saxons and scattered their army. Karl XII chose not to pursue but laid siege to the nearby fortress of Thorn, which Augustus had garrisoned with 6,000 of his best infantry. When Karl proposed to storm the fortress with only 600 men, his officers protested. At that time Karl XII is alleged to have uttered these words: *Where my soldiers are, there also will I be. As for Sweden, I should be no great loss to her, for she has had little profit out of me hitherto.*[46] He was persuaded not to undertake the reckless attack, and the army settled down to a six-month siege. It was successful in the end and cost only 50 Swedish casualties. In addition to the garrison, the booty included 84 cannons and 1,000 stands of arms. The walls of the fort were razed and the city had to pay a contribution of 60,000 riks-dollars. The following year the Swedes, through excellent use of their cavalry, produced another victory at Ponitz.

Karl XII was still fixed on destroying Augustus and his influence in Poland. His pacification campaign went on to capture Cracow and Poznan, and Ebling was occupied in 1704. In July that year Karl saw to it that his candidate, Stanislaw Leszynski was elected king of Poland and Lithuania.

Since Karl did not have sufficient forces to also effectively counter the Russians in the far north, they were allowed to pick off Swedish possessions one at a time. Dorpat was captured in July 1705 and Narva the following month. All the Swedish inhabitants of Narva were massacred by the Russians.[47] A Russian army under Scottish General George Ogilvie occupied Courland in 1705 but avoided any major engagement with Karl XII. The

Swedish king chased the Russians out of Lithuania but halted when he reached Pinsk in July 1706.

The Swedish cavalry had proven a decisive arm in several battles, and the best example is the Battle of Fraustadt on February 3, 1706. At this time Karl XII was besieging the fortress of Grondo where Ogilvie had been forced to retreat with his whole army corps. Peter was determined that Grondo be held, otherwise the road into Russia would be open to the Swedes. Ogilvie was ordered to withdraw from Grondo by the tsar after the news of Fraustadt. After he threw all his guns into the river Ogilvie managed to escape from Grondo in the direction of Kiev through the Pripet Marshes as ordered.[48]

General Rehnskiöld had been left behind to secure Poland. Tsar Peter implored Augustus to make a diversionary attack in the west to relieve the pressure on Grondo. To accommodate his ally, Augustus crossed the Oder with 15,000 troops while the Saxon General Johann Matthias von Schulenburg with 20,000–30,000 men, composed of Russians and Saxons, approached from the west simultaneously. Augustus was so sure of victory that he sent his minister to Berlin to request that Prussia not provide a safe refuge for the escaping Swedes.[49]

General Rehnskiöld had only 8,000 men, mostly cavalry, and he was therefore heavily outnumbered by both Augustus and Schulenburg. He could not let them join and decided to strike at the stronger force under Schulenburg. Despite being outnumbered by more than three to one, he attacked the Saxons and Russians in strong positions, deliberately chosen to resist the feared Swedish cavalry by being anchored on two villages. Attacking at full gallop, the Swedes put the Saxon cavalry on the wings to flight. They then pressed in on the center in a double envelopment while the Swedish infantry attacked the center. The result was disastrous for the Saxons. Of the combined Saxon-Russian army of 30,000,[50] eighty percent were killed or captured. Those killed were estimated at 7,000–8,000.[51] The Russians who were captured were massacred, undoubtedly in revenge for the Russian massacre of Swedish civilians at Narva.

Augustus did not try his own luck against the Swedes, and withdrew his army. Karl XII was so impressed by Rehnskiöld's victory that he immediately promoted him to field marshal.

Peter the Great was furious and worried. Portions of a letter he wrote to his Foreign Minister Fedor Golovin are quoted by Massie:[52]

*All the Saxon army has been beaten by Rehnskjold and has lost all its ar-
tillery. The treachery and cowardice of the Saxons are now plain: 30,000
men beaten by 8,000! The cavalry, without firing a single round, ran away.
More than half of the infantry, throwing down their muskets, disappeared,
leaving our men alone, not half of whom, I think, are now alive. . . By giving
money* [to Augustus] *we have only brought ourselves misfortune. . . .*

After the Blenheim and Ramillies campaigns (1704–1706) the maritime
powers appeared to have the upper hand in the War of the Spanish Succession, and Karl XII felt they would no longer be sensitive to a Swedish invasion of Saxony. The maritime powers were also worried about the possibility
of an alliance between Saxony and Prussia. William III sent John Churchill,
Duke of Marlborough, to Berlin to dissuade King Frederick I by threats,
bribes, and promises alike to convince the king to prepare to fight France.[53]

Karl XII decided to strike at Saxony, and the Swedish army crossed the
border into Silesia on 22 August 1706. They were greeted as liberators by
Protestant Silesians. By the time the Swedes reached the Saxon border a state
of panic existed in the electorate. Augustus and his family fled in various directions. The Saxon governing council, empowered to govern in Augustus' absence, resolved not to fight. They were war weary after losing 36,000 of their
troops trying to keep Augustus on the Polish throne. The primary cities such
as Leipzig and Dresden were quickly occupied without resistance, and Karl
XII dictated his terms to the Saxons at his headquarters in Altranstädt Castle.

The main terms were simple and the Saxons accepted them in the Treaty
of Altranstädt, signed on 13 October 1706:

1. Total and permanent abdication by Augustus of his claim to the Polish
   crown.
2. Augustus' recognition of Stanislaw as the king of Poland.
3. Saxony to break its alliance with Russia.
4. Surrender to the Swedes all Swedish nationals in Saxon service or
   prisoners.
5. Saxony to pay all the costs of the Swedish army wintering in Saxony.

At age twenty-four the Swedish king was at the apex of his career. In six
years of continuous campaigns against Danes, Saxons, Poles, and Russians he

had never lost a battle, and his reputation in Europe had never stood higher. But he had also spent six years that proved precious to Russia. Karl XII now settled down for the winter while contemplating his next moves.

KARL XII IN SAXONY

Karl XII and his army spent the winter of 1706–1707 and much of the following year in well-deserved rest in Saxony at the expense of their former enemy. In an unbroken string of victories Karl XII had eliminated two of the three enemies ranged against Sweden in the Great Nordic War—Denmark and Saxony. However, Russia still remained, and the Swedish king was determined to deal with that power next. The Swedes also did not sit idle in Saxony. They were constantly drilling, and reinforcements were arriving in preparation for the next campaign.

Two events during Karl XII's stay in Saxony are worth mentioning. The appearance of the Swedish army in the heart of Germany sent earthquake-like tremors through Europe. During the winter of 1706–1707, numerous emissaries arrived in Saxony trying to divine Karl XII's intentions now that he was only some 300 kilometers from the Rhine. Louis XIV proposed an alliance that would tip the European balance in his favor. The two countries would then divide the German states between them. Silesia begged the Swedes to remain and defend them against the Empire. Karl went so far as threatening to march on Vienna if the Lutherans in Silesia were not granted religious freedom. Voltaire reports that Emperor Joseph is alleged to have commented to a representative of the Pope who was angry at the effrontery of the Swedish king: *You may think yourself happy that the King of Sweden did not propose to make me a Lutheran; for if he had, I do not know what I might have done.*[54]

The most famous emissary was John Churchill, Duke of Marlborough (1650–1722). The maritime powers were anxious not to have Karl XII align himself with France, and, judging from the instructions Marlborough had received before he set out on his mission, to prevent such an eventuality they were willing to go far.

The two-day meeting between the two most successful generals of the age tells one much about the difference in their personalities. Marlborough, commander-in-chief of British forces, showed up splendidly attired. Karl XII appeared in the same blue coat he always wore.

Karl XII told Marlborough that he had his hands full in dealing with

Russia, a war he expected to last two years. He had no desire to be the arbiter of Europe. It appears Marlborough agreed to support Sweden with respect to its problems both with Denmark and the Empire, to recognize Stanislaw as king of Poland, and guarantee the Treaty of Altrastädt. Marlborough, an experienced diplomat as well as general, was careful not to put his promises on paper, thereby affording him some deniability when it came to his assurances concerning Stanislaw and Altrastädt, items that would not sit well with his allies, especially the Dutch. His mission was judged a success since he had assured himself, after discussions with Karl XII and some of his officers, and stealing a glance at a map the Swedish king either intentionally or inadvertently left on his desk, that the Swedes would be busy with the Russians for the next two years and had no intention to involve themselves in affairs in the west.[55] Karl XII had asked that a document detailing what had been agreed to be provided. Such a document was delivered to the king after he had left Saxony.

The alarm in the west was somewhat, but not totally, put to rest. If the Swedes were quickly victorious, as was expected, there was nothing to prevent them from turning west and dictating terms to both sides.

NEGOTIATIONS

That Peter the Great was worried when he became convinced that Karl XII would invade Russia, and that he would be left to face him alone, is best illustrated by his feverish search for allies and the massive peace offensive he launched. As most accounts of the peace offensive differ to some extent, I have chosen to rely mostly on Massie's research, his 2012 edition being the most current.

Peter's peace offer eventually included the return of Dorpat, Livonia, and Estonia with the exceptions that he wanted to retain Schlusselburg, the Neva river valley, St. Petersburg, Narva, and Reval. This was totally unacceptable to Karl XII. While some members of the Riksdag and the administration in Stockholm urged acceptance as they had done with respect to earlier peace offers from Augustus, the king politely refused. He viewed it as only "kicking the can down the road," not the permanent solution he was seeking.

In his peace offensive, the Russian tsar approached both sides in the War of the Spanish Succession, first the maritime powers and the Empire. He promised to provide 30,000 troops for their fight against France if they could convince Sweden to accept his peace offer. The Dutch did not reply to his request and he thereupon approached Denmark and Prussia. The attempt to get these countries involved failed. He then approached France, promising to provide troops for use against the Empire, the Netherlands, and England if they could mediate a peace. Louis XIV accepted, but his offer of mediation was politely refused by the Swedish king, who stated that the Russians could not be trusted to keep their promises.[56]

Peter's final attempt, which had begun before 1707, was to seek the help of England. For this purpose he was willing to give huge bribes to Marlborough and others—even though, due to his enormous wealth, he was skeptical of Marlborough accepting a bribe. The English duke nevertheless arranged for the Russian emissary to travel to London and meet Queen Anne. The queen told the Russian that, provided that her current allies Holland and the Empire agreed, she was prepared to make an alliance with Russia through it becoming a member of the Grand Alliance. Marlborough kept Russian hopes alive by promising to use his influence with the Dutch. This was at the same time that Marlborough had his two-day meeting with the Swedish king and made the promises mentioned earlier in this chapter.

English duplicity went even further according to Massie. A Russian ambassador-at-large in Europe, Heinrich von Huyssen, claimed that a different approach to Marlborough was under consideration. *The Duke had said that he would be willing to arrange English help for Russia in return for a substantial Russian gift of money and land for him personally.*[57] Peter, when informed, said Marlborough could have any one of three fiefs and 50,000 ducats per year for life. Nothing came of this offer.

Tsar Peter also sought the support of the Empire for a new candidate for the Polish throne. His suggested candidates included James Sobieski, the son of the former king, Eugène of Savoy, and finally Francis Rakoczy. Sobieski declined and the emperor, wary of offending Karl XII, made the excuse that Eugène was preparing for another campaign and therefore not available. Rakoczy did accept but only on condition that the Polish Diet make a request for him.

Karl XII's principal subordinates had assumed that the Swedish army would proceed north to retake the territories seized by the Russians. When they learned the king's real intent, Bain reports that they all objected except for Field Marshal Rehnskiöld.[58] I have not found this claim made by other sources.

The Swedish army was ready for its greatest test in mid-August 1707. In the late afternoon of 27 August 1707, Karl XII himself rode out of Altrastädt to catch up to his main army which had already departed. Accompanied by only seven officers he detoured and rode into Dresden, the enemy capital, to pay a surprise visit to his cousin Augustus. Surprise was achieved; the Swedish king found his relative in his dressing gown. Quickly donning something more appropriate, the two relatives embraced before taking a ride along the Elbe. Now that Augustus had been punished, Karl harbored no ill feelings. He also visited his aunt, Augustus' mother. It was the last time he would see either.

The king's foray into the enemy capital practically alone gave his subordinates a sense of alarm at his recklessness. They told the king that they were ready to besiege Dresden had he been made a prisoner. The next day Augustus held an unscheduled council meeting in Dresden. This led Baron Henning von Stralenheim, a Swedish diplomat in the field with the king, to comment to Karl XII: *You see they are deliberating upon what they should have done yesterday.*[59] We don't know what caused the king to make the detour to Dresden; it appears to have been a sudden impulse to see his relatives.

NOTES

1. Hatton, *op. cit.*, p. 35.
2. Augustus and Karl XII were first cousins. Karl's mother's sister, Anna Sofie, who died in 1717, was married to Johan Georg III of Saxony and Augustus was their son.
3. Frost, *op. cit.*, p. 227.
4. Peter Englund, *The Battle that Shook Europe: Poltava and the Birth of the Russian Empire* (New York: I. B. Turis & Co, 2011—originally printed in 2003), pp. 33–34.
5. Montross, *op. cit.*, p. 369.
6. Joseph Cummins, *Great Rivals in History: When Politics Gets Personal* (New York: Metro Books, 2008), p. 135.
7. This war is often called the War of the Grand Alliance. In America it was known as King William's War. On one side was France, supported by Irish and Scottish factions; while on the other side were the Dutch Republic, England, the Holy Roman Empire, Spain, and Piedmont-Savoy. The war was settled by the Treaty of Rijswijk in 1697.

The main gain for England was French recognition of William III of Orange as King of England, Scotland, and Ireland.

8. Gustaf Jonasson, *Karl XII och hans rådgivare: den utrikspolitiska maktkampen i Sverige 1697–1702*(Stockholm: Svenska bokforlaget, 1960), pp. 20–27.

9. Hatton, *op. cit.*, p. 133.

10. The Flintrännen channel was very shallow and the larger Swedish warships were left behind. Five ships touched bottom but were re-floated.

11. For a detailed discussion see Jonasson, *Karl XII*, pp. 168–173.

12. Frost, *op. cit.*, p. 229.

13. Herman Brulin, *Sverige och Frankrike under nordiska kriget och spanska successionskrisen åren 1700–1701* (Uppsala: Almqvist & Wiksells boktryckeri, 1905), pp. 60f and pp. 186–187.

14. Jonasson, *Karl XII.*, p. 181 and Brulin, *op. cit.*, pp. 99–101.

15. Hatton, *op. cit.* p. 146.

16. Jonasson, *Karl XII.*, p. 209.

17. Hatton, *op. cit.*, pp. 146–148.

18. Stiles, op. cit, p. 125 quoting from a Historical Association 1984 pamphlet that was a condensation of Hatton's massive biography of Karl XII.

19. Hatton, *op. cit.*, p. 149.

20. *Ibid*, p. 150, quoting Generalstaben, *Karl XII på slagfältet*, editor Bennedich, volume II (published 1918–1919), 304.

21. Hatton, *op. cit.*, p. 150.

22. Peterson, *op. cit.*, Kindle edition, loc. 5908, reports that there were 560 senior western officers with the Russian army, including 140 colonels.

23. For example Montross, *op. cit.*, p. 370. Fuller, *op. cit.*, volume II, p. 165 describes Peter the Great and his field marshal as fleeing the field in panic.

24. Robert K. Massie, *Peter the Great: His Life and World* (New York: The Modern Library, 2012), pp. 401–402 and Hatton, *op. cit.*, p. 152.

25. Massie, *op. cit.*, p. 404.

26. Thomas E. Griess, series editor, *The Dawn of Modern Warfare*. The West Point Military History Series (Wayne, New Jersey: Avery Publishing Group Inc., 1984), p. 90.

27. Massie, *op. cit.*, p. 407.

28. *Ibid*, pp. 408–409.

29. *Ibid*, p. 412.

30. Hatton, *op. cit.*, p. 153 quoting Generalstaben, *Karl XII på slagfältet*, volume II, p. 353.

31. Reinhard Wittram, *Peter I. Czar und Kaiser,*(Göttingen: Vandenoeck & Ruprecht, 1964), vol. I, p. 241.

32. Massie, *op. cit.*, p. 412.

33. *Ibid*, p. 413.

34. Fuller, *op. cit.*, volume II, p. 166 writes that a decision to invade Russia at this time *would have been an act of sheer folly.*

35. Hatton, *op. cit.*, p. 158.

36. Wittram, *op. cit.*, volume I, pp. 243–245.
37. Montross, *op. cit.*, p. 370. One of his illegitimate children was Maurice de Saxe (1696–1750), the famous Marshal General of France. He was also a noted writer on the art of war—*Mes Rêveries* being the best known. Maurice's mother was Countess Maria Aurora of Königsmarck.
38. Based on a report by General Steinau in July 1701, referenced by Hatton, *op. cit*, p. 165 and note 29, p. 564.
39. Massie, *op. cit.*, p. 424.
40. Hatton, *op. cit.*, pp. 165–166, quoting Generalstaben, *Karl XII på slagfältet*, volume II, p. 397.
41. Jonasson, *Karl XII*, pp. 229–231 and p. 239.
42. Hatton, *op. cit.*, pp. 168–169.
43. Massie, *op. cit.* p. 427.
44. Virginia Cowles, *The Romanovs* (New York: Harper & Row Publishers, 1971), pp. 44 & 49.
45. Frost, *op. cit.*, p. 272.
46. Bain, *op. cit.*, p. 117.
47. Dupuy & Dupuy, *op. cit.*, p. 615.
48. Massie, *op. cit.*, p. 495.
49. Bain, *op. cit.*, p. 137.
50. While Frost, op. cit., p. 275, puts the size of Schulenburg's army at 18,000, Massie, *op. cit.*, p. 495 places the number of Russian and Saxon troops at Fraustadt at 30,000 as does Peter the Great in a letter to his foreign minister.
51. Frost, *op. cit.*, p. 276, quoting Generalstaben, *Karl XII på slagfätet*, volume II, pp. 444–476.
52. Massie, *op. cit.*, p. 495.
53. Montross, *op. cit.*, p. 371.
54. Voltaire (François Marie Arouet), *History of Charles XII*. Translated from the French by Tobias Smollett. (New York: The Colonial Press, 1901), p. 90.
55. Hatton, *op. cit.* pp. 224–227.
56. Massie, *op. cit.*, p. 513.
57. *Ibid*, p. 515.
58. Bain, *op. cit.*, p. 159.
59. Voltaire, *op. cit.*, pp. 92–93.

9

The Russian Campaign— Karl XII's Exile and Death

When a general makes no mistakes in war,
it is because he has not been at it long.
MARSHAL TURENNE

CHANGES IN WARFARE SINCE GUSTAV ADOLF

W hile the military system of Gustav Adolf served as the basis for European warfare in the eighteenth century, few were able to apply it fully. While the external aspects of his ideas were copied, most practitioners failed to understand his flexible employment of the combined arms team on the battlefield. Arnold J. Toynbee refers to *an historical cycle of invention, triumph, lethargy and disaster.*[1]

Walter Goerlitz writes that *the strategy of the time was that of a chess board which concentrated on felicitous maneuvering and avoided, wherever possible, the more painful decisions of a direct encounter.*[2] One of the foremost military historians of that age, Count Wilhelm von Schaumberg Lippe, writes in his *Mémeoires sur la Guerre Défensive* that the aim of the art of war should be to avoid war altogether, or when that was not possible, to lessen the evil aspects of war.[3] Roger Boyle, Lord Broghill and Orrery, wrote in the 1670s:

> *Battells do not now decide national quarrels, and expose countries to the pil-*
> *lage of the conquerors, as formerly. For we make war more like foxes, than*
> *like lyons, and you will have twenty sieges for one battell.*[4]

As so often in history, economics dictated how wars were fought. The professional armies of the western powers were expensive instruments that could not be quickly replaced. Long periods of training were required to perform the mathematically prescribed deployments and maneuvering with precision. The infantry under Marlborough and Eugène of Savoy (1663–1736) fought in long thin lines often several kilometers in length. The infantry were trained to march directly into several sets of triple deployments, one behind the other and each three or four ranks deep. These lines were expected to retain their perfect alignment even during the heat of battle. The soldiers were drilled to carry out intricate movements and to keep strictly in step in their *ingenious wheeling and maneuvering*.[5]

It is not surprising that in such an environment there were few advances in weapons technology. Identifiable progress was primarily in refinements of weapons already in existence. The flintlock musket with the ring bayonet remained the basic infantry weapon, with only minor alterations.

There was practically no change in artillery. The Swedish technology of the early seventeenth century quickly spread across Europe, spurred on by a lively export from Sweden to the arms merchants in Amsterdam of at least 1,000 pieces annually starting in the 1650s. The weapons manufacturers in other countries were quick to copy.

Cavalry had a diminished role. They were used primarily as skirmishers, to fight enemy cavalry, as flank security, and for raiding the enemy's lines of communications.[6]

The most notable achievement was in the field of siege craft—both the construction of fortifications and in breaking through them. The credit for these achievements belongs to Marshal Sébastian le Prestre de Vauban (1633–1707). Space forbids going into his accomplishments, but two books are recommended for those who wish to pursue this subject further.[7]

The new fortresses created problems that were not easy to solve. As pointed out by Parker, a fortress or walled town with a strong garrison and supported by strategically located strongpoints was too dangerous to bypass and had to be taken.[8] Most of the pitched battles therefore took place between the besiegers and armies sent to help the besieged. The number of sieges increased while the number of pitched battles declined dramatically. Marlborough fought only four major battles during his ten campaigns but was involved in thirty sieges.[9]

The expanse of the battlefield and the extent of campaigns were dictated by three factors—the reduced role of cavalry, the limited range of weapons, and logistics. Supplies were gathered in a limited number of magazines. The location of these magazines and their distances from the battlefield dictated the scope of campaigns and put a limit on wars.

What did the Swedes think about the western form of warfare in the early eighteenth century? They were not very impressed, to say the least. Frost writes that the Swedish General Staff *had nothing but contempt for the linear tactics of contemporary European armies.*[10] In the view of the Swedes, western warfare was too defensive and precluded any final decisions by arms.

Frost believes that the differences between western linear tactics and those of the Swedes are overdrawn and that western tactics were not as defensive as depicted. However, as an excellent historian, Frost qualifies his statements by pointing out that western observers were baffled by Swedish tactics.[11]

There were considerable differences between the western approach to warfare and that of Sweden, driven largely by Karl XII's war aims based on two centuries of endless wars in the Baltic. Swedish war aims were the total defeat of its enemies, not the acquisition of a fort, city, or even a province, and the Swedish army was trained and organized to achieve those objectives. In short, the Swedish forces were geared for offensive war.

The Swedish army was as well equipped as its western counterparts. They were superbly trained and had a high level of discipline. This discipline was not based on severe corporal punishment or death as in the armies in the west, but on exemplary leadership. Karl XII shared the life of his soldiers, including sleeping in the open, eating the same rations as his men, and enduring the same hardships as they did. This example was followed by the other officers in the army. The king and his officers exposed themselves to hostile fire as much as the men. The king was invariably to be found at the hottest place on the battlefield, and his rashness was often deplored but the men liked it. He was truly loved and respected by his men, and this was sufficient to instill in them a discipline and aggressive spirit that seldom made disciplinary measures necessary.

The Swedes retained the pike while it had been discarded by western armies. This was not because modern infantry weapons, including bayonets, were lacking—in fact Frost points out that the Swedish bayonet was superior to many found in the west.[12] The Swedes simply considered that the pike still had a role to play.

During Gustav Adolf's time the Swedish infantry attack on enemy infantry was conducted at a steady pace behind continuous musket salvos delivered by each forward rank as one passed through the other, moving ever closer to their enemy. The Swedish infantry regulations under Karl XII had the infantry engaging the enemy infantry on the run, in some cases without unslinging their muskets. There was no pretension of any fire and maneuver, as the first—and in most cases the only salvo—was delivered as close to the enemy as possible. At the battle of Fraustadt on 13 February 1706, some of the infantry did not let loose even a salvo as it attacked headlong in one wave through three artillery salvos and one musket salvo before they stormed the enemy infantry line with sword, pike, and bayonet.

In a slow, traditional approach by the infantry, stopping momentarily to fire salvos, the enemy's stationary infantry should have been able to deliver 4 to 5 well-directed musket salvos and several artillery salvos at the attackers while they were in the killing zone to their front. In a dead run the enemy only had time to fire one, or at the most two, musket salvos. Having thousands of screaming Swedes approach at a dead run was enough to unnerve the best trained and battle-hardened infantry and make their fire inaccurate. Running at the enemy could theoretically reduce casualties and this may well be what was behind Swedish thinking.

Karl XII, while making some use of artillery, appears to have put less faith in firepower than his predecessors, and this is a definite divergence from the combined arms doctrine of Gustav Adolf. Marlborough, while walking through the Swedish camp in Saxony, was surprised at the scarcity of artillery.

At the Battle of Klissow in 1702, Karl XII, having only four guns at the outset, launched his attack on the Saxons without waiting for the rest of the artillery to arrive. In the invasion of Russia, Karl XII brought a total of 72 guns to support an army three times as large as Gustav Adolf had brought to Germany, supported by over 80 guns. Gustav Adolf had 200 guns at Frankfurt on Oder and 150 at the Battle of Werden. At Poltava, Russian artillery dominated the battlefield while most of the Swedish artillery was with their baggage train.

Unlike the western armies, Sweden still placed great emphasis on the cavalry arm. The Swedish cavalry charged theoretically in "knee to knee" formations mounted on large horses that must have been a disconcerting view to enemy formations.

Frost's observation that *the spectacular results of these aggressive tactics* [by the

Swedes] *played an important part in their success, since they ensured that morale remained high,* is on the mark.[13] An unbroken string of victories over a decade instilled a great sense of loyalty to and blind faith from the troops in Karl XII as a military leader. The king's simple life in the field and his reckless courage endeared him to his men. This military virtue of an army is labeled by Carl von Clausewitz as one of the most important moral powers in war.[14]

As with any military commander who loses a battle, particularly one as history-changing as Poltava, there is no lack in the literature of criticism and reasons for the ultimate defeat. I am reminded of the famous saying by Marshal Turenne that *when a general makes no mistakes in war, it is because he has not been at it long.*

KARL XII'S STRATEGY

In examining and judging Karl XII's strategy we must do so based on what the king knew or should have known when he launched his invasion of Russia. Military strategy must specify the ends—objectives to be achieved; military strategic concepts—the ways in which these objectives are to be achieved; and finally military resources adequate to achieve the objectives.

Napoleon was one of Karl XII's severest critics. In his memoirs dictated from his exile in St. Helena, Napoleon bluntly claimed that Karl XII was merely a brave soldier who knew nothing about the art of war.[15] It must be kept in mind that Napoleon was writing for posterity after his own disastrous Russian campaign, which he wanted to put in the best of lights.

Napoleon's arguments are not that the goal was unreasonable or that the resources were inadequate, as so many other writers have contended. He noted that Karl XII had 80,000 of the best troops in the world available for the invasion. He focused on the military strategic concepts, claiming that these were wrong. Napoleon's severest criticism is aimed at Karl splitting his forces and not following the example of Hannibal by abandoning all lines of communication and establishing a base in Russia.

This is strange criticism coming from a military leader who did just that in 1812; he captured Moscow but lost his army and empire in a disastrous winter retreat with inadequate provisions. Napoleon's criticism of Karl XII turning south instead of continuing on to Moscow, only ten days march away, has more logic. Clausewitz also levels mild criticism at Karl XII for not going after Russia's center of power: its capital.[16]

Napoleon, who took basically the same route as Karl XII initially, kept a copy of Voltaire's history of Karl XII on his nightstand or desk throughout his invasion in 1812.[17] While dismissing Voltaire's arguments with annoyance, he assured his subordinates and advisers that he would not repeat the mistakes of the Swede.[18]

We must look at the situation as it existed at the time of the invasion. The Swedes, based on past experience, had little respect for the Russian army. For Karl XII, the Russian weaknesses were demonstrated at the Battle of Narva. The king had concluded that the Swedish Baltic provinces could not be secured except by eliminating the Russian menace. This was to be done by dictating a lasting peace in the Russian capital. Karl XII believed strongly that this was achievable, as did most observers.[19] Near panic gripped Moscow when Peter the Great began to strengthen the Kremlin defenses. Fuller writes: *There was nothing astonishing in this, for Charles's [Karl XII's] prestige now stood so high that, with the exception of a few clear-sighted observers, all Europe predicted that he would crush the Tsar and dictate peace from the Kremlin.*[20]

While Sweden had begun the war on sound financial footing, it now found itself in the usual financial straits, and this made a long defensive war unthinkable.[21] The usual source for loans—the maritime powers—had dried up as they were fully engaged in the War of the Spanish Succession. Karl XII was well aware of these facts and concluded that the only reasonable course of action was to deliver a quick and decisive blow at the Russians in their homeland, and for this he had adequate supplies. In view of Peter the Great's feverish attempts to rebuild and transform his army, Karl may have concluded that time was not on Sweden's side since Russia would be more difficult to deal with 10–20 years in the future.

When it comes to the concept of operations selected by the Swedish king, there are some reasons for criticism. The direct route he chose through Lithuania—rather than the more northerly one—was obviously chosen to avoid leaving Poland to the mercy of the Russians who had already begun large-scale raids in that country. It was a logical decision but the logistical support that Karl XII arranged proved disastrous.

There was one thing the Swedes had not counted on: one of the severest winters on record in Russia. As in the case of 1812 and again in 1941, "General Winter" came to Russia's assistance. Karl XII was to learn, as Napoleon and Hitler did, that an army without sound logistics is at a distinct disadvantage when operating against a patient enemy willing to trade space for time.[22]

THE RUSSIAN CAMPAIGN IN 1707

As always, there is some disagreement in the sources as to the number of Swedes who participated in the invasion of Russia. The army which moved against the tsar is traditionally numbered at 33,000 to 43,000. Hatton concludes that the strength of the Swedish main army was not far from 44,000.[23]

More troops were on their way from Sweden to Livonia but had not yet joined the main army. An army of 14,000 under General Georg Lybeker, stationed in Finland, was expected to be brought into action by attacking St. Petersburg to tie down Russian forces. Furthermore, Karl XII expected to be joined by 11,400 troops under General Adam Ludwig Lewenhaupt in Livonia.

Karl XII left General Lewenhaupt in Livonia with the mission of bringing supplies forward. Lewenhaupt was to follow the main army when called forward. It would have been wiser to bring those supplies and Lewenhaupt's troops along at a distance that could be supported by the main army in an emergency. The fact that this might have slowed the Swedish invasion is not convincing. The Swedes were not in a hurry, spending a long time waiting for the Vistula to freeze, and the arrival of fresh troops from Sweden via Livonia, and then going into winter quarters near Grondo. Even a large supply train would not have slowed them down. To allow that train to move on its own far behind the main army through hostile territory with the flanks wide open for hundreds of kilometers was a reckless decision. If those supplies had accompanied the main army there would have been no reason to turn south to the Ukraine; it would have allowed the Swedes to proceed directly to Moscow. Downing writes that *Defeat came to Charles XII deep in the Ukraine as a result, at least in part, of a glaring weakness of indelningsverket: its lack of a rationalized system of supply.*[24] It would also, as suggested by Napoleon, have kept the Swedish forces concentrated. As it was, only about 50 percent of available forces took part in the actual campaign.

There were another 22,000 men in various parts of the Swedish empire and 17,000 in Sweden. These forces were roughly equal to the main operational army in number but it was not planned that they would take part in the main campaign.[25] No Swedish king had commanded an army of this size and quality.

The Swedes had been outfitted with new uniforms, and contemporary sources report that they made an imposing sight as tens of thousands headed eastward in their blue and gold uniforms. The population of Silesia came out to greet them as liberators by the thousands as they crossed that state from Saxony on their way to Poland.

Karl XII was aware as he marched east that there was unrest in Peter's empire, which began with a revolt in Astrakhan in 1705, but whether that played any part in his calculations is doubtful. He also knew that Peter's brutal and unpopular reforms of the army were far from complete and that the regular army was still relatively small. He also knew about the discontent among the Cossacks, which led to an uprising in 1707–1708, and the eventual defection of Ivan Mazepa, a leader among the Ukrainian Cossacks. News of the events in the east came primarily from Polish sources. King Stanislaw Leszcynski, while he had urged against the Swedish invasion of Russia, had stated his desire to incorporate all of the Ukraine into his kingdom.

Peter the Great had assembled an army of about 70,000 to meet the Swedes. At the beginning of the Swedish move from Saxony he was not sure what route they would take, but like so many others, he believed they would move to recapture their lost territories and then move toward Moscow after capturing Pskov.

Peter the Great had already taken action in January 1707 to make the invasion difficult for the Swedes. He had ordered a belt of devastation intended to prevent the invaders from living off the countryside. This area extended into broad swatches of Poland where he sent Cossacks and Kalmuks with instructions to destroy everything that could be useful to the Swedes.

Feverish activities were undertaken to strengthen fortifications, and the near panic this brought about in Moscow caused both Russian merchants and foreigners to flee with their families. It was not only the Swedes who were feared but a general revolt in Moscow where the people were bitter and resentful at continuous increases in taxes.[26]

Peter the Great spent two months during the summer of 1707 in Warsaw, partly because he was ill. He left as soon as he learned that the Swedes were marching east. At a council of military commanders held by Peter and General Alexander Danilovich Menshikov (who became a field marshal in 1709), it was decided not to offer the Swedes battle in Poland because the Russian infantry was not fully ready and Peter refused to risk its destruction.

The Swedish Invasion Route

Menshikov was given the mission of delaying the Swedes at river crossings.

In October 1707 Peter traveled to St. Petersburg to ensure that its defenses were in order. Massie reports that Peter was almost overcome in early winter by anxiety and depression. He was not completely well during the winter months as news flowed in about Cossack revolts in the southern part of his realm. While he was in St. Petersburg he married Catherine, a person who was able to calm his anxiety. They traveled to Moscow in late November to celebrate Christmas and inspect the fortifications being built.

Peter left Moscow on 6 January 1708 and proceeded to join his army. On the way he learned that the Swedish army was advancing rapidly across the wintry landscape of Poland. He therefore hurried to Grondo. The ability of the Swedes to move quickly in winter further raised his anxiety. The Swedes had crossed into Poland at Rawicz, a town that had been burned to the ground by the Russians. Menshikov, who had caused all the destruction, stayed away from the Swedish army which advanced in six parallel columns.

Karl XII initially headed directly for Warsaw but just before reaching that city he turned north. He stopped at Posen and set up a temporary camp while he waited for reinforcements to arrive from Sweden via Livonia. He detached 9,000 troops—6,000 dragoons and 3,000 infantry under General Ernst Detlow von Krassow—to bolster the forces of King Stanislaw.

As winter approached and the Swedish king had not made any move, the Russians in the vicinity gained more confidence and became lackluster. They concluded that the Swedes would remain in their camp until spring. However, this was not Karl XII's intention. He was training his new troops and waiting for the fall rains to stop.

In this part of the invasion we see a change in Karl XII's tactics. He temporarily set aside his usual fast and furious frontal attack, and turned to maneuvering. He allowed the Russians to establish defensive positions behind rivers and then outflanked them by crossing the rivers away from their defenses. This would force them to withdraw without a battle.[27] One may question the wisdom of this method of not going for an early decisive battle, but it brought results.

At the end of November 1707, after waiting for two months, the Swedes left their camp at Posen and marched 80 kilometers in a northeasterly direction to the great bend in the Vistula. The river was wide and there were no Russians on the far bank. Despite a heavy snowfall, the wide river was still flowing and drifting ice made it impossible to build a bridge. The Swedes had to wait another month for the river to freeze. By 28 December the river had frozen to a thickness of three inches. By using straw and planks sprayed with water the ice froze sufficiently to support the artillery and supply wagons, allowing the Swedes to make a successful crossing between 28 and 31 December.[28]

The whole army was east of the Vistula by New Years Day, 1708. This forced General Menshikov to evacuate Warsaw and withdraw behind the Narew River.

THE RUSSIAN CAMPAIGN IN 1708

Karl XII again outflanked the new Russian position, but with less ease than at the Vistula. He decided to approach the Russian positions by a tortuous trek through some of the worst terrain in eastern Europe, the heavily forested Masurian Lake area, full of marshes. The troops and animals suffered greatly on this march and we see the first outbreak of guerrilla warfare and Swedish reprisals.[29] This would not have been the kind of terrain for the use of supply trains, but they could have set up camp waiting for the main army to secure crossings that would have allowed them to take a more direct route.

The Swedes exited the nightmarish march at the town of Kolno, about

20 kilometers southwest of Grondo. They were observed by Russian cavalry but all they could do was to report the situation to General Menshikov. The Russians were forced to retreat from their positions along the Narew River.

Karl XII used different tactics in forcing the third river line, the Neman. Whatever route Karl XII selected in his continual march, he had to pass through the Lithuanian frontier town of Grondo. Peter the Great had arrived in that town to stiffen the resolve of a frustrated Menshikov, who had been outwitted by the Swedes in every defensive position. The Russians, knowing that the Swedes needed Grondo so as to use the road to avoid the surrounding swampy and forested areas, were pouring troops into the town.

Karl XII decided to attack immediately before the enemy had a chance to establish themselves securely. He left the army to follow and rode ahead with only 600 men of the Guards Cavalry. Finding the bridge, which had not been destroyed, guarded by 2,000 troops commanded by a German Brigadier named Mühlenfels in Russian service, he immediately attacked without waiting for the arrival of the rest of the army. Some of the Swedes headed directly for the bridge while others rode across the ice to attack the Russian rear. In the confused hand-to-hand combat, Karl himself killed two Russians. The Swedes captured the bridge and camped for the night at the town walls, waiting for the rest of the army—not knowing that Peter the Great was within the town, only a few hundred yards away.[30]

Believing that the whole Swedish army had arrived, the tsar and General Menshikov fled the town before daylight, heading for Vilna. When he found that Karl XII only had a small detachment in Grondo the tsar sent General Mühlenfels back with 3,000 cavalry to recapture the town and hopefully Karl XII. The Russians might have succeeded in their stealthy post-midnight approach except for two alert sentries who raised the alarm. The Swedes were so surprised that the king did not have a chance to put his boots on before he entered the pitch black fight which forced the Russians to withdraw. General Mühlenfels was captured but escaped. He was recaptured by the Swedes on his way back to Germany and joined them.[31]

The apparent ease with which the Swedes had crossed three defended river lines and traversed all of Poland had political repercussions. England, which had earlier been reluctant to recognize Stanislaw as the Polish king, now quickly gave that recognition. The recalcitrant Polish nobles also gave their support to Stanislaw. Western Europe gave Peter the Great little chance of survival. The Swedes went into winter quarters at Radoskovichi northwest of Minsk. After covering 800 kilometers in one campaign it needed a rest.

Peter the Great went to Vilna after his flight from Grondo. He was still not sure where the Swedes were heading, but if they went toward Minsk there could be no question but that they were aiming for Moscow. When the Swedes took up winter quarters at Radoskovichi, Peter ordered a 200-kilometer zone of devastation from Pskov to Smolensk. He conducted one of the first, most thorough and successful scorched earth campaigns in military history.[32] When Karl XII went into winter quarters, Peter traveled to St. Petersburg. He again became very ill, and judging from his correspondence with various officials it appears that he believed the end was near.

While in his winter camp, Karl XII ordered General Lewenhaupt to Radoskovichi. Lewenhaupt was ordered to bring a vast amount of food, powder, and ammunition, to scour the Livonian countryside for horses, and to junction with the Swedish army during midsummer.

The Swedish camp came alive with activities in late April 1708. Training was intensified and foraging brought in sufficient food for a six-week campaign. A primary reason for going into winter quarters was that there was no feed for the horses after frost and snow covered the ground and until grass began to grow in spring.

The Swedish army was still in good shape. Their main army had twelve regiments of infantry and sixteen regiments of cavalry for a total of 35,000 men. The Swedish forces in Livonia and Finland and those left in Poland still had a function to play, and some of these were expected to join the main army during summer. The entire campaign front still had 70,000 troops.[33]

The Russian army was considerably larger, numbering some 110,000. It was spread out in an arch around the Swedish winter camp from Vitebsk in the north to Mogilev in the south. The main army consisted of 26 regiments of infantry and 33 regiments of dragoons, numbering together 57,500 men. The main army was under the command of Marshal Sheremetev and General Menshikov. General Heinrich Goltz with large cavalry formations covered the Minsk-Smolensk road and patrolled the Berezina River. They were expected to absorb the first shock of the Swedish attack if the Swedes continued eastward. An army of 24,500 under General Apraxin had the mission to defend St. Petersburg. General Bauer with 16,000 men covered the Swedish army in Livonia. Finally, a force of 12,000 under General Golitsyn was stationed near Kiev to cover Ukraine. These forces could of course be shifted around as the situation dictated.[34]

Sheremetev and Menshikov had decided to make their first stand on the Berezina River line. The Russians occupied this line on a forty mile front. The most obvious crossing point was at Borsiov, and 8,000 Russian troops under Goltz were dug in at that location.

By 6 June the grass was sufficiently high to provide fodder for the horses, and Karl XII broke out of the winter camp with Minsk designated as the army's mustering point. When heading from Minsk towards Berezina heavy rain set in, making the roads soft and difficult for the supply wagons to follow the army. Miles of planks had to be laid to make the roads passable.

Karl XII again decided to turn the enemy flank, this time from the south. He sent General Sparre's cavalry in a feint against Borsiov, followed by the main army. After some distance the main army made a sharp turn eastward on side roads and reached the river at Berezina-Sapezhinskaya on June 16. Driving back a covering force of Cossacks and Russian dragoons, Swedish engineers constructed two bridges and the Swedes crossed the river with only minor losses. The Russians had again been outmaneuvered and they knew it. It was decided at a war council on 23 June to attempt to cover the towns of Mogilev and Shklov from behind the Vabich River.

Having been out-maneuvered four times by Swedish flanking movements at river crossings, the Russians spread their armies out along all possible crossing sites, and although they had a two-to-one superiority, they were spread thin. This left the attacker at an advantage since he could pick the time and place for the attack and achieve local superiority. Karl XII made excellent use of this opportunity.

Swedish reconnaissance revealed that what appeared to be the main Russian army of 30,000 had taken up position behind the Vabich River, near a place called Holowczyn.[35] Deserters confirmed that the Russians had decided to fight. The enemy was divided into two main concentrations. Sheremetev and Menshikov were to the north with thirteen regiments of infantry and ten regiments of cavalry; General Nikita Ivanovich Repnin was located to the south with nine regiments of infantry and three regiments of dragoons. There were other large concentrations of Russian forces on the flanks of these main concentrations. The Russians were dug in behind strong field fortifications. The two central groupings were separated by a marshy and heavily wooded area—considered impenetrable by the Russians—along a tributary stream that flowed into the Vabich River. This is where Karl XII decided to strike.[36]

Karl XII's army at hand numbered about 20,000 by 3 July, the date that the Swedes were ordered to prepare for battle as silently as they could. The troops had grown restless, not knowing why they were not ordered to cross the very fordable river and scatter the Russian rabble to their front. The king was anxious for the Russians not to change their positions and therefore carried out a number of feints along their whole front.

Karl XII had decided to personally deliver the main attack against General Repnin to the south of the marsh while Field Marshal Rehnskiöld would lead the Swedish cavalry against General Goltz' cavalry expected to come to Repnin's assistance from the south. There was a mist rising from the river on the night and morning of the battle, and this gave the Swedes some natural concealment. Some of the heaviest Swedish artillery had been moved into position during the night directly across from the Russians at the crossing site. At the first light these guns opened a thunderous salvo at the surprised Russians. At the same time Karl XII plunged into the river at the head of 7,000 of his infantry.

The river was deep enough so that in places it reached to the shoulder but, with muskets over their heads, the soldiers calmly crossed despite heavy enemy fire. Exiting the river on the Russian side the king regrouped his forces. To his surprise the Russians stood and fought, but were not willing to come to hand-to-hand combat. The battle developed into a firefight as the Swedes steadily advanced, delivering their own salvos at the Russians. This was not the normal pattern of Karl XII's many battles.

By 0700 Repnin realized he was the object of the Swedish main attack and called for help. A 1,200-strong force of dragoons from Goltz came to his assistance, trying to drive into the right flank of the Swedish infantry. Rehnskiöld, on the opposite side of the river, went into immediate action with 600 of the Guards cavalry. After splashing across the stream, they fell on the Russian dragoons in a bloody engagement. As additional Swedish cavalry squadrons joined the fight Goltz' troops were forced to retreat into the woods. In the meantime the Swedes poured additional infantry across the river. Repnin's forces retreated, rallied, and retreated again. They were finally scattered into company-size units which withdrew through the woods, leaving behind their camp and artillery. It was not a Russian rout, as they maintained good order. The casualties in this battle were 975 dead and a reported 675 wounded on the Russian side while the Swedes had 267 dead and 1,000 wounded.[37] Repnin was court-martialed for his failure at Holowczyn. Karl XII for unknown reasons considered this his finest victory.

Karl XII next turned to meet Marshal Sheremetev's army but that officer had already left the field and retreated toward Mogilev and the Dnieper. This was in accordance with earlier instructions from the tsar to avoid a decisive battle. The road to the Dnieper was now clear for the Swedes and they reached that river at Mogilev on 9 July. The king sent strong reconnaissance forces across but no resistance was encountered. Here Karl XII hesitated. He remained on the western bank with the main army for almost a month— from 9 July to 5 August. The troops were perplexed.

The reason for the pause was the failure of Lewenhaupt's supply train to arrive, something that was of increasing concern to the king. The instructions given to Lewenhaupt at the meeting with the king at Radoshkovichi was to bring enough supplies for a six-weeks campaign. The troops he was bringing forward would also augment Karl's army in the move to Moscow. It had been calculated that if Lewenhaupt left at the beginning of June he could traverse the 650 kilometers in two months.

Lewenhaupt was not able to leave until the last days of June with 2,000 wagons and 8,000 horses, escorted by 7,500 infantry and 5,000 cavalry. He did not personally join the train until 29 July. At that time they should have neared a junction with the main army but they had only covered 250 kilometers and were still 400 kilometers short of their meeting point at Mogilev.[38]

Karl XII was in a quandary. If he knew, as I believe he did, that Lewenhaupt had not yet reached the Dnieper, he should have turned around to link up with the supply convoy. This was a difficult decision to make since he had successfully crossed five great watersheds and he may have been reluctant to give up two of them. Furthermore, a turnabout at this time might cause morale problems among his own troops, encourage the Russians, and appear to an adoring following in western Europe and Poland as a serious setback. Karl had also realized that the Swedes were not fighting the same Russians as at Narva. The Russian army now showed a steadiness that surprised him, particularly the infantry. On the other hand, the linking up with the supply train would still give him time to reach Moscow, about 500 kilometers away.

After all, he had already covered more than 1,200 kilometers.

The Swedish king became involved in some short-range and desultory maneuvering while waiting for Lewenhaupt. By 21 August the Swedes had reached Cherikov on the Sozh River, only to find Russian cavalry and infantry in position on the far bank. A sharp infantry engagement took place on 30 August as a Russian force of 13,000 attacked the Swedish rearguard under General Axel Roos. Learning from the Swedes, the Russians approached the Swedish force through a swamp near the town of Molyatychy. The Russians broke off the fight after Swedish reinforcements arrived, having suffered twice as many casualties as the Swedes.[39] Karl believed this indicated that the Russians were finally ready for a battle, but the next day a reconnaissance found the Russian positions empty.

The Swedish army began a slow move in the direction of Smolensk. The Russians were still carrying out a thorough destruction ahead of the invaders. The smoke from burning villages and farms was at times so thick that it blotted out the sun. Whether Karl XII intended to proceed as far as Smolensk is not known. The key to the decision was Lewenhaupt's supply train. In view of the Russians' scorched earth policy, to try to go on without the supplies was out of the question.

Karl XII had basically two choices: return to the Dnieper and wait for the supply train or turn south away from Smolensk and Moscow into the province of Severia. Although the Swedish king appeared to believe that Lewenhaupt would show up, the time was running out for him to make a decision. He found a withdrawal to the Dnieper repugnant while a march into Severia would continue his offensive. In that province they were just beginning to harvest their crops. Karl could march on Moscow after his troops were replenished and he was reinforced by Lewenhaupt.

The final decision to turn south was made at a prolonged conference after the Swedes reached Tatarsk. We don't know who took part in this conference besides Field Marshal Rehnskiöld and Karl Piper, a senior Swedish official who accompanied the king on the Russian campaign. There were no disagreements recorded.

The importance now was to get to Severia before the Russians. Speed was of the essence. A special vanguard of picked infantry and cavalry numbering 3,000 under General Anders Lagercrona were given rations for three weeks and ordered to proceed rapidly to seize the bridges and towns that would open the area for the Swedes and thereupon deny them to the Russians. The provincial capital of Starodub was to be seized. The distance that had to be covered was 200 kilometers.

The Swedish army began its southward march on 15 September. We now know that Lewenhaupt on that date was 50 kilometers west of the Dnieper and therefore 150 kilometers from Tatarsk. The column reached the Dnieper on 18 September and there Lewenhaupt received the messages from the king ordering him to turn south to the new rendezvous point at Starodub. We can only speculate what the impact would have been on the campaign if the main Swedish army had retrograded to the Dnieper. It took until 23 September for the tired soldiers to get the wagon train across the river.

Lewenhaupt now became aware that Russian forces were moving against him. The Russians had followed the progress of the supply train and they now saw an opportunity to destroy it since it was separated by 150 kilometers from the main Swedish army. The strength of the Russian forces, under the personal command of the tsar, was 14,625, not the 50,000 claimed by Creasy.[40] The force under Lewenhaupt numbered 12,500.

Lewenhaupt was desperately trying to reach the town of Propoisk on the Sozh River. If he could cross that stream there was a possibility he could reach the main army. But the heavy wagons were slow to move over the muddy roads, and it became obvious that a fight was imminent. There were no good options but he chose to make a stand with his wagons instead of sending them ahead while fighting a rearguard action. This may have been a mistake.

The Swedes spent the whole day of 27 September in battle formation waiting for a Russian attack that never came. Lewenhaupt finally dissolved his battle formation and proceeded several kilometers along the road and again formed up for battle for the night. On the morning of 28 September there was still no attack and the Swedish column reached the village of Lesnaya, a few hours march from Propoisk. Had it not been for the stop on the 27th there was a chance the Swedes could have crossed the Sozh to relative safety, the fords over that river having already been secured. Lewenhaupt was under enormous pressure and may have chosen the wrong solution, but the fault lies with Karl XII for not waiting for his supplies or returning to the Dnieper to link with the column.

The battle began shortly after noon on 28 September. The fighting continued until nightfall when a snowstorm brought it to a halt. Although his lines were unbroken, Lewenhaupt decided to retreat and began burning the supply wagons. The cannons were buried in pits. In the shimmering light of the burning wagons there was mass confusion and discipline began to break down as the Swedish soldiers began plundering their own wagons. Infantrymen took off on horses that had been used to pull wagons, while others fled into the woods. When the survivors reached the crossing site at Propoisk they found the bridge burned by those who had fled earlier and the rest of the wagons had to be burned as Cossack and Kalmuk cavalry arrived and killed another 500 Swedes on the riverbank.

The disaster was complete. Lewenhaupt had not only lost the wagon train but half his force. His total loss was 6,307, and of these over 3,000 were taken prisoners. Many of those who fled into the forest died or were eventually captured. Amazingly, about 1,000 found their way back to Riga after an 800-kilometer trek. The Russian losses were 1,111 killed and 2,856 wounded.[41]

Karl XII did not blame Lewenhaupt. He may have realized that despite lingering and waiting for him, he had not waited long enough. The most disconcerting lesson was that the Russians had been victorious in a battle in which the two sides were about equally matched; it demonstrated the new fighting quality of the Russian troops. However, it was not an open battle. The detailed description sounds more like an ambush where the dismounted Russian dragoons and cavalry were pouring short-range fire into the Swedish troops protecting the wagon train along a rather narrow trail.

More good news for the Russians arrived while Tsar Peter was in Smolensk in mid-October. General Lybecker in Finland with 14,000 troops was supposed to carry out a diversionary attack against St. Petersburg from the Karelian Isthmus. He crossed the Neva River on 29 August 1708, but false information planted by the Russians convinced him that St. Petersburg was too heavily fortified to be taken. In the end, General Lybecker's aimless and desultory campaign in Ingria achieved nothing but the loss of 3,000 soldiers and 6,000 horses.

In the south, General Lagercrona's mission had been to seize key towns in Severia, including the provincial capital of Starodub, before the expected Russian troops appeared. However, due to a series of tragic mistakes in routes and failure to secure the capital, all key towns were occupied by the Russians.

The main Swedish army, which used the crossings seized by Lagercrona on the Sozh and Iput rivers, was suffering immensely as it crossed the primeval wooded area between the Sozh and Iput. Men and animals expired after weeks of hunger, and dysentery was ravaging the army. When it was learned that Lagercrona had failed to seize the empty capital, despite pleas from his colonels to do so, Karl exclaimed, "Lagercrona must be mad!"[42] On 11 October Lewenhaupt, with less than 7,000 starving survivors, stumbled into the Swedish camp in front of the town of Mglin. Karl XII had already decided that his army was in no shape to try to take Mglin, and that Severia was lost with Marshal Sheremetev's army pouring into the province. The Swedish king broke camp the same day as Lewenhaupt's survivors arrived, and headed for the Desna River which formed the boundary between Severia and the Ukraine.

The Swedish king's plunge into the Ukraine has often been attributed to rashness, but the condition of his army left no other choice. The fertile Ukraine, rich in both cattle and grain, offered the Swedes what they needed most for the winter that was just around the corner. Turning south also offered the prospects of an alliance with the ongoing Cossack rebellion.[43] Under the circumstances it was the right decision.

The Swedish king had sent an advance guard under Colonel Karl Gustav Kreutz (later General) to secure the bridge across the Desna River into the Ukraine and take the town of Novgorod-Seversky. Kreutz arrived at the border on October 22 only to discover that the Russians were there first and had destroyed the bridge. However, the main Swedish army continued its southern advance to the Desna and the Ukraine, the homeland of General Ivan Mazeppa, Hetman of the Ukrainian Cossacks.

There is a long and complicated history of Polish-Swedish contacts with Mazeppa that is not covered in this book. Appeals from the hetman for the Swedes to come to his aid had reached Karl XII. Mazeppa with 2,000 Cossacks arrived in the Swedish camp at Larinowka while preparations were being made to cross the Desna. The hetman also brought the news that General Menshikov was headed towards Mazeppa's capital of Baturin.

The Swedes forced a crossing of the Desna on 2 November at Mezin against determined Russian resistance. They were too late to save Baturin, which was stormed by Menshikov's troops on 3 November and burned to the ground to prevent its capture by the approaching Swedes. This was a serious setback for the Swedes who had hoped to capture its well-stocked magazines as compensation for the loss of Lewenhaupt's wagon train.

The Swedish army went into winter quarters southeast of Baturin, but Tsar Peter was not about to allow the Swedes a restful stay. The coldest winter in Europe's memory had now begun. It was in Peter's interest to weaken the Swedes as much as possible during the winter, and they undertook what could be called hit-and-run tactics. They would appear to threaten a place but withdraw as soon as the Swedes approached. The Swedes captured some towns taken over by the Russians and drove the tsar out of his headquarters in Lebedin. Although the two armies had been within half of mile of each other at the town of Hadyach, Peter withdrew rather than face the Swedes. The winter campaign was meantime taking its toll on the Swedes, as many died or became incapacitated with frostbite. The cancellation of the Christmas services in 1708 because of the bitter cold was an unheard of event in the Swedish army. The Russians suffered even more and lost more men.[44]

THE RUSSIAN INVASION IN 1709

After the worst of the cold spell was over the Swedes attempted to capture the hilltop fort of Veprik. The first attempt was repelled with 400 Swedes killed and another 600 wounded. The casualties were heaviest among the officers, and Field Marshal Rehnskiöld was among the wounded. Veprik surrendered to the Swedes on the night of 7–8 January 1709.

Leaving Field Marshal Rehnskiöld in charge of the winter camp, Karl XII carried out a merciless winter campaign against the Russians, capturing several towns and—taking a page from Peter—laying waste the countryside to provide more security for the Swedish encampment. In a lightning raid on Menshikov's headquarters, Karl XII nearly captured the Russian general, who managed to flee, but the raid killed 400 of his men while only two Swedes were killed.[45] An early thaw began in mid-February, turning the ground to mud. Campaigning for both Russians and Swedes was impossible.

Rumors from the north reported that a large Russian army was now heading for Poland. This, combined with the fact that the king of Poland and General Krassow would probably not arrive, prompted Count Karl Piper to recommend a retreat to Poland. The advice was rejected by Karl XII. He had in effect decided to move the Swedish camp to new positions between the Psiol and Vorksla rivers. The main army went into quarters in March and April along the Vorksla, two miles south of Poltava, a fortress that commanded the road to Moscow.

The Swedes began a siege of Poltava on 1 May but made little headway. The siege followed what may have been a peace feeler by Peter the Great in the guise of a prisoner exchange. The message was carried by Erik Johan Ehrenroos, who had been captured at Lesnaya. The message was simply that Peter was inclined to make peace but would not give up St. Petersburg. The reply was sent back by Ehrenroos on 1 May and it ignored the peace offering.[46]

Karl XII's search for allies had meantime proved fruitless. The Khan of the Crimean Tartars was ready to provide support, but he was a vassal of the sultan in Constantinople who had decided not to get involved and forbade the Khan from doing so. The rebellion by the Zaporozhian Cossacks was put down by the Russians in May 1709.

The Russians were eager to prevent the Swedes from capturing the Poltava fort because its vast stores of supplies would provide those sorely needed by Karl XII's men. They made an unsuccessful attempt to force their way across the Vorskla River. At a Russian war council it was decided to cross the river far enough from Poltava to avoid the Swedish defenses, and the spot selected was Petrovka. The operation was given urgency by a message from the fort's commandant that he would not be able to hold out much longer. The Swedes were, however, aware of the Russian plan and their own plan called for allowing a large portion—but not all—of the enemy army to cross before attacking.

THE BATTLE OF POLTAVA

The Swedish king had received a foot wound on 17 June from a musket fired from an island in the river while he was reconnoitering the bank. The wound was sustained around 0800 hours but the king continued his rounds before returning to his headquarters around 1100 hours where he fainted while trying to get off his horse. The musket ball struck the heel of his left foot and traveled the length of his sole before it exited.

Rehnskiöld, with ten cavalry and eight infantry regiments, had been given the mission to execute the agreed upon plan against the Russian crossing. The king would remain at Poltava but would join the field marshal to take part in the battle as soon as the situation at Poltava allowed. This was before he was wounded.

After he was wounded but still able to issue orders, he left it up to his field marshal whether or not to fight at Petrovka.[47] The field marshal consulted his senior commanders and all agreed not to fight the battle, not only because of the king being wounded but also because the Russians were already well entrenched. Some historians have criticized the field marshal's decision and claimed the failure not to attack the Russians at Petrovka contributed to the disaster that followed. While he was recovering from his wound, Karl XII received definite word that neither Stanislaw nor General Krassow was coming, since they were fully engaged in Poland.[48]

The Russians began building a second fortified camp just north of Poltava. It was fortified on three sides while the side facing the river was left open as no threat there existed. It was a strong camp but had the disadvantage that if forced to retreat the Russians would have to retrace their steps back to Vorskla since only one track led directly to the river from the encampment.[49] A battle had become inevitable after the Russians brought their main army across, and neither side had good withdrawal routes, being virtually surrounded by rivers.

The Russian camp was built in the form of a quadrilateral, with strong redoubts that would channel the attacks and keep the attacking columns in a deadly crossfire as long as possible. The southern side was difficult to attack because of ravines and woods. The western side faced an open plain with a forest behind it. Between this forest and the one on the south side was a piece of open ground. The Russians built six redoubts and were in the process of building four more when the battle started.[50]

The Swedish strength consisted of 8,200 infantry, 7,800 cavalry, 1,000 irregular Wallachians, 1,300 siege-work troops with 2 guns, a baggage train protected by 2,000 cavalry and 28 guns, an unknown number of Zaporozhian Cossacks, and 1,800 cavalry along the lower Vorskla. The Russian forces consisted of 25,500 infantry with 73 pieces of artillery, 9,000 cavalry with 13 pieces of artillery, a redoubt force of 4,000 infantry with 16 artillery pieces, vthe Poltava garrison of 4,000 infantry with 28 cannons, an outpost at Yakovtsi with 2,000 troops equally divided between infantry and cavalry, and an unknown number of Cossacks.[51]

The appalling picture painted by the above order of battle is not only in the fact that the Swedes were heavily outnumbered in infantry, but that they had no artillery placed to assist in the battle. Of their 30 pieces, two were with the besiegers of Poltava and the other 28 were with the baggage train! The Russians, on the other hand, had 130 artillery pieces.

The Swedes were outnumbered almost 3 to 1, the enemy had complete dominance in artillery, and the Swedes were going against a well entrenched foe which normally requires a superiority of 3 to 1. Only an unabashed believer in miracles could expect the Swedes to prevail under these circumstances. Since the king had decided to be carried onto the battlefield on a litter, he failed to appoint a single overall battle commander, and the orders were issued in such a hurry that by the time they got to battalion and company level there was not enough time to become familiar with them. Finally, the personality and tactical eye of the king was not present to give his troops the morale lift they sorely needed.

The Swedes had expected to launch a surprise attack at first light on June 28, and for that purpose some of the troop movements took place shielded by the woods to their rear. However, the Russians learned about the Swedish plans and moved strong cavalry forces behind their redoubts. When the Swedes realized that their surprise had been discovered they hurried their preparations. Orders went out to change from a line formation to a column in approaching the enemy positions. This caused further confusion. The Russian artillery had already opened fire on the Swedes. Rehnskiöld commanded the Swedish right and Roos the center, while Lewenhaupt commanded the left.

The Swedes easily captured the first two redoubts but bitter fighting ensued for the rest, and the attackers were severely mauled. The dust raised by the cavalry and the smoke from artillery and muskets ruined visibility. One part of the Swedish army under General Roos became separated from the rest, attacked and surrounded by cavalry, and relief forces were unable to break through. Having failed to take all the T-shaped redoubts the Swedes began to withdraw.

The Russians now came out of their entrenchments and prepared to attack. The Swedes decided to take the initiative with their own attack. The king, who was consulted, suggested that it was best to first get rid of the enemy cavalry. This was probably the best thing to do in this impossible situation, but when Rehnskiöld told him it was impossible the king is alleged to have muttered, "Well, you must do as you will."[52]

The Swedes thereupon launched an infantry attack while posting their cavalry in the rear. The depleted Swedish infantry lines—no more than 4,000 strong—faced 18,000 Russian infantry supported by over 70 field guns. The

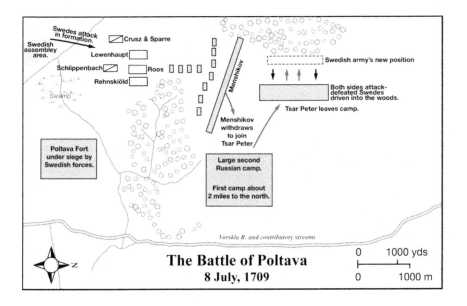

Swedes attack in formation.
Swedish assembly area.
Crusz & Sparre
Lewenhaupt
Schlippenbach
Rehnsköld
Roos
Swamp
Menshikov
Swedish army's new position
Both sides attack-defeated Swedes driven into the woods.
Tsar Peter leaves camp.
Menshikov withdraws to join Tsar Peter
Poltava Fort under siege by Swedish forces.
Large second Russian camp.
First camp about 2 miles to the north.
Vorskla R. and contributory streams
The Battle of Poltava
8 July, 1709
0   1000 yds
0   1000 m

Cossacks were asked to bring their 28 guns forward but it was too late.

The Swedish right drove the Russians back and captured some field guns which they turned against their enemy. However, a gap had developed between some of the regiments, and Russian infantry poured into that gap. Panic began to set in among the Swedish infantry, and Lewenhaupt's attempt to halt the stampede failed. Rehnsköld, who tried to come to Lewenhaupt's aid, was captured. Most of the Swedish infantry which had crossed the field against the Russian lines was destroyed.

Roos, who had earlier become separated from the main Swedish army after he lost 1,100 men in attacking the redoubts, withdrew to the south, not knowing where the main army was. He was pounced upon by Russian cavalry and infantry and forced to surrender his remnants.

The battle was over but the killing continued. With Rehnsköld and Piper captured, Lewenhaupt was left in command. Karl XII was in the middle of the debacle and tried his best to stem the stampede, but his feeble voice could not be heard above the din. The murderous fire was like a great scythe bringing down men, horses, and trees. Twenty-one of the king's twenty-four litter-carriers were killed, and the litter was finally shattered. It looked like the king would be captured but an officer stopped, dismounted, and lifted Karl into the saddle, only to have the horse shot from under him. Another horse was provided but now his wound was fully reopened and bleeding profusely.[53]

The Swedish cavalry, which was basically intact, covered the remnants of the infantry in their withdrawal to the camp at Pushkarivka. The reserve regiments, artillery, and Mazeppa's Cossacks were placed in defensive positions around the camp. The two infantry regiments besieging Poltava managed to fight their way through the Russian lines to the camp. Most of the defeated army had reached the camp by noon. The Swedes had left some ten thousand on the battlefield, 6,901 dead and 2,760 prisoners. The Russian losses were relatively light: 1,345 killed and 3,290 wounded. It was almost the exact opposite of previous Swedish-Russian encounters.[54]

No immediate pursuit was launched by the Russians, as their troops were almost as confused as the Swedes, and Peter wanted to celebrate the victory. The Swedish army had been defeated but it had not surrendered. About 16,000 Swedes gathered at Pushkarivka to join the approximately 6,000 Cossacks already there.

Future plans had to be laid and they boiled down to a retreat to Poland to join Stanislaw and Krassow by one of several routes known to the Cossacks. The first leg of the retreat was a withdrawal to Perevolotjna, at the junction of the Vorskla and Dnieper rivers. The route would then go north to the Vorskla fords, cross the river and move south along the Dnieper to the Khan's dominions and join the king at Ochakov on the Black Sea from where the entire army would return to Poland.[55] The baggage was sent ahead and the infantry and cavalry followed under the command of General Kreutz. Horses were gathered for the infantry to increase the speed. The march continued through the heat of the day of 28 June and through most of the night. The whole army arrived safely at Perevolotjna on 30 June.

The first order of business was to get the Cossacks, starting with the leadership, across the Dnieper to safety since the Russians would not show them any mercy. To do otherwise would be a stain on Swedish honor. Second, the wounded king had to be spirited away to safety in Turkey, despite his own arguments to stay with the army. Lewenhaupt chose to remain with the army after he gave the king his word that he would continue the fight; but he chose his words carefully.[56] The Cossack leaders were moved across the river on 30 June, followed by the king and his group the following day.

General Menshikov appeared with 6,000 dragoons and 2,000 Cossacks early on 1 July and asked for a parley. Kreutz was sent to find out what terms the Russians were offering. He came back stating that Menshikov offered normal surrender terms. Lewenhaupt consulted his colonels and they asked what the king's last order had been. Lewenhaupt gave a rather evasive answer that he had only asked the army to "defend itself as long as it could." Lewenhaupt directed the colonels to poll the soldiers if they were willing to fight. This was contrary to all Swedish army practice. The answer from the soldiers was that they would fight if the others did.

The surrender—termed by some as shameful—took place at 1100 hours on 1 July: *1,161 officers and 13,138 non-commissioned officers and men filed into Meshikov's camp and laid down their arms.*[57] Englund gives higher figures for the Swedes who were surrendered (see below). Only few ever saw their homeland again. It should be noted that several of the Swedish regiments had seen little action, particularly the cavalry which was virtually intact. The Swedes actually outnumbered Menshikov's tired troops, and an inspiring and resolute combat leader would have opted for a daring attack rather than captivity. Lewenhaupt was no such leader. The 5,000 Cossacks who had remained with Lewenhaupt were not included in the capitulation, and most grabbed horses and rode away, but some were caught, tortured in the most brutal manner, and killed.

Englund gives precise and startling figures of the losses sustained by the Swedish army—which had numbered 49,500 the previous summer. He notes that almost exactly 20,000 entered captivity and when the roughly 2,800 taken prisoner during the battle are added, he arrives at a grand total of about 23,000 prisoners.[58]

Karl XII reached the Bug River on 7 July and entered the Ottoman Empire on 10 July, eventually joined by about 1,800 of his troops. They were granted asylum and treated as welcomed guests. The last action was that of the rearguard on the other side of the Bug when it was caught by Russian cavalry. The 300 Swedes surrendered, but an equal number of Cossacks fought to the last man.

IMMEDIATE CONSEQUENCES OF POLTAVA

It is not surprising that the consequences of a battle historians have long considered one of most decisive in history would be great and long-lasting. Here we will only deal with the immediate effects.

The results of the battle shocked Europe; in a matter of days the whole political situation on the continent had been changed. However, the Great Northern War dragged on, inconclusively, for another decade, which caused great fiscal strain and disaffection in war-weary Sweden.

The scavengers moved in to carve up the carcass of the Swedish Empire. Denmark seized Schleswig, Bremen, and Verden, but turned some of those territories over to Hannover in order to gain its alliance. Danish forces also invaded southern Sweden but were defeated by General Magnus Stenbock in the Battle of Helsingborg in February 1710, forcing them to withdraw across the Sound. Stenbock then proceeded to Germany where he defeated the Danish army at the Battle of Gadebusch in 1712. He was thereafter set upon by much stronger allied forces and compelled to surrender in 1713. Russia occupied Poland, Karelia, Livonia, Estonia, and Ingria. Augustus (who was reinstated as King of Poland), moved against Pomerania with a Saxon-Polish army but was stopped. The Saxons and Russians were also repulsed from Stralsund in 1713. A Russian fleet defeated a Swedish squadron in the Gulf of Finland in the Battle of Hangö in 1714.[59] However, they did not yet feel strong enough to offer an open challenge to the Swedish navy. There were still some teeth left in the old lion.

Karl XII stayed in exile for four years, trying to convince the sultan to attack Russia. He had some success as Turkey entered the war in October 1710 and moved an army of 200,000 under Grand Vizier Baltaji Mehmet to the Russian frontier. This move by the Ottoman Empire was also encouraged by the French.[60]

An overconfident Tsar Peter invaded Moldavia with 60,000 men, was outmaneuvered by the Turks, and driven back to the Pruth River where his starving army was surrounded in July 1711. Peter had never been in greater peril; however, luck was with him. Rather than forcing Peter to surrender Mehmet entered into negotiations which led to the Treaty of Pruth on 21 July 1711. Among the terms of the treaty was a promise by Peter to withdraw from Poland, stay out of Polish internal affairs, and provide Karl XII a safe passage back to Sweden. Forcing Peter to surrender on the Pruth would have had unimaginable historical consequences.

Karl XII was bitterly disappointed, and stayed in Turkey for the next three years. He wisely did not believe Peter the Great would keep his promise of safe passage any more than he did regarding the Polish provisions. The Swedish king kept insisting that his host should renew the war. Karl was finally placed under house arrest after a fierce hand-to-hand struggle on 1 February 1713. He remained under virtual arrest until he departed the following year. While General Sparre and 1,200 Swedes who had been in Turkey took a separate route, Karl XII in the company of two aides made the dangerous journey, incognito, across the unfriendly states of Europe to enter Stralsund on 11 November 1714.[61]

Will and Ariel Durant present a different version of these events. They write that Karl XII was encouraged to return by the Turks who gave him gifts, money, and a military escort.[62] If Karl was given a military escort, it could only have been as far as the border with the Holy Roman Empire in Hungary. For the rest of the journey through Hungary, Austria, and into Germany southeast of Nuremberg, the king probably traveled incognito. Karl XII stayed in Stralsund helping to fight off a siege, but headed back to Sweden in December 1715 after an absence of more than 15 years.

THE INVASION OF NORWAY AND DEATH

Once back in Sweden, Karl XII raised a new army of 20,000 men to meet a planned invasion by Denmark and Norway, but Denmark abandoned her offensive plans in 1716. Karl seized the initiative and invaded Norway in March 1717 with 8,000 troops. He may have hoped to win an easy victory and use Norway as a bargaining chip with his enemies. Karl approached the Norwegian capital from the north but found out that Akerhus fortress was too strong to capture. He began his return march to Sweden on 29 April. The final nail in the invasion coffin was delivered by Norwegian Admiral Peter Wessel Tordenskjold, who on 8 July captured the Swedish supply fleet at the Battle of Dynekil.

Karl XII tried his luck again in 1718, this time with 48,000 troops at his disposal. General Karl Gustav Armfelt led 10,000 troops against Trondheim while the king, with the rest of the Swedish forces, laid siege to Fredrikstend fortress, which had 1,300 defenders. Traverse and parallel trenches were dug that brought the Swedes closer and closer to the walls. While on an inspection visit to the forward trenches on 30 November 1718, the king was hit in the head by a Norwegian sharpshooter's round fired from the fortress and was immediately killed.[63] The Durants write that *He died as he had lived, stupefied with bravery. He was a great general, and won unbelievable victories against great odds; but he loved wars to intoxication, never had victories enough . . .*[64]

Since a coup had been considered by the war-weary Riksdag, there immediately arose various conspiracy theories lasting until the present day claiming that the king was assassinated. His body was exhumed in 1916 for an autopsy, and another one was requested in 1998, but I am not aware of any conclusive results. The whole Swedish army returned to Sweden, but 3,000 of Armfelt's force froze to death in a snowstorm during the second week of January 1719.

The war continued for more than two years. Russian and Danish raids against the Swedish mainland were worrisome and seen as a prelude to an invasion. This alarmed both France and England. England was especially fearful that critical naval supplies might be lost. Diplomatic pressure from France and England put an end to any invasion plans Peter the Great may have had. Although the end to a direct Russian threat must have seemed incredible to the Swedes, Downing notes that such happenings were part of the hydraulics of the state system and quotes Kenneth N. Waltz: *In international politics, success leads to failure. The excessive accumulation of power by one state or coalition of states elicits the opposite of others.*[65] Downing also notes that Sweden was not only given diplomatic assistance but also financial aid to help it through its difficulties.

Karl XII's death was not officially mourned in Sweden. Peter the Great, on the other hand, declared a one-week period of mourning at the Russian court when he received the news that his rival had been killed.[66]

THE END OF THE GREAT NORTHERN WAR

The Great Northern War was finally settled in a series of treaties between 1719 and 1721. In the two Treaties of Stockholm, Sweden first ceded Bremen and Verden to Hanover on 9 November 1719. In return she received a substantial payment from England. The second treaty, on 21 January 1720, settled the war with Prussia. Sweden ceded most of Pomerania to Prussia.

The war with Denmark and Norway was settled in the Treaty of Frederiksborg on 3 July 1720. Denmark gained full control of Schleswig and Holstein, while Sweden was forced to break its alliance with Holstein and pay Denmark 600,000 riks-dollars in damages. The portions of Pomerania occupied by Denmark were returned to Sweden.

The war with Russia was settled by the Treaty of Nystad (Finland) on 10 September 1721. The bulk of Finland was restored to Sweden, but the transfer of Estonia, Livonia, Ingria, and parts of Karelia to Russia was recognized. Russia paid Sweden 2,000,000 silver thalers as compensation.

I have never seen accurate figures of the human cost to Sweden of winning and maintaining an empire over more than a century. With respect to the Great Northern War we find widely different figures. Jill Lisk writes that Sweden lost 30 percent of its manpower during the war.[67]

Stiles challenges the 30 percent figure and writes that, at most, 30,000 perished in military service. She uses census figures from 1750 and notes that there was a 9 percent decline in the population, but attributes it to bad harvests, epidemics, and the plague in the years 1710–1712.[68] She fails to mention how the population broke down by gender, which would be important. It appears she also did not factor in the two generations of births between 1697 and 1750 or explain why Norway, which experienced similar problems with harvests and epidemics, did not show a corresponding loss in population.

Hatton and Peterson, while using the same base figure as Stiles, show even lower casualty figures due to 8,000 prisoners being returned, claiming that the loss in military service amounted to only 22,000. At the same time Peterson notes a 129,000 drop in the Swedish population, from 1,376,000 in 1697 to 1,247,000 in 1718. He, like Stiles, attributes the population drop to bad harvests and epidemics while apparently not allowing for births in those years.[69]

The 22,000 figure for 21 years of war with virtually constant campaigning, numerous battles, and untold skirmishes are difficult to accept, and fail to tally with reported battle losses mentioned in this and the previous chapter, including deaths from cold and sickness which devastated the Swedish army in Livonia and Russia. Many thousands of Swedish soldiers also froze to death. For example 3,000 died in the retreat from Norway in 1718–1719, and a much larger number died during the 1709 winter in Russia.

Since Karl XII did not have any children, the crown passed to his sister Ulrika Eleonora. Ulrika had little interest in politics and abdicated in 1720 in favor of her husband, Fredrik of Hesse, who became Fredrik I as king and ruled the country until 1751 when the crown passed to Ulrika Eleonora's nephew of the Holstein-Gottorp family which ruled Sweden until 1818 when the current dynasty, the Bernadotte family, assumed the throne.

Sweden's age of military/political greatness had come to an end. However, the country was still respected for its military prowess for some time to come. It is my belief that all warring nations, small and large, reach a point of exhaustion—burn-out if you will. Sweden had almost reached such a point in 1720, but not quite. Over the next 90 years, she fought three more wars against Russia (1741–1743; 1788–1790; and 1808–1809). The Swedes also fought a war with Friedrich the Great's Prussia from 1757 to 1762. Finally, Sweden participated in the War of the Fourth Coalition against France and its allies from 1806–1807.

In the end, Finland and what remained of Pomerania passed to Russia and Prussia, respectively, during the Napoleonic wars, while Sweden gained Norway in compensation until that union was dissolved in 1905.

NOTES

1. Arnold J. Toynbee, *A Study of History*, Somervell Abridgment (Vols. 1–6) (New York: Oxford University Press, 1947), p. 336.
2. Goerlitz, *op. cit.*, p. 7.
3. *Loc. cit.*
4. As quoted in Parker, *The Military Revolution*, p. 16.
5. Goerlitz, *op. cit.*, pp. 6–7.
6. Jeremy Black, "The Military Revolution II: Eighteenth-Century War" in Townshend, *op. cit.*, p. 41.
7. Christopher Duffy, *The Fortress in the Age of Vauban and Frederick the Great, 1660–1789.* (London: Routledge, 1985), particularly volume II. Reginald Blomfield's *Sébastian le Prestre de Vauban, 1663–1707* (New York: Barnes and Noble, 1971) is also very informative.
8. Parker, *The Military Revolution*, p. 16.
9. *Loc. cit.*
10. Frost, *op. cit.*, p. 276. Frost has an excellent description of the Swedish army in 1707 at the end of the Polish and Saxon campaigns on pp. 271–278.
11. *Ibid*, pp. 277–278.
12. *Ibid*, p. 274.
13. *Ibid*, p. 276.
14. Carl von Clausewitz, *On War*. Edited by Anatol Rapport. (Baltimore: Penguin Books, 1968), p. 257.
15. Edward Shepherd Creasy, *Decisive Battles of the World* (New York: The Colonial Press, 1899), p. 288.
16. Clausewitz, *op. cit.*, pp. 389–390.
17. Adam Zamoyski, *Moscow 1812: Napoleon's Fatal March* (New York: Harper Perennial

Publishers, 2005), p. 337.

18. *Ibid,* pp. 92 and 193.

19. Voltaire, *op. cit.*, p. 91.

20. Fuller, *op. cit.* volume 2, p.168.

21. Frost, *op. cit.*, pp. 280–281.

22. Gunther E. Rothenberg, *The Art of Warfare in the Age of Napoleon* (Bloomington: Indiana University Press, 1980) pp. 129–130 and Creveld, *Supplying War*, pp. 62–70.

23. Hatton, *op. cit.*, p. 233.

24. Downing, *op. cit.*, p. 206.

25. Hatton, *op. cit.*, pp. 233–234 and note on p. 234.

26. Massie, *op. cit.*, pp. 523–524 based on reports by the Austrian envoy to Moscow.

27. *Ibid,* p. 527.

28. Hatton, *op. cit.*, p. 249.

29. *Ibid*, p. 251.

30. Massie, *op. cit.*, p. 530.

31. Englund, *op. cit.*, p. 245 and Hatton, *op. cit.*, note on p. 252. Muhlenfels was captured at Poltava, and Englund describes the atrocious death he suffered at the hands of Peter the Great.

32. Andersson, *op. cit.*, p. 232; Fuller, *op. cit.*, Volume 2, p. 172; Hatton, *op. cit.*, pp. 277–293.

33. Massie, *op. cit.*, p. 537.

34. *Ibid*, pp. 537–539.

35. It later turned out that the strength was 38,000.

36. Massie, *op. cit.*, p. 541 and Hatton, *op. cit.*, pp. 258–259.

37. Massie, *op. cit.*, pp. 543–544.

38. Hatton, *op. cit.*, pp. 261–262 and Englund, *op. cit.*, p. 48.

39. Swedish casualties were 300 killed and 500 wounded while the Russians suffered 700 killed and 2,000 wounded.

40. Massie, *op. cit.*, p. 551 and Creasy, *op. cit.*, p. 290.

41. Massie, *op. cit.*, pp. 552–553.

42. Hatton, *op. cit.*, p. 271.

43. Fuller, *op. cit.*, Volume 2, pp. 169–175, Hatton, *op. cit.*, pp. 300–306, and Downing, *op. cit.*, p. 207.

44. Hatton, *op. cit.*, p. 279.

45. Massie, *op. cit.*, p. 577.

46. Hatton, op. cit., p. 285.

47. Soon after receiving the wound the king developed a serious fever, and blood-poisoning set in. The king's life hung in the balance between 19 and 21 June, his doctors giving him but a few hours to live.

48. Fuller, *op. cit.*, volume II, p. 175.

49. Englund, *op. cit.*, p. 59. Englund, I have found, gives a recent (2003) and detailed account of the battlefield and the actual battle. Another good source that puts the battle in perspective is Sarauw's *Die Feldzüge Karl's XII* (Leipzig: B. Schlicke, 1881).

50. Fuller, *op. cit.*, volume II, pp. 177–178.

51. Englund, *op. cit.*, p. 86.

52. Hatton, *op. cit.* p. 299.

53. Massie, *op. cit.*, p. 617.

54. Hatton, *op. cit.*, p. 300.

55. Massie, op. cit., p. 626.

56. This promise was given by Lewenhaupt with only General Kreutz present. The king later wrote that it was his mistake not to also have given the order to the other generals and colonels.

57. Hatton, *op. cit.*, pp. 305–306.

58. Englund, op. cit., p. 246.

59. Nickolas V. Riasanovsky, A History of Russia. Third Edition. (New York: Oxford University Press, 1977), p. 248.

60. *Ibid*, pp. 247–248.

61. Peterson, *op. cit.*, loc. 6440.

62. Will and Ariel Durant, *The Story of Civilization* (New York: Simon and Schuster, 1963), volume VIII, p. 388.

63. Ersland and Holm, *op. cit.*, volume 1, p. 244.

64. Durant, op. cit., volume VIII, p. 389.

65. Downing, *op. cit.*, p. 210.

66. Joseph Cummins, *Great Rivals in History*, p. 145.

67. Lisk, *op. cit.*, p. 194.

68. Stiles, *op. cit.*, p. 108.

69. Hatton, *op. cit.*, pp. 516–517 and Peterson, *op. cit.*, loc. 6570-6571.

Summary/Conclusions

The intent of this book was laid out in the Preface, and how this intent was to be fulfilled was detailed in the Introduction.

My first objective in writing this book was to fill a void in the military historiography. Because the period covered is more than a century, and in order to keep this book to a reasonable size, there are many aspects that I could deal with only in summary.

My second objective was to probe the subject of how an agrarian country with a population of, at the most, only 1.5 million could rise to become the major military power in Europe for nearly a century. This aspect is addressed throughout the nine chapters. In the context of the elements of national power discussed in the Preface, I define national power as the aggregate capability of a nation to achieve its national interests and to influence the behavior of other states.

Many people, if not most, when looking at Sweden, would immediately rule out any possibility of that nation achieving great power status. Nevertheless, in the early 17th Century we have seen how Sweden assembled, for that period, an enormous army and defeated major European powers or combinations of those powers, or fought them to a draw.

The fact that Sweden had very few, if any, of the elements that we associate with great power status not only does not negate those elements, but rather demonstrates that they can be overcome or compensated for. The failure to consider Sweden a candidate for great power status is partially due to a lack of understanding of the historical background of the Scandinavian societies.

There are few societies in Europe that were more martial than those of Sweden, Norway, Denmark, and Finland. During the first millennium of their histories, they were constantly involved in internal strife, in war among themselves, or in overseas adventures. It should therefore not be a surprise that we find a dynasty that came to power in 1521 having a series of what we commonly refer to as warrior kings.

The Swedes have always had strong interests in the Baltic area going back to the earliest history of that region. While the first two generations of the Vasa Dynasty laid the foundation of the Swedish empire, the focus of this book was on its two greatest warrior kings—Gustav Adolf and Karl XII. The former presided over Sweden's rise to European great power status, while the latter saw the empire crumble at the beginning of the 18th Century.

Though both kings were heavyweights in military history, their personalities were highly different, and history treats them very differently. One is considered a military genius—and that he was—while the other is considered the epitome of rashness, bordering on insanity. There is something wrong with this picture. Was it not more daring for Gustav Adolf to enter into a life and death struggle with the Holy Roman Empire and its allies with only 13,000 troops and no allies than it was for Karl XII to go after Russia with 80,000 of the best and most highly trained troops in the world?

Gustav Adolf owes much of his high reputation to the fact that he was glorified as the savior of Protestantism. In truth, he was fighting for the same political goal as Karl XII—control of the Baltic.

The severest criticism of Karl XII is that, in the words of Napoleon, he was no tactician or strategist, just a brave soldier. My conclusions are different. If Karl XII had followed the advice of Napoleon and severed his lifeline to the homeland as Hannibal did, he would surely have shared the fate of both the Carthaginian and Napoleon. Carthage did not have naval superiority and Hannibal therefore had no choice but to establish a base in the Italian Peninsula. The Romans did not lay waste their provinces as did Peter the Great, and this provided a way for the Carthaginian to sustain himself for years.

Now let us look at some of the elements of national power and see how Sweden handled its problems in these areas.

GEOGRAPHY

Sweden was both unlucky and blessed by geography. She was separated from Denmark, Germany, Poland, and Russia by the Baltic Sea. Naval power was therefore important for protecting her long coastline, for controlling trade in the Baltic, for maintaining communications with her armies on the continent, and for an outlet to the west. The unlucky part of Sweden's geographic location was that she shared a long border with Norway, a country that was in the enemy camp during the whole period, and the fact that Denmark and Norway possessed the strongest fleet in Europe, at least during the opening decades of the 17th Century. These were the reasons Sweden invariably dealt with Denmark-Norway first when facing an enemy coalition. She had to make her line of communications and back door safe. It was a failure of policy for the Nordic countries not to have established some form of cooperation as envisioned by the Kalmar Union (discussed in the Introduction). This geographic problem was never overcome.

POPULATION

Sweden was handicapped by a population of insufficient size to support an empire. When Gustav Adolf launched his invasion of the Holy Roman Empire, the Swedish population was from 1.3 to 1.5 million. About one hundred years later the population was 1,247,000. This decline of 60,000 to 250,000 does not take into account the four generations born during this period and shows the burden posed by the population problem.

SOCIETAL FACTORS

Sweden had a homogenous population. Furthermore, it had a population used to harsh climatic conditions and centuries of almost constant warfare. It was a warlike society in the period covered by this book.

ECONOMICS

The economy was a problem that Sweden grappled with during the whole period covered by this book. Economic considerations, then as now, dictated strategy. While the first Vasa king, by adopting the Protestant religion and taking over the properties of the church, put Sweden on a sound financial footing, it was not enough to undertake the expansion it did in the 17th Century. The Swedish army was in a deplorable condition when Gustav Adolf assumed power in 1611. All efforts to increase domestic revenues prior to 1630 failed. At most, domestic revenues and toll revenues could support a military establishment of 50,000, but fell far short of what was required to support an army of 175,000 men.

Gustav Adolf adopted a policy relying on foreign resources—part of a policy that stated that war should pay for itself. Subsidies were obtained from nations that wanted the power of the Holy Roman Empire curbed but not willing to do so themselves. Heavy monetary "contributions" were levied on both friends and enemy states. Sweden also obtained contributions in kind in a very organized manner. Its quartermasters spread throughout Germany, inventoried the resources required, and requisitioned them—organized plunder as some have called it. However one looks at it, it was part of the philosophy that "war should be made to pay for itself." This system worked well during campaigns in a rich country like Germany, but was a failure in the Baltic and Poland.

The impact was dramatic. Swedish taxpayers had to find 2,800,000 silver dollars for the German war in 1630. By 1633 that amount had dropped to 128,000. It has been estimated that after the Battle of Breitenfeld contributions and subsidies were ten to twelve times as large as Sweden's ordinary budget. Still, 35 percent of Sweden's domestic revenues went to the military in the closing years of the Thirty Years War—mainly to pay for the navy, home defense, and operations outside Germany.

Sweden also lacked manpower resources to fight a continental war. Like most countries in that period, Sweden relied heavily on allied levies and mercenaries. At the time of Breitenfeld only about 25 percent of the Swedish army was composed of Swedes and Finns. That ratio declined after the Battle of Lützen to less than 18 percent, and it declined further in the later years of the Thirty Years War. Throughout most of that war the Swedes and Finns only provided a nucleus, albeit an important one. That the Swedes suffered substantial losses can be shown by the fact that the population in 1718 was somewhat smaller than the estimate for 1600. It was therefore in resources—financial and manpower—that we find an important key to how the Swedes overcame the shortage in those areas during their rise to great power status.

MILITARY

In the military establishment fashioned by Gustav Adolf we find another key to Sweden's ability to rise to great heights. It was, in short, a military revolution, and Sweden led the way both in the development of weapons and their tactical use. They ended up with a highly trained, expertly led, and exceedingly motivated army.

This important advantage was rather short-lived as far as technology was concerned. Other nations were quick to copy, as it was impossible to keep some of the weapons from falling into their hands. This spread was greatly assisted by armament magnates who freely exported great quantities of weapons, including some that had taken decades for the metallurgical industries to perfect. By the later years of the Thirty Years War, opponents had caught up with Sweden in weaponry.

SITUATION IN THE EARLY 1700S.
We will now consider briefly how things changed by the time Karl XII made his supreme effort against Russia. The recruiting base remained the same, with Swedish and Finnish troops forming a nucleus. There continued to be heavy reliance on mercenaries but not so much on allies since there were none, or very few. The wars conducted by Karl XII's immediate predecessors were aggressive in nature, and you don't make many friends by doing so. The failure of the Scandinavian nations to make common cause rather than nibbling at each other only increased nationalist sentiments that had persisted since the failure of the Union of Kalmar.

War could no longer pay for itself since operations were taking place in areas much less prosperous than Germany. Attempts to repeat the "contribution" approach only led to resentment and resistance. The military and land reforms carried out by Karl XII's father and grandfather increased the taxpayer base but failed to address, because of popular opposition, domestic and foreign exploitation of resources. The reforms also failed to set up a rational and functional logistics service or a logistic command.

Financing warfare fell back on Swedish taxpayers and foreign loans. The land reforms that had been carried out resulted in a less cooperative magnate class than we find in the days of Gustav Adolf. He wooed the Riksdag and the magnates and received their cooperation. Karl XII was much more aloof and received very little support from those segments of Swedish society. The fall of mineral prices in the second half of the 17th Century severely reduced state income from export and the mining industries. Finally, the normal source of foreign loans dried up during Karl XII's reign since the countries most relied on for loans were deeply involved in their own wars.

There was no longer a technological gap between Sweden and its opponents. However, Sweden still held an edge in the discipline of its troops and their offensive method of warfare. Leadership still remained superb.

LESSONS

It is very unlikely that the Swedish case could be replicated, but there are some things that are pertinent for policy makers and military planners and practitioners.

Throughout the wars covered in this book, the advantages of a well-directed offensive over defensive operations in the tactical sphere are obvious. This is nothing new, but reinforces what most military practitioners have come to know through experience.

The importance of both tactical and strategic intelligence is underscored. It was a lesson the Swedes had to learn the hard way since they were operating in areas with unfriendly civilians. Without good intelligence, armies are groping in the dark.

Wars cannot be won unless the armies are backed up by a good and functioning logistics system. Gustav Adolf struggled with this in Germany, and would not move unless the operation could be logistically supported. Karl XII was negligent in failing to arrange logical logistical provisions for his invasion of Russia and paid a heavy price.

The importance of the concentration of striking power is demonstrated both in the Russia invasion and in the operations in Germany during the Thirty Years War. It caused more problems for Gustav Adolf than for Karl XII. When you end up with a striking force of perhaps 20,000 out of a field army of 150,000, there is something wrong with the strategic positioning.

Leading from the front is a great troop motivator, but it can be taken too far and both warrior kings were guilty of risking having their commands leaderless at critical times. It is not necessary for the commander to personally lead tactical reconnaissance parties. Gustav Adolf lost a number of his best and most experienced commanders leading from the front at Alte Veste. Consequently, he faced Field Marshal Wallenstein at Lützen with a whole set of new senior commanders.

There are three lessons for the policy level. First, no war can be fought and won without proper financing. It is so important that no war should be contemplated if the cost will damage national security. It is the lifeblood of the defense establishment. In our days, with tight resources and heavy debts, it has become perhaps the greatest threat to our national security.

The second is that countries that request aid from another country should be expected and required to "contribute" resources—both financial and/or manpower. The prosperous nations with shared values and who therefore benefit from the use of military resources of others should be asked to help finance those efforts. This is an old problem but one that has for the most part only received lip service. Long-term plans and efforts need to keep this uppermost in mind now that resources have become strained.

Tight control must be exercised on modern arms sales and the transfer of advanced technology, both by the government and by industries. Most technological advances have in some ways been paid for by taxpayers, and we need to make sure that these advancements are not squandered away for political or monetary reasons. This is especially true for companies that benefit from government contracts.

Appendix I

*Brief Biographic Sketches of Source
Authors Most Frequently Referenced.*[1]

AHNLUND, NILS GABRIEL (1889–1957). Ahnlund was a Swedish historian, born in Uppsala, Sweden. As an historian, Ahnlund wrote on a variety of subjects but his main works deal with the period of Sweden's great power status and relations between Germany and Sweden. I have used one of his books as a reference.

BAIN, ROBERT NISBET (1854–1909). Nisbet was a British historian and linguist who worked for the British Museum. He could use over twenty languages and authored several books on Scandinavian, Russian, and Polish history. I have used one of his books as a reference.

CREVELD, MARTIN VAN, born in Rotterdam in 1946, is an Israeli military historian and theorist. He holds degrees from the London School of Economics and the Hebrew University of Jerusalem, where he has been a member of the faculty since 1971. He is the author of 17 books. I have used two of these as references for this work.

DELBRUCK, HANS (1848–1929). He was a German historian, and one of the first modern military historians. Delbruck's many writings are chiefly concerned with the history of the art of war. I have used two of his books as references.

DUPUY, TREVOR NEVITT (1916–1995). Dupuy graduated from West Point in the class of 1938. He spent much time in Burma during World War II. He was one of the original members of Supreme Headquarters Allied Powers Europe (SHAPE) under Generals Dwight D. Eisenhower and Matthew Ridgeway. Dupuy retired from the Army in 1958 and helped found the Harvard Defense Studies Program, directed by Henry Kissinger. He also served at the Ohio State University and Rangoon University in Burma. Dupuy committed suicide by gunshot in 1995 when he learned he had terminal pancreatic cancer. He formed the first of his research companies dedicated to the study and analysis of armed conflict in 1962. During his lifetime Trevor Dupuy wrote or co-wrote—often with his father R. Ernest Dupuy—more than 50 books. I have used three of his books as references.

ENGLUND, PETER. A Swedish author and historian who was born in 1957. He has been the permanent secretary of the Swedish Academy since 1 June 2009. I have used one of his books as a reference.

ERSLAND, GEIR ATLE (born 1957) & HOLM, TERJE H. (born 1951). They are military historians who co-authored volume 1 of a 3-volume set. Volume 1 includes the period when Norway and Denmark were united.

FROST, ROBERT I. Robert Frost, born c. 1960, is a British historian and academic. He attended the University of St Andrews, the Jagiellonian University in Krakow, and earned his doctorate in Slavonic and East European Studies at the University of London. As of 2009 he was Professor of Early Modern History at the University of Aberdeen, Scotland. I have made frequent use of one of his books as a reference.

FULLER, JOHN FREDERICK CHARLES (1878–1966). Fuller was a British Army officer who rose to the rank of Major General. He was a military historian and strategist, notable as an early theorist of modern armor warfare. He was a prolific writer on military history and strategy. I have used one of his books as a reference.

HATTON, RAGNHILD (1913–1995). She was born in Bergen, Norway and died in London. Educated in Bergen and Oslo, she moved to London when she married an English businessman named Harry Hatton. She completed her PhD degree in 1947 and eventually became professor of International History at the London School of Economics. I have made frequent use one of her books as a reference.

LIDDELL HART, SIR BASIL (1895–1970). British army officer who was invalided in 1924 and retired as a captain in 1927. He was military correspondent of the *Daily Telegraph* from 1925 to 1935 and military adviser to the *Times* from 1935 to 1939. Liddell Hart was a noted British military historian and strategist known for his advocacy of mechanized warfare and the theory of indirect approach. I have used two of his books as references.

MASSIE, ROBERT K. III was born in Lexington, Kentucky in 1929 but moved to New York. He studied US and European history at Yale and Oxford University, respectively, on a Rhodes Scholarship. In addition to working as a journalist,

Massie was the president of the Authors Guild from 1987–1991. He has concentrated his writings on the House of Romanov and is a Pulitzer Price recipient. I have used one of his books as a reference.

MONTROSS, LYNN (1895–1961). Montross was born in Nebraska and lived in Colorado before moving to Washington, D.C. He studied at the University of Nebraska before spending three years with the American Expeditionary Force in World War I. He was a free-lance writer for the Chicago Daily News and is one of the foremost post-World War II western military historians. I have used one of his books as a reference.

PARKER, GEOFFREY. He was born in 1943 and is a British historian specializing in Spanish history, military history of the early modern era, and the role of climate in world history. He earned his doctorate from Cambridge University. Parker has taught at the Universities of Illinois, St. Andrews, Yale and Ohio State. I have used four of his books as references.

ROBERTS, MICHAEL (1908–1996). Roberts was an English historian specializing in the early modern period and particularly known for his many studies of Swedish history. He has authored many books and received several Swedish honors, and was elected a member of the Royal Swedish Academy of Letters, History and Antiquities. I have used six of his books as references.

WILSON, PETER H. Wilson became Professor of History at the University of Hull in 2007. He previously worked at the universities of Sunderland and Newcastle-upon-Tyne and also taught at High Point University, North Carolina, in 2011, and has been a fellow at the University of Münster, Germany. He did his BA at Liverpool and PhD at Jesus College Cambridge. He is a specialist in early modern German history, particularly the political, military, social, and cultural history of the Holy Roman Empire between 1495 and 1806. I have made frequent use of two of his books as references.

NOTES

1. Sources used for this appendix include Encyclopedia Britannica, institutional listings, and information contained in author's own works.

Appendix II

Selected European Rulers 1500–1721[1]

SWEDEN AND FINLAND

Hans II	1497–1501
Sten Sture	1501–1503 (2nd Regency)
Svante Nilsson	1504–1511 (Regent)
Sten Svantesson	1512–1520 (Regent)
Kristian II	1520–1523
Gustav I Vasa	1523–1560 (Regent from 1521)
Erik XIV	1560–1568
Hans III	1568–1592
Sigismund III	1592–1599
Karl IX	1599–1611
Gustav II Adolf	1611–1632
Kristina	1632–1654
Karl X Gustav	1654–1660
Karl XI	1660–1697
Karl XII	1697–1718
Ulrika Eleonora	1719–1720

DENMARK AND NORWAY

Hans	1481–1513
Kristian II	1513–1523
Frederik I	1523–1533
Kristian III	1534–1559
Frederik II	1559–1588
Kristian IV	1588–1648
Frederik III	1648–1670
Kristian V	1670–1699
Frederik IV	1699–1730

POLAND/LITHUANIA

Johan I Albrecht	1492–1501
Alexander	1501–1506
Sigismund I	1506–1548
Sigismund II Augustus	1548–1572

Henry of Valois	1573–1574
Stefan Batory	1576–1586
Sigismund III Vasa	1587–1632
Wladyslaw IV Vasa	1632–1648
Johan II Casimir Vasa	1648–1668
Michael Wisniowiecki	1669–1673
Johan III Sobieski	1674–1696
Augustus II of Saxony	1697–1705
Stanislaw Leszcynski	1705–1709
Augustus II of Saxony	1709–1733

RUSSIA

Ivan III Vasiljevitsch	1462–1533
Ivan IV—The Terrible	1533–1584
Theodore (Fedor) I	1584–1598
Boris Godunov	1598–1605
Theodore II	1605
Gregor Otrepjef	1605–1606
Vasilii V Shuiskii	1610–1612
Vadislav of Poland	1610–1612
Michael Romanov	1613–1645
Alexei Mikhailovich	1645–1676
Theodor (Fedor) III	1676–1682
Ivan V	1682–1689
Peter I	1689–1725

SPAIN

Ferdinand II	1479–1516
Charles V	1516–1556
Philip II	1556–1598
Philip III	1598–1621
Philip IV	1621–1665
Charles II	1665–1700
Philip V	1700–1746

HOLY ROMAN EMPIRE

Maximilian I	1493–1519
Charles V	1519–1556

Ferdinand I	1556–1564
Maximilian II	1564–1576
Rudolph II	1576–1612
Matthias	1612–1619
Ferdinand II	1619–1637
Ferdinand III	1637–1657
Leopold I	1658–1705
Josef I	1705–1711
Charles VI	1711–1740

BRANDENBURG/PRUSSIA

George William	1619–1640
Frederick William	1640–1688
Frederick III	1688–1713 *(became King Frederick I of Prussia in 1701)*
Frederick William I	1713–1740

NETHERLANDS (HOLLAND)

Wilhelm I	1575–1584
Maurice	1585–1625
Frederick Henrik	1625–1647
Wilhelm II	1647–1650
Jan de Witt	1650–1672
Wilhelm III	1672–1702
None	1702–1747

FRANCE

Louis XII	1498–1515
Franz I	1515–1547
Henry II	1547–1559
Franz II	1559–1560
Charles IX	1560–1574
Henry III	1574–1589
Henry IV of Navarre	1589–1610
Louis XIII	1610–1643
Louis XIV	1643–1715
Louis XV	1715–1774

ENGLAND

Henry VII	1485–1509
Henry VIII	1509–1547
Edward VI	1547–1553
Mary	1553–1558
Elizabeth I	1558–1603
Jacob I	1603–1625
Charles I	1625–1649
Oliver Cromwell	1653–1658
Richard Cromwel l	1658–1659
Charles II	1660–1685
Jacob II	1685–1688
Wilhelm III of Orange	1689–1702
Anna Stuart	1702–1714
George I	1714–1727

NOTES

1. Paul Holt, *Historisk Årstalsliste Med slægtsoversigter*. Ninth Edition. (København: P. Haase & Søns Forlag, 1963).

Appendix III

Field Marshals (or equivalent ranks, i.e. hetmen) Mentioned in this Book

HOLY ROMAN EMPIRE	YEAR OF APPOINTMENT
Johann Tserclaes, Count of Tilly (1559–1632)	1618
Albrecht von Wallenstein (1583–1634)	1625
Gottfried Graf von Pappenheim (1594–1632)	1625
Baltsar von Marradas (1560–1638)	1626
Hans Georg von Arnim (1583–1641)	1627
Rudolf von Tiefenbach (1582–1653)	1631
Johann von Aldringen (1588–1634)	1632
Matthias Gallas (1584–1647)	1632
Heinrich von Holk (1599–1633)	1632
Hans Casimir von Schaumburg († 1649)	1632
Archduke Ferdinand of Austria (1608–1657)	1634
Rudolf von Colloredo (†1657)	1634
Ottavio Piccolomini (1599–1656)	1634
Melchior Graf of Hatzfeld (1593–1658)	1634
Friedrich, Duke of Savelli († 1649)	1638
Archduke Leopold Wilhelm of Austria (1614–1662)	1639

SWEDEN	
Karl Karlsson Gyllenhielm	1616
Herman Wrangel	1621
Gustaf Horn	1628
Åke Henriksson Tott	1631
Dodo Knyphausen	1633
Johan Banér	1634
Alexander Leslie	1636
Lennart Torstensson	1641
Karl Gustaf Wrangel	1646
Lars Kragg	1648

Gustaf Adolf Lewenhaupt	1655
Hans Christoff von Köningsmarck	1655
Arvod Wittenberg	1655
Gustaf Otto Stenbock	1656
Henrik Horn	1665
Clas Åkesson Tott	1665
Otto Wilhem von Köningsmarck	1676
Nils Bielke	1690
Karl Gustav Rehnskiöld	1706
Nils Gyllenstierna	1709
Magnus Stenbock	1713

RUSSIA

Charles Eugene de Croy (1651–1702)	1700
Fedor Golovin (1650–1706)	1700
Boris Sheremetev (1652–1729)	1701
Alexander Menshikov (1673–1729)	1709
Anikita Repnin (1668–1726)	1725

POLISH-LITHUANIAN COMMONWEALTH

Stanislaw Zolkiewski	1588–1613
Stanislaw Koniecpolski	1618–1632
Krzysztof II Radziwill	1615–1640
Janusz Radziwill	1654–1655
Wincenty Gosiewski	1654–1662
Pawel Jan Sapieha	1656–1665
Stanislaw Lanckoronski	1654–1657
Stefan Czarniecki	1664–1665
Jan Sobieski	1666–1688

FRANCE

Henri of Turenne (1611–1675)	1643
Sebastien Le Prestre of Vauban (1633–1707)	1703

The British did not use the field marshal rank until 1736.

Bibliography

Ahnlund, Nils. *Gustavus Adolphus the Great*. New York: History Book Club, 1999— originally published in 1940.

Akermann, Jurgen. *Jurgen Akermann, Kapitan Beim Regiment Alt-Pappenheim, 1631*. Whiteface, Montana: Dessinger Publishing, 2009. A facsimile reprint.

Alnæs, Karsten. *Historien om Norge*. Five volumes. Oslo: Gyldendal Norsk Forlag A/S, 1996.

Andersson, Ingvar. *A History of Sweden*. Translated from the Swedish by Carolyn Hannay. London: Weinfeld and Nicholson, 1956. I also used the 1962 edition published in Stockholm by Natur och Kultur.

Årgren, Sven. Karl XI:s indelingsverk för armén. Bidrag till dess historia åren 1679–1697 (Uppsala, 1922).

Asch, Ronald G. The Thirty Years War: The Holy Roman Empire and Europe, 1618–48. New York: St. Martin's Press, 1997.

Atkingson, Charles Francis. *Thirty Years War*. Kindle Edition.

Axelrod, Alan. *Little-Known Wars of Great and Lasting Impact: The Turning Points in Our History We Should Know More About*. Beverly, Massachusetts: Fair Winds Press, 2009.

Bain, R. Nisbet. *Charles XII and the Collapse of the Swedish Empire, 1682–1719*. Nabu Public Domain Reprints, 2010.

Barudio, Günter. *Gustav Adolf, der Grosse: eine politische Biographie*. Frankfurt am Main: S. Fischer, 1982.

Barudio, Günter. *Der Teutsche Krieg, 1618–1648*. Frankfurt am Main: S. Fischer, 1985.

Bély, Lucien (ed.). *L'Europe des traits de Westphalie: esprit de la Diplomatie et diplomatie de l'esprit*. Presses universitaires de France, 2000.

Blomfield, Reginald. Sébastian le Prestre de Vauban, 1663–1707 (New York: Barnes and Noble, 1971).

Bray, R. S. *Armies of Pestilence: The Impact of Disease on History*. New York: Barnes & Noble Books, 2000.

Brulin, Herman. *Sverige och Frankrike under nordiska kriget och spanska successkrisen åren 1700–1701*. Upsala: Almqvist & Wiksells boktryckeri, 1905.

Buchner, Volker & Buchner, Alex. *Bayern im Dreissigjärigem Krieg*. Dachau: Bayerland GmbH, 2002.

Chemnitz, Philipp Bogislaw von. *Königlich Schwedischer in Teutschland geführter Krieg.*

Four volumes first published in Stettin in 1648. Stockholm: 1653. New Swedish edition published in 1855–1859 in six volumes.

Childs, John. "The Military Revolution I: The Transition to Modern Warfare" in *The Oxford Illustrated History of Modern War*, edited by Charles Townshend. New York: Oxford University Press, 1979.

Christiansen, Eric. *The Northern Crusades*. New York: Penguin Books Inc., 1997.

Clausewitz, Carl von. *On War*. Edited with an Introduction by Anatol Rapoport. Baltimore, Maryland: Penguin Books Inc., 1968.

Cowles, Virginia. *The Romanovs*. New York: Harper & Row, Publishers, 1971.

Creasy, Edward Shepherd. *Decisive Battles of the World*. New York: The Colonial Press, 1899.

Creveld, Martin van. *Command in War*. Cambridge, Massachusetts: Harvard University Press, 1985.

Creveld, Martin van. *Supplying War: Logistics from Wallenstein to Patton*. New York: Cambridge University Press, 2004.

Cummins, Joseph. *Great Rivals in History: When Politics gets Personal*. New York: Metro Books. 2008.

Cummins, Joseph. *History's Greatest Wars: The Epic Conflicts that Shaped the Modern World*. Beverly, Massachusetts: Fair Winds Press, 2009.

Davis, Paul K. *100 Decisive Battles from Ancient Times to the Present: The World's Major Battles and how they shaped History*. New York: Oxford University Press, 2001.

Defoe, Daniel. *Memoirs of a Cavalier: A military Journal of the Wars in Germany, and the Wars in England. From the Year 1632 to the Year 1648*. Edited with Introduction and Notes by Elizabeth O'Neill, 1922. Kindle Edition.

Delbrück, Hans. *History of the Art of War: The Dawn of Modern Warfare*, Volume IV. Translated by Walter J. Renfroe, Jr. Lincoln, Nebraska: University of Nebraska Press, 1990.

Downing, Brian M. *The Military Revolution and Political Change: Origins of Democracy and Autocracy in Early Modern Europe*. Princeton, New Jersey: Princeton University Press, 1992.

Duffy, Christopher. The Fortress in the Age of Vauban and Frederick the Great, 1660–1789. London: Routledge, 1985.

Dunn, Richard S. *The Age of Religious Wars, 1559–1715*. New York: W. W. Norton & Company, 1979.

Dupuy, Richard Ernest and Dupuy, Trevor N. *The Encyclopedia of Military History from 3500 B.C. to the Present*. New York: Harper & Row, 1970.

Dupuy, Colonel Trevor N. *The Military Life of Gustavus Adolphus: Father of Modern War*. New York: Franklin Watts, Inc., 1969).

Dupuy, Colonel Trevor N. *The Evolution of Weapons and Warfare.* New York: The Bobbs-Merrill Company, Inc., 1980.

Durant, Will and Durant, Ariel. *The Story of Civilization.* Ten volumes. New York: Simon and Schuster, 1963.

Durant, Will and Durant, Ariel. *The Lessons of History.* New York: Simon and Schuster, 1968.

Englund, Peter. *The Battle that Shook Europe: Poltava and the Birth of the Russian Empire.* New York: I B. Tauris & Co Ltd, 2003.

Ersland, Atle and Holm, Terje H. *Norsk forsvarshistorie.* Three volumes. Bergen: Eide Forlag, 2000.

Erslev, Kristian. *Dronning Margarethe og Kalmarunionens Grundleggelse.* Kjøbenhavn: J. Erslev, 1882.

Ferguson, Robert. *The Vikings: A History.* New York: Published by the Penguin Group, 2009.

Frost, Robert I. *The Northern Wars 1558–1721.* New York: Longman, 2000.

Fuller, J. F. C. *A Military History of the Western World.* Three volumes. New York: Da Capo Press, 1999.

Gardiner, Samuel Rawson. *The Thirty Years War 1618–1648.* Kindle Edition.

Goerlitz, Walter. *History of The German General Staff 1657–1945.* Translated by Brian Battershaw. New York: Praeger, 1957.

Gordon, Patrick. *Tagebuch des Generals Patrick Gordon wärend seiner Kriegsdienste unter den Sweden und Polen.* Moscow, 1969.

Gottfried, Robert S. *The Black Death: Natural and Human Disaster in Medieval Europe.* New York: The Free Press, 1983.

Griess, Thomas E., editor of The West Point Military History Series. *The Dawn of Modern Warfare.* Wayne, New Jersey: Avery Publishing Group, 1984.

Guthrie, William P. *The Later Thirty Years War: From the Battle of Wittstock to the Treaty of Wesphalia.* eBook edition. Westport, Connecticut: Greenwood Press, 2003.

Harbottle, Thomas. *Dictionary of Battles.* Revised and Updated by George Bruce. New York: Stein and Day, 1974.

Hatton, R. M. *Charles XII of Sweden.* New York: Weybright and Talley, 1969).

Haythornthwaite, Philip J. *Invincible Generals,* Bloomington, Indiana: Indiana University Press, 1991.

Hittle, James D. *The Military Staff: Its History and Development.* Originally published in 1944. Third edition. Harrisburg, Pennsylvania: The Stackpole Company, 1961.

Hollway, Don. "Triumph of Flexible Firepower" in *Military History,* February 1996.

Holt, Paul. *Historisk Årstalsliste: Med slægtsoversigter.* Ninth Edition. København: Haase & Søns Forlag, 1963.

Howard, Michael. *War in European History*. Third Edition. New York: Oxford University Press, 2009.

Jonasson, Gustaf. *Karl XII och hans rådsgivare; den utrikespolitiska maktmapen i Sverige 1697–1702*. Stockholm: Svenska bokforlaget, 1960.

Jones, Gwyn. *A History of the Vikings*. New York: Oxford University Press, 1968.

Keegan, John and Holmes, Richard. *Soldiers: A History of Men in Battle*. New York: Viking Penguin Inc., 1986.

Lee, Stephen J. *The Thirty Years War*. Lancaster Pamphlets. New York: Routledge, 2001.

Liddell Hart, B. H. *Great Captains Unveiled: From Genghis Khan to General Wolfe*. Novato, California: Presidio Press, 1989.

Liddell Hart, B. H. *Strategy*. New York: Praeger Publishers, 1972.

Lisk, Jill. *The Struggle for Supremacy in the Baltic: 1600–1725* New York: Funk & Wagnalls, 1968.

Lockhart, Paul Douglas. *Denmark 1513–1660: The Rise and Decline of a Renaissance Monarchy*. New York: Oxford University Press, 2007.

Lockhart, Paul Douglas. *Denmark in the Thirty Years' War, 1618–1648: King Christian IV and the Decline of the Oldenburg State*. Selingsgrove: Susquehanna University Press, 1996.

Lukowski, Jerzy and Zawadzki, Hubert. *A Concise History of Poland*. Second Edition. New York: Cambridge University Press, 2006.

Lundkvist, Sven. "Die schwedishen Kriegs und Friedensziele 1632–1648" in Repgen, editor. *Krieg und Politik: Europäische Probleme und Perspktiven*. Munich, 1988.

Lundkvist,"Svensk krigsfinasiering 1630–1635," in 1966 *Historisk Tidssfrift*.

Lynn, John A. *The French Wars 1667–1714*. London: Osprey Publishing, 2002.

Machiavelli, Niccolo. *The Prince*. Edited and translated by Peter Bondanella. New York: Oxford University Press, 2008.

Mann, Golo. *Wallenstein, Sein Leben erzählt*. Frankfurt am Main: S. Fischer Verlag, 1971.

Massie, Robert K. *Peter the Great: His Life & World*. New York: The Modern Library, 2012.

Moberg, Vilhelm. *A History of the Swedish People*. Two volumes. Translated by Paul Britten Austin. Minneapolis: University of Minnesota Press, 2005.

Monro, Robert. *Monro, His Expedition with the Worthy Scots Regiment Called MacKeys*. Whiteface, Montana: Kessinger, 1999. This is a reprint of the original.

Montross, Lynn. *War Through the Ages*. New York: Harper & Row, 1960.

Ogg, David. *Europe in the Seventh Century*. Eighth Edition, Revised. London: Adam & Charles Black, 1961 [First Published 1925].

Öhman, J. *Der Kampf um den Frieden. Schweden und der Kaiser im Dreissigjährigen Krieg.* Vienna, 2005.

Opitz, Walter. *Die Schlacht Bei Breitenfeld Am 17 September 1631.* First published in 1892. This is a facsimile reprint of the original. Whitefish, Montana: Kessinger Publishing, LLC, 2010.

Pagden, Anthony. *Worlds at War: the 2,500-year Struggle Between East and West.* New York: Random House, 2008.

Palma, R. Matthew. "Battle of Lützen: Victory and Death for Gustavus Adolphus" in *Military History*, October 1988.

Paret, Peter, editor. *Makers of Modern Strategy From Machiavelli to the Nuclear Age.* Princeton, New Jersey: Princeton University Press, 1986.

Parker, Geoffrey. *Europe in Crisis 1598–1648.* Malden, Massachusetts: Blackwell Publishers, Inc., 2001.

Parker, Geoffrey. *The Military Revolution: Military Innovation and the Rise of the West 1500–1800.* Second Edition. New York: Cambridge University Press, 1999.

Parker, Geoffrey, editor. *The Thirty Years War.* New York: Routledge, 1997.

Peltier, Louis C. and Pearcy, G. Etzel. *Military Geography.* Princeton, New Jersey: D. van Nostrand Company, Inc., 1966.

Peterson, Gary Dean. *Warrior Kings of Sweden: The Rise of an Empire in the Sixteenth and Seventeenth Centuries.* Jefferson, North Carolina: McFarland & Company, Inc., 2007.

Phillips, Brig. Gen. Thomas R., editor. *Roots of Strategy: A Collection of Military Classics.* Harrisburg, Pennsylvania: The Military Service Publishing Company, 1955.

Polisensky, J. V. *The Thirty Years War.* Translated from the Czech by Robert Evans. Berkeley: University of California Press, 1971.

Pratt, Fletcher. *The Battles That Changed History* Mineola, New York: Dover Publications, Inc., 2000. Rabb, Theodore K. *The Struggle for Stability in Early Modern Europe.* New York: Oxford University Press, 1975.

Repgen, Konrad. *Krieg un Politik, 1618–1648: europäische Probleme und Perspektiven.* München: R. Oldenbourg, 1988.

Riasanovsky, Nicholas V. *A History of Russia.* Third Edition. New York: Oxford University Press, Inc., 1977).

Roberts, Michael. *Gustavus Adolphus: A History of Sweden, 1611–1632.* Two volumes New York: Longmans, 1958.

Roberts, Michael. *The Early Vasas. A History of Sweden 1523–1611.* London: Cambridge University Press, 1986.

Roberts, Michael. *The Swedish Imperial Experience 1560–1718.* New York: Cambridge University Press, 1979. I have used both the 1973 and 1979 editions.

Rotenberg, Gunther. *The Art of Warfare in the Age of Napoleon*. Bloomington: Indiana University Press, 1980.

Sarauw, Christian Frederik Conrad. *Die Feldzüge Karl's XII: ein quellenmässiger Beitrag zur Kriegsgeschichte und Kabinetspolitikk Europa's im XVIII Jahrhundert*. Leipzig: B. Schlicke, 1881.

Sprague, Martina. *Sweden: An Illustrated History*. New York: Hippocrene Books, Inc., 2005.

Steinberg, S. H. *The Thirty Years War and the Conflict for European Hegemony 1600–1660*. New York: W. W. Norton & Company, Inc., 1966.

Stiles, Andrina. *Sweden and the Baltic 1523–1721*. London: Hodder & Stoughton, 1992.

Sweden. Armén. Generalstabens krigehistoriska avdeling.

Sveriges krig 1611–1632. Six volumes. Stockholm, V. Petterson, 1936–1939. Also Generalstaben, *Karl XXII* in two volumes. Since I have been told that only thirteen copies exist world-wide, I have not had direct access to them.

Tallett, Frank. *War and Society in Early-Modern Europe 1495–1715*. New York: Routledge, 2001.

Toynbee, Arnold J. *A Study of History*. Somervell abridgement in two volumes. New York: Oxford University Press, 1947 volume 1 and 1957 volume 2.

Townshend, Charles, editor. *Modern War*. New York: Oxford University Press, 1997.

United States Air Force Academy. Transformation in Russian and Soviet Military history. Proceedings of the Twelfth Military History Symposium USAF Academy 1986. Washington, D.C.: United States Air Force, 1990.

United States National Defense University. *The Art and Practice of Military Strategy*. Edited by George Edward Thibault. Washington, D.C.: National Defense University, 1984.

Voltaire (François Marie Arouet). *History of Charles XII* Translated from the French by Tobias Smollett. New York: The Colonial Press, 1901. This is the second volume of the two-volume limited edition (this being 366 of 1,000 published) *The Worlds Great Classics*.

Wedgwood, C. V. *The Thirty Years War*. Foreword by Anthony Grafton. New York: New York Review of Books, 2005.

Wells, H. G. *The Outline of History*. Two volumes (New York: Doubleday & Company, Inc., 1961)

Wilson, Peter H. *The Thirty Years War: A Sourcebook*. New York: Palgrave Macmillan, 2010.

Wilson, Peter H. *The Thirty Years War: Europe's Tragedy*. Cambridge, Massachusetts:

The Belknap Press of Harvard University Press, 2009.

Wittram, Reinhard. Peter I, Czar und Kaiser. Göttingen: Vandenhoeck & Ruprecht, 1964.

Zamoyski, Adam. *Moscow 1812: Napoleon's Fatal March*. New York: Harper Perennial Publishers, 2005.

Index